COMPARATIVE POLITICS

Comparative Politics

Theory and Methods

B. Guy Peters

NEW YORK UNIVERSITY PRESS
Washington Square, New York

First published in the U.S.A. in 1998 by
NEW YORK UNIVERSITY PRESS
Washington Square
New York, N.Y. 10003

This book is printed on paper suitable for recycling and
made from fully managed and sustained forest sources.

Library of Congress Cataloging-in-Publication Data
Peters, B. Guy.
Comparative politics : theory and methods / B. Guy Peters.
p. cm.
Includes bibliographical references and index.
ISBN 0–8147–6667–6 (alk. paper). — ISBN 0–8147–6668–4 (pbk. :
alk. paper)
1. Comparative government. I. Title.
JF51.P42 1998
320.3—dc21 98–18784
CIP

Printed in Hong Kong

Contents

List of Figures and Tables

Figures

Tables

List of Key Texts

Preface

This book represents the culmination of an effort on my part to improve thinking about questions of comparative research in political science. One part of this was a pedagogical effort at my home institution as well as at Oxford. I found that even many of the best graduate students were beginning their dissertation research without a firm sense of the issues of comparative research in political science. Many of the students were well equipped with a statistical arsenal to attack any data set they might confront, but they were not thinking about more fundamental, and logically prior, questions such as conceptualisation, measurement and the selection of cases. Further, they still tended to think too much in terms of stark dichotomies of methods and approaches, despite the work of many leading methodologist pointing to the commonality of methods of research.

A graduate course on the subject at Pittsburgh, and a short seminar at Oxford, ameliorated some of these problems for two sets of students, but it was obvious that if these students were encountering these problems then there were almost certainly others who were as well. My publisher, Steven Kennedy, suggested that this book might be an appropriate response to the perceived need to encourage more explicit concern with questions of comparison and the comparative method. After several iterations, this manuscript is finally ready to go to press.

One thing that may require some explanation is the comparative politics 'hall of fame' that is included in the form of 'Key Texts' boxes throughout the text, largely at the prompting of Steven Kennedy. The selection is idiosyncratic on my part, but the intention is to give the reader a sense of what has been happening in this area of inquiry and where it may be going now. Most of the pieces were selected for their theoretical contributions, although several were chosen because they illustrate well the use of a particular mod of inquiry, For each of the selections included there is a description of the contribution made, as well as some critique, As is repeatedly stressed throughout the text, there is no perfect method for investigation, and likewise there is no perfect theory for guiding those investigations.

A number of people deserve thanks for helping me to bring the book to this point. One is Steven Kennedy. Another is Vincent Wright of Nuffield College, Oxford. Vincent has been, in addition to a wonderful friend, a source of advice and guidance in the preparation of the manuscript. Seeing how he deals with these questions with his own graduate students has also helped me clarify some of the points. Gillian Peele at Lady Margaret Hall, Oxford, team-taught the seminar with me at Oxford and provided a number of insights into the material. Students at Pittsburgh and at Oxford have helped me to refine some of the presentation of the material and have raised questions that needed to be answered in the text. Finally, my wife Sheryn has suffered through yet another series of deadlines and worries about a book. Thanks to you all.

B. Guy Peters

Acknowledgements

The author and publishers acknowledge with thanks permission from the following to reproduce copyright material: *Comparative Political Studies*, for Figure 1.1 and Figure 4.1, from A. Lijphart, 'Typologies of Democratic Systems' (1968); *Comparative Politics*, for Figure 4.1, from T. L. Karl, 'Dilemmas of Democratization in Latin America' (1990); Simon & Schuster, for Figure 4.2, from J. Paige, *Agrarian Revolution* (1975); *Comparative Political Studies*, for Table 1.1, from D. Berg-Schlosser, 'African Political Systems' (1984); Institute for East–West Studies, for Key Text 4.1, from P. C. Schmitter and T. L. Karl, 'The Types of Democracy Emerging in Southern and Eastern Europe and in South and Central America', in P. M. E. Volten (ed.), *Bound to Change* (1992). Every effort has been made to contact all the copyright-holders, but if any have been inadvertently omitted the publishers will be pleased to make the necessary arrangement at the earliest opportunity.

1

The Importance of Comparison

Comparative politics is central to the development of political theory. For most sciences, experimentation is the way to test theory, but for political science, comparison is the principal method. Political science can be an experimental science only rarely, and then almost always in highly contrived circumstances. Researchers are sometimes able to have students or other more or less willing subjects participate in games or experiments, but those exercises tend to be far removed from most real questions about governing. Therefore, comparing what happens when different countries, for their own reasons, modify constitutions, or party systems, or whatever, provides useful information about the probable consequences of different political orders.

The real world of governing and politics is too important to permit social scientists to manipulate an institution here and a law there just to see what might happen. It may sometimes appear to the populations of some poor countries that wealthier governments and international organisations are indeed experimenting with their political lives, as one reform after another is imposed on them from abroad. For example, international organisations are requiring many less developed countries to implement a variety of reforms such as privatisation as conditions of receiving assistance. Those reforms are, however, almost always based on an implicit, if not explicit, comparative analysis of government, and the institutions being advocated appear to the foreign government or international organisation advocating change to be associated with more successful governance in their own or in similar governments.

There is some question of whether political science would want to be a more experimental science, even were it possible. When a scientist conducts an experiment the purpose is to hold as many factors as possible constant, in order to permit a single independent variable to operate upon a single dependent variable. Unfortunately (or fortunately), the real world of politics is not that sterile and controlled, and there are a host of seemingly extraneous factors that influence the way people vote, or policies are made, or interest groups lobby. Thus, any great investment in experimentation might rob the discipline of much of its descriptive richness and attention to complexity, which are important for understanding what makes politics in France so different from politics in its neighbour Italy, much less politics in Nigeria. A great deal of political life involves the interaction of numerous forces, so that any artificial isolation of *the* causal factor would almost certainly be misleading as well as less interesting.

Real countries present both problems and benefits for comparative politics. The benefits are obvious. Within those real countries occur the real, complex and convoluted sequences of events that are of so much interest to the student of the subject. On the other hand, the complexity of real political life means that variables come to the researcher in large bundles of factors that are almost inextricably intertwined. It is then up to the researcher to disentangle the sources of variance, to contextualise the findings, and to provide as useful a 'story' about politics as he or she can.

If the claims of political science to be an empirical method are based largely on comparative analysis, so too is a good deal of the substance of normative political theory based implicitly on comparison. Normative political theory is directed at identifying and producing 'the good life' in the public sphere, and to some extent arguments about the desirability of different forms of government are based on the comparative observations of the propounders of those theories. Certainly, not all normative political theory is that instrumental in its advocacy of particular solutions to the problem of government, but much of the analysis has been. Thomas Hobbes had observed that the absence of effective government – his 'state of nature' – during the period of the English Civil War produced less desirable social outcomes than might occur under more effective government. From that observation, he extrapolated to argue for strong government, even at the possible expense of some civil liberties. Even when there are no real-world observations of a particular version of 'the good life', normative analysts often engage in mental experiments based upon their generalised empirical knowledge of politics, drawn largely from informal comparative analysis. This comparison could be conducted across time as well as across countries.

The real world of comparative government is therefore the laboratory for political scientists to determine what works and what does not, as well as to demonstrate important theoretical relationships among variables. It is a laboratory in which the 'experiments' are designed by other people – politicians, civil servants, interest group leaders – for their own purposes and not for those of social scientists. Therefore, the difficult but yet crucial task for the comparative analyst is to devise the methods necessary to construct meaningful theoretical and analytic statements about government and politics within those complex and largely unplanned settings. We must develop the methodologies for entering into the real world of politics in a number of different settings, and extracting meaningful information. That information needs to be descriptively accurate, but it also need to be more than that. Those statements must also link observations made in one political system with similar observations made in another, or link the observations in one system with general propositions about politics. For a researcher to be able to say what happens in a single country may be interesting, but it is generally insufficient to mean that he or she is really engaged in the study of comparative politics.

Studying the single country can however be argued to be comparative analysis if it is guided by implicit comparison with other systems, or if the research has a strong connection to theories based on comparison (Verba, 1967). Indeed, carefully selected and crafted studies of individual countries can be crucial for testing theory (see Key Text 5.1). One country may be the crucial case for testing a hypothesis – if the proposition works there then it will work anywhere – so that the case-study is the most efficient means of addressing the theoretical proposition. For example, élite theory and élite pacts have become important means of explaining the success of democratisation in transitional regimes (Burton and Higley, 1987; Higley and Gunther, 1992; Zhang, 1994; Hagopian, 1990). These pacts involve members of the contending political factions reaching agreements to govern peacefully, even in the face of intense disagreements between them, not only on policies but also on the structure of government itself. If élite pacts were found to function to manage a deeply divided society, for example, in Lebanon, then they might be expected to have the potential to work almost anywhere. Lebanon was discussed as an example of conflict management through consociationalism prior to the outbreak of the Civil War. It now remains to be seen if other means of conflict management can work.

The virtue of comparative analysis, especially when the analysis is limited to a single case or a few cases, is that it forces greater specificity on the researcher. What are the factors in a country that produce certain observed patterns of behaviour? If the study is conducted outside a comparative framework, it is easy for the researcher to make a number of assumptions about the exceptionalism of the case. In a more comparative mode of analysis, the similarities as well as the differences become evident, and the researcher must think more clearly about the root causes of the performance of the system. Comparative analysis can also be useful even when one is thinking about political behaviour within one's own country. What is it that makes British or American politics different from those of other countries, and what evidence would a researcher need to muster in order to substantiate that argument about the differences? What are the 'shadow cases' that would be most useful when making judgments about British politics? Are they the Commonwealth countries, the USA, or the countries of continental Europe?

We do not need to apologise at all for the contributions of comparative politics, despite the obvious disability of moving the study forward and of making it even more useful for analysts and perhaps indeed for practitioners in the 'real world'. This body of research has been able to cope with immense changes in the surrounding political world – decolonisation and political development, the development of regional bodies such as the European Union, democratisation in Latin America, Southern Europe, and Central and Eastern Europe, and the emergence of the 'little tigers' in Asia – and has something important to say about these changes. There has also been the gradual accretion of a rich store of knowledge about individual political systems, which can serve not only as grist for theoretical exercises but also simply for a better understanding of those systems. Finally, there have been interesting and important theoretical developments. These developments have not been uncontroversial, but again, they have added to the store of weapons at the disposal of those political scientists who go into the field attempting to understand politics and political behaviour in a comparative manner.

In this book, the concentration on the development of theory is in contrast to the roots of comparative political analysis, which lie more in the description of formal, legal institutions and in prescribing governmental structure based on ideas of democracy and 'good government'. This theoretical development in the discipline has been praised by some, especially those who fought so hard to break the domination of formalism (Eckstein, 1963). It has also been condemned by more traditional scholars (MacIntyre, 1978), who argue that the differences among countries are so subtle, and so ingrained in cultural and historical factors, that they are not subject to 'scientific' analysis; however, while attempting to be sensitive to the difficulties of comparison and to the subtleties of national differences, we will nevertheless operate within the more scientific paradigm.

Forms of Comparative Analysis

The task of understanding politics comparatively is made all the more difficult by the number of the different forms of analysis that are commonly labelled 'comparative politics' in textbooks and in political science curricula. On the one hand, there are studies of an individual country (other than that of the author and the intended audience) that are labelled 'comparative'. At the other end of the spectrum are studies in which individual countries are submerged in a multitude of other countries, and become 'data points' in a statistical analysis much more than they are vital political entities. Both types of studies have their appropriate place in the discipline, despite efforts by scholars from the other camp to weed them out, and both can claim to make important contributions to the study of comparative politics. The problem lies in attempting to understand both methods of analysis within that single rubric of 'comparative', and to understand the contributions each type can make.

Despite their apparent dissimilarity, all these approaches to comparative politics must confront a fundamental trade-off between the respective virtues of complexity and generalisation. That is, the more an approach (the case method for example) takes into account the context and the complexities of any one political system, or a limited range of systems, the less capable that research strategy will be of producing generalisations about politics. Similarly, the more an approach (such as statistical modelling) attempts to furnish generalisations and to test broad theories about politics, the less nuance about particular political systems it is able to permit in its analysis.

This trade-off is inherent to the research process of comparative politics, and to some extent to other component parts of the social sciences, and the researcher must make decisions about where along that underlying continuum of specificity to place a particular piece of research. Dogan and Pelassy (1984: 127) note that 'at times comparativists will emphasise similarities, at times differences. They will tend to look for differences in contexts that are roughly similar, or . . . will try to find analogies in contrasting political systems.' Research also can be strengthened by the interaction of the two styles of comparison, although that makes difficulties for any individual scholar.

Another way to think about these fundamental trade-offs in comparative analysis is to contrast configurative and statistical methods of analysis (see Lijphart, 1971). In the configurative approach, the primary purpose is the thorough description of a case or cases, so that the consumer of the research will be capable of comprehending the logic of political life in that limited number of settings. That understanding of the case will be, however, rather deep, or 'thick', and would include a number of aspects of social and political life found in those systems. The anthropologist Clifford Geertz (1973) used the phrase 'thick description' to describe interpretative work in his discipline. By this, he meant using detailed description as the precursor of interpretation and theory development in the social sciences. The descriptions generated in a configurative analysis tend to range across institutional and micro-political 'variables', rather than just on the specifics of a case. That description would also involve an understanding of the social, cultural and economic context of politics. This is the kind of comparative analysis associated with the scholar who devotes his or her career to the study of one or a few countries, but feels very much at home in the culture and politics of that limited sample of countries. The understanding developed through the extended analysis of the single case becomes almost intuitive, so that conveying it to others may become very difficult. One of the standard descriptions of science is that its findings and methods must be 'intersubjectively transmissible'. If the findings are excessively intuitive, they do not necessarily contribute to political science.

One of the more interesting, and confounding, features of comparative analysis from the configurative perspective is that researchers from different countries may apply their own particular national lens to the same data. This is true not only in terms of the selection and treatment of the cases, but also in the implicit comparison with the home country (see Wiarda, 1981). Tocqueville's (1946) magisterial study of politics in the United States was written very much with the French society and French politics of his time in mind. The strong position of American political science in the field of comparative politics has meant that a large proportion of single country studies use the United States as the implicit if not explicit comparison. Edward Page (1990), however, has documented a British tradition in comparative politics that tends to be less theory-conscious and less quantitative than American configurative studies. Given that the individual scholar is the principal research 'instrument' in this type of study, there may be a great deal of extraneous and error variance added to these studies (see Key Text 9.1), and the study may be comprehensible only in the national context within which it was written.

Statistical explanation has a fundamentally different purpose. It attempts to test propositions about the relationship among political variables across countries and in a variety of settings. To some extent, the characteristics of these settings other than those explicitly included in the model are assumed to be irrelevant, so long as they do not confound measurement of the variables in which the researcher is interested, or introduce other forms of extraneous and error variance (see below, pp. 30–2). Further, statistical explanations tend to leave unmeasured a number of factors that might be central to the more descriptive and convoluted explanations provided through configurative analysis. To the extent that cultural factors are a part of the statistical explanation, they tend to be included only as residual explanations, and to appear only when all other measured factors prove inadequate to explain the dependent variable in question. In fairness, there have been some attempts to measure cultural factors more explicitly, and to include them in the statistical models. For example, the wealth of data coming from the World Value Study is used increasingly to both describe national political cultures and to attempt to explain other political phenomena (Inglehart, 1997; Kaase and Newton, 1995).

At the extreme, statistical analysis ceases to identify countries as countries, but instead conceptualises them as packages of variables. Two major students of comparative politics, for example, argued that the ultimate purpose of the comparative exercise should be to eliminate proper names of countries and to think primarily in terms of concepts and variables (Przeworski and Teune, 1970: 30). That view is probably too extreme for most students of comparative politics, even those interested in quantitative analysis. The variable-driven perspective on comparison does, however, point to the need to direct some scholarly attention away from the specifics of thick description of individual countries into the development and testing of hypotheses that are meaningful cross-nationally. As we will point out below (pp. 139–54), however, more formalised comparative analysis need not, and should not, abandon totally the traditional concern with real cases and real countries, nor need it be entirely quantitative in order to be able to 'test' hypotheses.

Quantity and Quality

Although the familiar configurative, case-study approach to comparative politics and the statistical approach to the same phenomena may appear extremely different, the fundamental logic of research comparison that undergirds them is actually very similar. As King *et al.* (1994; see also Kritzer, 1996) have pointed out very forcefully, any meaningful differences between quantitative and qualitative research are almost always exaggerated by the advocates of both styles of enquiry. Conducting either style of social research properly depends upon the same issues of research design, each is prey to the same potential errors, and each requires interpretation that goes beyond their available data. In particular, both types of research face the task of developing research designs that maximise the observed variance in their dependent variables that is a function of the presumed independent variable or variables. Further, the research design – whether quantitative or qualitative – also must minimise error variance, or the observed variance resulting from random sources such as measurement error and unreliability.

As well as error variance, dealing with extraneous variance is a crucial problem for research design. Qualitative researchers often do not think in terms such as independent and dependent variables, but their research problems can certainly be expressed in that manner. A scholar using the case-study method must be sure that the causes to which he or she is attributing the observed outcomes are indeed the 'true causes', and not a function of other factors that might as easily produce the observed outcomes. While statistical research can cope with the problem of other possible causes by introducing control variables to identify and quantify the confounding causes, qualitative research must deal with the confounding factors through careful research design, greater attention to the proper selection of cases, and fairness to all causes when doing the research. Of course, if the statistical researcher does not identify, via theory or personal insight, the appropriate control variables then the analysis will be no more effective in sorting out confused causality than will the qualitative analysis. There is a fundamental dilemma here for the researcher. He or she needs a theory to guide the research if it is to be truly comparative, but that theory may colour the research. We all have a tendency to see what we want to see, or what we set out to find.

The argument that quantitative and qualitative research are more similar than dissimilar is not uncontroversial. Advocates of both styles of enquiry argue for the superiority of their own method. In addition, scholars who have no particular methodological axe to grind raise some doubts about the similarity of the methods in practice. For example, Ronald Rogowski (1995) argues that the admonitions of King *et al.* (1994) not to select cases on values of the dependent variable (see below, pp. 36ff) are apt for statistical analysis, but would make much case-research less useful than it is. The strength of much case-analysis is that it samples (*sic*) purposefully on the dependent variable to be able to test theory in the most difficult setting. Likewise, Collier (1995) expresses some doubts about the assumed goal of generalisation implied by the wedding of the methodological traditions.

Although Rogowski and Collier do raise some questions about the similarity of quantitative and qualitative analysis as presented by King *et al.*, they are still working in the same positivist, empirical tradition of analysis. There are other scholars who would argue that qualitative, interpretative analysis is the only real way to consider comparison (MacIntyre, 1978). For these scholars, all this discussion of variance would be irrelevant; what is important is individual interpretation of political events. This volume obviously takes a more positivist position, and argues that we really need to remove, as much as possible, the individual and his or her idiosyncracies from the research if we want to be able to make statements about politics that are more general, more usable, and testable.

Types of Comparative Studies

The study of comparative politics is an extremely diverse intellectual enterprise. This diversity is both a strength and a weakness of comparison On the one hand, Wiarda (1986: 5) argues that the field is so diverse that it can scarcely be called a field at all. On the other hand, Verba (1986: 36) argues that the heterogeneity of the field will continue, and that this diversity is a source of strength rather than of weakness. Verba argues that the openness of the field to various theories and methodologies helps to maintain its vitality and its capacity to cope with a rapidly changing political world. Any premature closure of content or method might therefore, it is argued, inhibit intellectual progress.

At least five types of studies are classified as being components of comparative politics. We can question whether some of these studies are truly 'comparative', given that they either focus on a single country other than that of the scholar doing the study or that they are so general that individual countries get lost. All five types of research do, however, find themselves treated as part of comparative politics within the discipline. These five types are:

(1) Single country descriptions of politics in *X*, whatever *X* may be (examples are Anderson, 1982; Fitzmaurice, 1981; Rose, 1989; Lal, 1986; Ramage, 1995);
(2) Analyses of similar processes and institutions in a limited number of countries, selected (one expects) for analytic reasons (Bendix, 1964; Moore, 1966; Skocpol, 1979; Lipset and Rokkan, 1967; Tilly, 1975; 1993; Collier and Collier, 1991);
(3) Studies developing typologies or other forms of classification schemes for countries or subnational units, using the typologies both to compare groups of countries and to reveal something about the internal politics of each political system (Lijphart, 1990; Elazar, 1987; Bebler and Seroka, 1990);
(4) Statistical or descriptive analyses of data from a subset of the world's countries, usually selected on geographical or developmental grounds, testing some hypothesis about the relationship of variables within that 'sample' of countries (Lange and Garrett, 1985; Ames, 1987; Kaase and Newton, 1995; Hydén and Bratton, 1992); and
(5) Statistical analyses of all countries of the world attempting to develop patterns and/or test relationships across the entire range of political systems (Banks and Textor, 1963; Banks, 1971; Rummel, 1972; 1979; Russett, 1964; Sullivan, 1996).

Although these are very different types of research exercises, requiring a variety of different research skills (both methodological and theoretical), they all claim to be viable components of comparative politics. Further, they all can claim rightfully to make some significant contributions to the development of that field of enquiry. There is often a tendency of scholars to select one mode of enquiry and defend it as the best viable approach to enquiry, or even the only one, but at least for this one social science a great deal is to be gained from each research strategy. Were there time and money enough, the optimal strategy would appear to be to move back and forth between large-scale statistical studies and the more descriptive analysis of individual countries, refining concepts and theories as one goes. Unfortunately, one individual scholar rarely has the skills necessary to do all those things, so that this iterative research agenda must be shared, often in an extremely uncoordinated and haphazard manner.

Single Country Studies

The single country case-study has perhaps the least claim to advancing the scientific status of comparative politics, although it is also perhaps the most common form of analysis in the discipline. The obvious weakness of this approach is that it is not really comparative, but rather is the explication of politics 'someplace else'. As Sartori (1991: 243) has said:

> a scholar who studies only American presidents is an Americanist, whereas a scholar who studies only French presidents is a comparativist. Do not ask me how this makes sense – it does not. The fact remains that a field called comparative politics is densely populated by non-comparativists, by scholars who have no interest, no notion, no training comparing.

Despite Sartori's negative views, comparative politics conventionally has been dominated by studies of politics 'somewhere else'. There are now any number of books labelled 'Politics in Country *X*'; an analysis of the electronic card catalogue at my university library revealed 371 separate books with such a title, or 'The Government and Politics of Country *X*', covering over fifty different countries, and even more monographs and case studies of particular periods of time, events, and/or institutions in a particular country. In almost every country, the politics of that country is taught as the basic class in political science, with comparative politics being politics occurring everywhere else – even if it only a single country. Governments of the United States and UK are rarely taught as components of comparative analysis in their home country, even though each is just another example of an industrialised democracy that needs to be understood comparatively.

Limitations of language, education and funding tend to force scholarship in the direction of the single country monograph, and, despite some almost inherent weaknesses, this style of research does make numerous important contributions. In the first place, these individual country volumes can be the grist for the mill for scholars more interested in direct comparison and theory. This is especially true if a series of books is written with a common theoretical framework in mind, or if any one country study is written in a self-consciously theoretical manner by itself. The series of country study books appearing in the 1960s and 1970s under the general editorship of Gabriel Almond and Lucien Pye provides a good example of the possibility of implicit comparison through a series of single country studies. These books included Rose (1989), Ehrmann (1992), Edinger (1977), Barghoorn and Remington (1986) and Kothari (1970). They were later compiled into Almond *et al.* (1973). Another example of a coherent series of books would be that on 'policy and politics' in a variety of developed political systems, including Ashford (1981, 1982), Heclo and Madsen (1987), and Tuohy (1992).

A second possible virtue of the single case-study is to explicate a concept that appears to be particularly evident in one national setting and to use the country study to develop that concept. For example, the Netherlands is (or at least was) an archetypical case of consociationalism. Lijphart's (1975a) analysis of Dutch politics provided a great deal of general information not only concerning that country, but also in particular about the Dutch approach to managing deep-seated social cleavages. That concept has since been applied, intellectually if not practically, to other political systems (see p. 94). Further, the consociational concept has been applied to the Netherlands several additional times to assess the degree of political change within that system (Mierlo, 1986; Toonen, 1996). Concept-defining studies such as Lijphart's may engender unwise conceptual stretching in the future (see pp. 86–93), but they also help fill the conceptual storehouse of comparative politics.

Another useful example of the concept-defining study would be Robert Putnam *et al.*'s work on Italy (1993) and the need for a 'social capital' or 'social infrastructure' in society for successful democracy. Putnam's research monitored the development of social capital – meaning membership in organisations of all sorts – across time and across different regions of Italy, finding that those regions without adequate 'social capital' found it difficult to have viable democratic institutions. This concept has proved to be useful well outside the boundaries of that one system. Putnam has used it to identify patterns of social and political behaviour in the United States that he finds potentially damaging to democracy there (Putnam, 1993). Similar analysis of social capital and the social basis of democracy has also been done for other European countries (Perez-Diaz, 1994), the United States (Putnam, 1995) and for some African countries (Gyimah-Boadi, 1996). The concept of social capital may generate some difficult empirical and theoretical questions (Tarrow, 1996), but it has proven to be useful for comparative political analysis.

Process and Institution Studies

Another long and honourable strand of comparative political analysis is to select a small number of instances of a process or an institution that appear similar (or at least appear 'comparable') in some important ways and then use those instances to illuminate the nature of either the process or the institution itself, or the politics of the countries within which it occurs. In practice, these case studies are often capable of saying a good deal about the process, as well as a great deal about the countries. Further, time becomes an important element of the analysis, pointing to additional possibilities of comparisons across time as well as across political systems.

The purpose of such studies is somewhat different from that of the whole-system comparisons already discussed. It is not to describe and (implicitly) compare whole systems, but rather to develop lower-level comparisons of a particular institution or political process. To some extent, these institutions and processes are assumed to be almost independent of the setting within which they occur. Thus, these scholars are employing comparative data to develop a theory (implicit or explicit) of aspect of political life. For example, the monumental historical studies mentioned above tend to develop theories of fundamental social revolution (Skocpol, 1979; Heper, 1991), or of the development of the welfare state (Flora and Heidenheimer, 1981), or of tax policy (Webber and Wildavsky, 1987). The particular settings within which these events occur are generally less important than the nature of the events themselves in the development of those theories.

Although less grand than the historical studies of social development, the comparative analysis of public policy formulation and implementation would be a clear case of applying a process model across a range of countries. Much public policy analysis in political science uses a process model, beginning with agenda-setting and ending with evaluation and feedback (Jones, 1984; Peters, 1994b). This model posits that the same stages will have to occur in all political systems, so that comparison can be made on just how the process unfolds in different settings. This process model is therefore very similar to the functionalist theories of politics (Almond and Coleman, 1960; Almond and Powell, 1966 – see Key Text 1.1). This approach argued that there were certain requisite functions that all political systems had to perform, and comparison therefore was focused on how this took place. Although the heyday of functionalist analysis was during the 1960s, much of its logic remains operative, albeit disguised, in contemporary thinking about governing.

Comparative studies of institutions are somewhat different, in that they often have a discernible functionalist bias built into them. Legislatures must legislate, and therefore they will tend to perform approximately the same tasks, although perhaps in markedly different ways. This presumed commonality of activity may, however, be overstated. Polsby (1975), for example, distinguishes 'transformative' legislatures from 'arena' legislatures. The former, most notably the Congress of the United States, actually make independent judgments about proposed legislation, and frequently impose significant transformations on the intentions of the political executive. Arena legislatures, on the other hand, are merely fora within which the constitutional formalities necessary for approval of the wishes of the executive take place – the British Parliament is a prime example (but see Norton, 1993). Legislative bodies of both these types of do legislate in some sense of the term, but are they really engaged in the same activity? The answer to that question may depend upon whether the researcher is interested in legislatures as institutions, or is more interested in the process of policy-making.

Typology Formation

A third way of approaching comparative politics is to develop classification schemes and/or typologies of countries, or perhaps of different components of the political system. For example, Lijphart (1968) attempted to classify democratic political systems according to the degree of fragmentation of their élites and the fragmentation of the mass political culture. This cross-classification (Figure 1.1) yielded four categories of democratic political systems. Lijphart later

Key Text 1.1 Gabriel Almond and Bingham Powell, and Structural Functionalism

One of the dominant approaches to comparative politics during the 1960s and into the 1970s was 'structural-functionalism'. This approach was largely borrowed form anthropology and sociology. The basic premise was that all societies (or polities in our case) had certain core functions that they had to perform. Polities could then be compared on the basis of how they performed those functions and what structures (institutions) they used to perform them.

The principal virtue of structural-functionalism was that it could be used to compare any political systems from the most primitive to the most advanced. All these political systems had to perform certain functions – things such as 'interest articulation', 'rule-adjudication' and 'political communication' in the Almond and Powell version of the approach. The acceptance and elaboration of this approach was in part a response to the critique of traditional comparative politics that it was culture bound and built entirely upon the experiences of wealthy European and North American societies.

Gabriel Almond had sketched the structural–functional approach to politics in his earlier book (1960) with James Coleman, but the Almond and Powell volume elaborated the approach. It added another category of comparison – capabilities such as extraction and regulation – that focused on the policy-making role of government. The Almond and Powell version of structural-functionalism also made the developmental aspects of the model clearer. In particular, they argued that three basic variables – cultural secularisation, institutional differentiation, and xxxx – could be used to measure the degree of political development.

The critiques of this approach have been numerous. It has been argued that Western cultural and political values were smuggled into a presumably value-free model of political development. It was also argued that by being so general this and similar approaches to comparison said nothing about the way in which politics actually worked in any real country. To the critics the analytic language merely got in the way of meaningful comparison rather than aiding in the process. Finally, the model told the person using it little or nothing about the way in which inputs were converted into outputs. The institutions of government such as legislatures and bureaucracies were merely parts of a 'black box' that would remain largely unopened until the resurgence of institutional analysis. Still, for an era in which there were massive changes occurring in African and Asian countries this general model did a great service.

FIGURE 1.1
Types of democratic systems

		Political elite	
		Competitive	*Coalescent*
Political culture and society	*Homogeneous*	Centripetal (United Kingdom)	Depoliticised (Sweden)
	Fragmented	Centrifugal (Italy)	Consociational (Netherlands)

Source: Derived from Lijphart (1968).

(1984) compared democratic systems using the rubric of consensual and majoritarian political systems. Majoritarian systems are those of the Westminster type, in which a single party is usually able to gain control of government, and in which politics is conducted in an adversarial manner. Consensus democracies, on the other hand, tend to have coalition governments, in which the style is cooperative and consensual, so that policies might vary less than in adversarial regimes.

Typologies imply the interaction of two or more variables to produce a classification system. For example, Lijphart's typology of democratic systems was more than a simple classification system. It required that each political system be classified on two variables, and that they then be placed in a group based on their scores on those two variables. Thus, a typology is the beginning of a theory about the subject matter used to classify the cases. It argues that there are at least two variables that are crucial for understanding the phenomenon being studied, and that it is possible to derive useful measures of those variables for purposes of classification. Further, the typology argues that a second, more useful, order of classification can emerge from integrating the first. The degrees of homogeneity of élites and masses may be interesting in themselves, but they become much more useful for explanatory and theoretical purposes when they are combined.

Other forms of classification (taxonomies) are not so elaborate, but rather may be only simple listings of the major types in a class. Taxonomies assume a scheme that uses variables to classify the cases (taxa), although unlike typologies these do not involve the interaction of the variables. For example, Sartori (1966) argued that political party systems in Western Europe fell into one of three categories: two-party, moderate multi-party, and extreme multi-party. Similarly, Peters (1995a) has argued that the relationships between bureaucracies and interest groups around the world can be seen as falling into four basic classifications: legitimate, clientela, parantela and illegitimate. Berg-Schlosser (1984) provided a classification of African political systems based on a number of political variables. He then uses this classification scheme (Table 1.1) to predict the economic and political performance of these systems, finding that more democratic regimes perform rather well in comparison with others. These various classification systems help to explain the behaviour of political systems, or parts of systems, and their capacity to perform their tasks of governing. Perhaps the extreme version of the taxonomic approach to comparison is to create a description of single type of political system in which the scholar is interested and then to use a simple dichotomy for analysis: a case is either '*X*' or 'non-*X*'. This method may be seen as a derivative of the methodology of 'ideal types' advocated by Max Weber (Gerth and Mills, 1958: 59–61) and used by him in studying religion, bureaucracy and modernisation. For example, O'Donnell (1978) developed the concept of 'bureaucratic authoritarianism' to describe the politics of major Latin American political systems. This concept was then used to analyse politics in the various countries in the region, and the dynamics of their development by comparing their actual performance with the conceptual model. This concept did prove useful for describing the Latin American cases, but has not been able to travel well outside that region (Bunce, 1995: 88–9).

TABLE 1.1

Classification of African political systems (early 1980s)

Polyarchic	Botswana, Djibouti, Mauritius, Gambia, Kenya, Lesotho, Nigeria, Senegal, Uganda, Zimbabwe
Socialist	Angola, Cape Verde, Congo (Brazzaville), Guinea, Mozambique, São Tome, Tanzania, Zambia
Authoritarian	Cameroon, Gabon, Ivory Coast, Malawi, Swaziland
Praetorian	Benin, Burundi, Central African Republic, Chad, Comoros, Equitorial Guinea, Ethiopia, Ghana, Guinea-Bissau, Liberia, Madagascar, Mali, Mauritania, Nigeria, Rwanda, Seychelles, Sierra Leone, Somalia, Upper Volta, Zaïre

Source: Berg-Schlosser (1984).

Regional Statistical Analyses

A fourth variety of comparative analysis encountered in the literature is the statistical study of a selected group of countries, usually the population of countries within a particular region. The purpose of this approach to analysis is to test some proposition about politics within that region. The goal is usually to make a generalisation only about that one region, and, if successful there to extend that analysis later to be a proposition about politics more generally. As with the single country study mentioned above, a particular region may be selected as the trial locus for analysis because the traits in question are manifested most clearly there.

Take, for example, the huge number of studies that have been undertaken concerning the welfare state in Western Europe (for example, Hicks and Swank, 1992; Esping-Anderson, 1990 – see Key Text 10.1; 1996; Leibfried and Pierson, 1995). These studies tend to examine the political and economic roots of the welfare state in these countries, as well as looking at patterns of expansion or contraction of public expenditures across time. Some scholars, for example, Esping-Anderson, may attempt to differentiate groups of countries within the broader European area, although most attempt to derive generalisations about the entire group of countries (see Castles and Mitchell, 1993). Clearly, the welfare state came into full flower in Western Europe and the nature of its politics and economics may be seen most clearly there.

Could, however, the same sets of variables that influenced development of social programmes in Europe also have influenced their development in North America (Kudrle and Marmor, 1981), or in Latin America, which in some ways was also an innovator in the welfare state (Rosenberg, 1976)? Thus, valuable as these studies may be for the analysis of a single region, their utility could be extended to creating more general theories about subsets of the political world, but defined in functional as opposed to geographical terms.

One problem that these regional studies present is that they tend to encourage conceptual stretching (see below, pp. 86–93), once they are extended beyond the original area of enquiry. The welfare state has a particular conceptual meaning for Europeans, and perhaps for Canadians, but the interpretation of that term may be substantially different in the United States. This difference may not be too much of a problem if we only examine aggregate data – for example, levels of public expenditure for social programmes – but may become severe if we attempt to understand comparative survey data on attitudes towards taxing and spending (see the 'beliefs in government' studies, for example, Borre and Scarborough, 1995). Even within Europe, it is not always certain that some fundamental political and social terms are interpreted the same way, especially between Northern and Southern Europe (Lijphart, 1990). Thus, while continents appear homogeneous on the map, and university departments often organise their teaching of politics in that way, there may be sufficient variation in political life to make comparative research difficult and perhaps even misleading.

Another way to say that this approach (and the next) encounter conceptual stretching is to say that they trade complexity for an attempt to generalise. The first two approaches to comparison tended to be very rich in complexity, and were able to deal with the nuances of the political systems in which they were working. In the third approach, the trade-off began to be evident. The creation of typologies and ideal types tends to collapse subtle differences among countries into simple dichotomies. This is an example of Sartori's (1990) 'degreeism', in which variables that are inherently continua are collapsed into dichotomies by selecting an arbitrary point along the dimension as a threshold value (see below, pp. 103–5). As we move into the regional and then global studies, the purpose of analysis becomes statistical hypothesis-testing, and the real and important differences among countries may be manifested only when the data from particular countries appear as 'outliers' in the distribution of residuals of a regression equation. If the case is clearly deviant, then the theory almost certainly provides no means of explaining it, and the researcher usually must resort to some variables not included in the theory, often something amorphous, such as 'political culture'.

Global Statistical Studies

The final option for comparative analysis that we will discuss is the global statistical study. This does for the entire population of countries what the regional studies do for a subset. They measure political and socio-economic variables and then apply statistical tests to the relationships among those factors. Some of the early instances of this style of research remain classics in the field. Perhaps the best example was *A Cross-Polity Survey* by Banks and Textor (1963), which attempted to classify all the (then) countries of the world on a number of political variables, and then created huge correlation matrices linking all those variables. A similar effort, the *World Handbook of Political and Social Indicators* (Russett, 1964; Taylor and Hudson, 1972), developed by the Yale Political Data Program, did much the same thing but used primarily aggregate, interval-level data as opposed to the nominal data of the *A Cross-Polity Survey.* Rudolph Rummel (1972; 1979) also engaged in a huge exercise in data collection, the *Dimensions of Nations* Project, although much of the emphasis was on the international behaviour (for example, war and other acts of aggression) of the countries rather than their domestic politics. More recently, Wallerstein (1980; Hopkins and Wallerstein, 1980) has taken a more radical approach, arguing that in essence the *N* of comparative politics is one – a single world system. Despite that claim, his work still tends to use nation-states as a unit of analysis, albeit within the context of a dominant world system.

These statistical exercises are about as far removed intellectually from the single country monographic study as they can be, but they still are often described as comparative political studies. The strategy of these excursions into data analysis was to accumulate as much data as possible, and then to utilise those data to identify some generic truths about politics across the entire range of countries, usually at a single point in time. For example, the *World Handbook* did include substantial amounts of time-series data on socio-economic variables, although somewhat less data on political variables. These studies performed some very important functions for comparative research in their time. For example, they pointed out that it was possible to apply the same ideas and measurements to the developing countries of Africa, Asia and Latin America as could be applied to Western Europe and North America. Perhaps even more basically, these studies attempted to demonstrate that it was possible to measure empirically some of the important aspects of government that had previously been left largely to normative analysis, for example, democracy (see also Cnudde and Neubauer, 1969; Bollen, 1980; 1990).

This style of research did make its contributions, but it also revealed a number of serious deficiencies. One of these is the measurement problem mentioned above in reference to regional studies (see below, pp. 93–4). Almost by definition, these global studies involve substantial conceptual stretching. It is difficult for any empirical measure of a concept such as 'democracy' to travel well across a range of cultures with a wide range of political and social histories. Even aggregate data may be somewhat suspect in these circumstances. For example, a measure such as gross national product may not tap adequately economic activity in any country with a large subsistence economy and a great deal of household production. Even in highly industrialised countries, there is a great deal of household production, but if it occurs at relatively equal levels across these countries then the measurement is not confounded seriously. When comparing these countries with very poor countries, however, there is marked measurement error. In addition, aggregate statistics can have their own social and cultural elements that may reduce their comparability across countries (Desrosieres, 1996). A concept such as unemployment, for example, appears to be directly comparable across systems, but may contain strong national biases in measurement (Moore and Richardson, 1989).

Thus, these research efforts may have produced a number of significant correlations statistically, but it is not always very clear what the substantive importance of these efforts was. Such problems of interpretation are even more true given that they have tended to encourage relatively mindless, atheoretical exercises in correlating all variables with all other variables, in the knowledge that there probably would almost certainly be some significant correlations. Rummel's use of factor analysis tended to carry this approach to higher levels of statistics, but not always a higher level of substance.

Summary

From the above discussion, it may appear that comparative politics is a hopeless enterprise. Each of the approaches considered above appears filled with flaws and insurmountable intellectual objections. On the one hand, that apparent hopelessness is very real, but yet it is no reason not to carry on doing comparative politics. Any approach or method we may select for conducting our research will have some real and important problems. However, these weaknesses do not mean that we should not choose it. What they *do* mean is that we need to be cognizant of the strengths and weaknesses of each candidate method and then to be wary of the results our analysis may give us. If we are aware of the inherent flaws of each method, we can compensate for those problems in interpretation, if not directly in the analysis.

The difficulties of each of these methods also points to the possibility and desirability of 'triangulation', or the use of multiple methods and approaches (Webb *et al.*, 1967; Roth, 1987) for research. For example, if a country is a deviant case on a statistical distribution, then the obvious comparative question is, Why are they? A researcher may then want to engage in a more detailed analysis of the one case, and in so doing not only illuminate that one case, but also illuminate and expand the theory being tested through statistical analysis. Unfortunately, relatively few researchers bother to extend their analysis in this direction. Most statistical researchers simply dismiss the outliers as deviant cases, so long as the overall results are statistically significant. At most, the outliers may receive a sentence or two. Likewise, the case-study expert on one country or a limited number of countries may never know whether his or her case is an outlier or not, because of not thinking in those statistical terms.

The Content of Comparisons

Up to this point, we have been looking at the various methodological approaches to comparative analysis. We should also point out that, despite its centrality in the field, cross-national analysis is not the only way in which to perform comparative political analysis. The logic of a comparative analysis is almost always exactly the same, regardless of what the geographical or temporal focus of the comparison may be. Each of the different possible foci and loci of analysis will, however, impose some costs and provide some benefits for the research exercise. The researcher must determine what advantages, in terms of testing or developing theory, can be gained by using one or another of the various sites and styles of comparison. He or she must also determine what are the costs, in terms of possible threats to validity, that are associated with each style of research.

Although we usually think primarily of cross-national comparisons – the whole system bias described by Lijphart (1975b: 166) comparative analysis across subnational units within a single nation-state is also a fruitful form of political analysis. Indeed, if we are interested in employing comparative analysis for the purposes of testing political theory then in many ways this form of analysis has even greater potential than has the cross-national one. The principal virtue of analysis across subnational governments is that it holds constant, or minimises, a number of factors that might otherwise confound it. For example, V. O. Key's classic analysis (1949) of politics in the Southern states of the United States points out how holding a number of factors constant enables the researcher to understand better the subtle differences in these political systems, even at a more descriptive level.

The comparative state policy literature (Dye, 1966; Sharkansky, 1968; Brace, 1993) further demonstrates how this locus of analysis enables researchers to uncover important relationships among variables that might not be possible at the national level. This style of comparative policy research has been emulated in other countries with both federal (Fried, 1976) and non-federal systems (Alt, 1971).

It would be easy to assume that the cultural and social factors that may confound comparative analysis can be eliminated in an analysis of units within a single nation-state. That is not necessarily true. For example, the states within the United States share many cultural and socio-economic features, but also have distinctive political histories and cultures that may influence policy choices and their internal politics (Elazar, 1987; Kincaid, 1990). Further, even though there may be relatively limited variance in some factors, in contrast to a comparison between the United States and, for example, Upper Volta, there may still be significant variance. That is, in a way, an opportunity, however, given that the greater commonality among the states may provide an opportunity for more precise and sensitive forms of measurement than would be possible in cross-national comparisons.

Cross-Time Comparisons

In addition to comparisons across geographical units, comparison can also be made within the same political unit across time. Even more than with the case of subnational units within a single country, this strategy holds (relatively) constant the cultural and social factors that may confound analysis of political relationships. Certainly, social and cultural patterns within a political system may change gradually across time, but time also can be included as one component of the analysis. This contextual change can be controlled for statistically (Achen and Shively, 1995), and also can be controlled for in qualitative research through a thorough understanding of the case. Most forms of comparative analysis focus on the characteristics describing political units and the relationships that exist among variables measured within those units. The cross-time method, however, looks at relationships among variables within individual units across time.

To the extent that cross-system comparisons are made with time-series analysis, those comparisons would be made across the patterns that are manifested within individual countries across time. If statistical analysis of developmental patterns is done within countries, the outcomes of that analysis, such as the degree of fit with the statistical model, or the slope of the regression line (as a measure of effect) could be compared. Diagnostics might also be used to determine if there had been significant changes in the relationships of variables across time. Less quantitative analysis might examine the apparent impact of different factors – independent variables – at different stages of the development process. This mode of analysis can establish some less formal sense of changing relationships among variables across time.

Analysis across time remains, for the most part, underutilised in political science. This is often a function of inadequate time-series data for other than a few variables, for example, voting or public expenditure. While governments have collected a great deal of economic data across time, they have been less helpful to the political science researcher, and methods such as survey research tend to have been poor at preserving time-series on all but a few key variables. It is important to note, however, that less statistical time-series analysis is making a major impact, in the hands of the 'historical institutionalists' (Thelen *et al.*, 1992; Pierson, 1996) and their considerations of the enduring impact of policy and institutional choices.

There are several ways to combine the cross-national and the cross-temporal modes of analysis. In particular, the pooled time-series approach to statistical analysis (Stimson, 1985; Alvarez, Garrett and Lange, 1991) includes data from a number of countries across a significant period of time. This method provides several benefits for comparative analysis, one of the most important of them being simply expanding the number of observations, thereby improving the capacity of researchers to make reliable statistical estimations. In addition, pooled time-series permits the analyst to test directly whether the principal source of variance is the country or some other factor. It may be that relationships of variables within countries are more significant in explaining outcomes than the differences across countries. The same factors that create the benefits for comparative analysis also create some statistical problems (see Key Text 6.1) but this still offers a means of expanding the reach of comparative analysis.

Finally, we come to the question of whether all comparisons involving time need to use exactly the same slices of chronological time. The most appropriate comparisons for theoretical development may be made with events and structures occurring in different time periods, albeit periods that are similar in their basic characteristics. For example, the contemporary problems of modernisation and democratisation in the countries of Eastern and Central Europe (Agh, 1994; Roskin, 1991; Rose, 1992) are functionally equivalent to the problems of Western Europe in the late nineteenth century, or to immediately post-colonial Africa and Asia. The researcher will have to establish the relevant criteria for comparability, and then attempt to extract the theoretical and substantive meaning from the comparison.

Summary

To be effective in developing theory, and in being able to make statements about structures larger than an individual or the small group, the social sciences must be comparative. We have been aware of this truism for some time, and a great deal of good comparative analysis has been available in all the social sciences, but especially in political science. Much of that comparative analysis has however been done, using more intuition about the logic of comparison than any self-conscious effort to compare effectively and efficiently. This volume is intended to identify the questions that a comparativist should at least think about before embarking on data collection and analysis, whether the data to be used are quantitative or qualitative. It also will discuss some of the techniques (in a non-technical manner) available to the researcher and what they can, and cannot, add to the study of comparative politics.

Although there is some agreement that comparative politics is essential to the development of the discipline, there is less agreement over what constitutes acceptable versions of this approach. Definitions of 'good research' are largely a function of who is being asked, and in what context. The traditional view of comparative politics emphasised the description of one or a limited number of political systems, and a place certainly remains in the discipline for that such research. More contemporary research is often more directly comparative, involving a number of countries, and uses a variety of quantitative techniques in place of the more detailed description common in traditional analysis. Both of these styles have their place, and increasingly the discipline is attempting to reconcile the research traditions and the research methods of both. Still, there are adherents of each who will argue for exclusivity rather than a more catholic approach.

As we assess the quality of comparative research, we must remember that 'quality' is to some degree a function of the goals being pursued by the researcher. One purpose of comparative analysis is to verify propositions, and to demonstrate that certain relationships among variables hold true in a wide variety of settings; the intention here is to demonstrate similarity and consistency. On the other hand, good comparative research, and indeed most comparative research, is concerned with differences and demonstrating that what occurs in one setting most certainly does not occur in another. This latter strategy of differentiation may appear to be only an old-fashioned description in new clothing. It can be as 'scientific' as the strategy of finding similarities, but merely looks for different types of propositions and different types of variables.

While there will be a number of questions raised, the answer to most of them is, 'It depends'. There is no perfect way to conduct comparative analysis, only strategies that are better or worse under given circumstances. Furthermore, almost any choice of a research strategy involves sacrificing some virtues in order to achieve more of others. What is perhaps most important, therefore, is to understand fully what values are being traded for what others in choosing any analytic approach. The researcher can then know where the analysis is likely to be weak, and where the results have to be regarded with even greater scepticism than is truly necessary for all social science research. Scepticism is almost always justified, but careful consideration of the probable impacts of the tools used for analysis helps to make the scepticism useful.

The one thing that should be universal in studying comparative politics, whether in one country or in many, and whether using statistical or qualitative methods, is a conscious attention to explanation and research design. What is the thing the researcher wants to explain – what is the 'dependent variable'? When the problem is clear, the question then becomes, What is the presumed 'cause' of the phenomenon in question? It is better for the development of the discipline of political science if that presumed cause is related to some broader theoretical concerns, but there may be interesting research in which that initial connection is tenuous at best. Finally, what evidence is needed to 'prove' the connection between cause and effect, and how can that evidence be mustered? How can we be as sure as possible about the quality of our evidence? These rather straightforward research questions are the foundations of research design, just as they might be the focus of historiography in a neighbouring discipline. This book is intended to help the reader answer these questions, although the style of answering them may be different from those usually encountered in many parts of the discipline.

2

The Logic of Comparison

We have already argued in brief that the logic of comparative analysis is different from the logic of other forms of social science research, especially from the statistical method that tends to dominate social research. This difference is evident in terms of the tendency of the unit of analysis for statistical research to be the individual, as opposed to the collectivity more commonly encountered in comparative research. It is seen more importantly in terms of the manner in which the two methods deal with the crucial question of controlling sources of extraneous variance. In the complex social world, there are any number of factors associated with the variance observed in any number of other variables. Finding significant statistical correlations among those factors is rarely a problem for social researchers. What is more of a problem is determining whether those correlations are empirically and theoretically meaningful; that is, can we say confidently that *X* causes *Y*, or whether they are merely the product of other, unmeasured, variables affecting the variables actually measured. In other words, the real difficulty for the social sciences is making convincing statements about the causation of political phenomena, given the complexity of interactions among the whole range of social phenomena and the number of external sources of variance.

Over a century and a half ago, John Stuart Mill (1846) was beginning to grapple with some of the same issues, although he did not call it comparative politics. Instead, he was concerned with the fundamental logical and philosophical problem of proving causation, an intellectual problem that persists to this day (Blalock, 1964; Asher, 1983; King *et al.*, 1994: 75–114). Many social scientists remain very sceptical about any claims of causation, believing that the complexity of the issues and the many interactions among variables make claims of causation suspect at best. In his analysis of causation, Mill presented three conditions that could be satisfied in order to demonstrate a causal connection between 'variables':

(1) *The Method of Agreement* To paraphrase Mill, this method argues that, if the several observations of the phenomenon under investigation (dependent variable) have only one of several possible causal circumstances in common, then the circumstance in which all the instances agree is the cause of the phenomenon.
(2) *The Method of Difference* Again paraphrasing Mill, this is the argument that, if there is an occurrence and a non-occurrence of a phenomenon (the dependent variable), and the circumstances in which these are observed (independent variables) are the same in all circumstances save one, then that one is the cause of the occurrence.
(3) *The Method of Concomitant Variation* If two variables tend to vary in the same pattern, then they are somehow linked, either causally or through some other pattern of connection (linked to some third variable).

These three methods for coping with the problem of causation were devised long before contemporary social science, and indeed Mill did not consider that his methods were appropriate for the social sciences. He (like many scholars now) believed that the complexity of the causal relationships encountered in social enquiry limited the possibility of discovering meaningful causal relations. Despite Mill's own cautions, his three approaches to solving the problem of causation will be echoed rather strongly in some of the research methods discussed later in the book (see Chapter 9), as well as in the discussion of fundamental problems of comparative analysis in this chapter.

The basic problem for Mill, as well as for the contemporary social researcher, is to isolate, as far as possible, a factor or a limited number of factors that appear to produce (or at least are strongly associated with) changes in the dependent variable. This problem is, in turn, a problem of identifying possible ways to exclude the numerous possible confounding factors in the relationship between variables a problem of the greatest theoretical importance. The identification of the confounding influences is also in part a function of having adequate theoretical guidance about where to look for the other variables (see Chapter 5). There are any number of possible causes for changes in political conditions – the secret is to use theory to identify the most likely sources of confounding variance.

Comparative Research Design

A more contemporary approach to the same problem addressed by Mill can be expressed in terms of the variance observed in the dependent variable in comparative research. The fundamental litany for social research, which will keep appearing in the course of this volume, is:

Maximise experimental variance, minimise error variance, and control extraneous variance.

This is a relatively easy phrase to repeat, but a substantially more difficult task to implement in comparative research designs. In each dependent variable that we utilise for comparative analysis, there is always some of each of these three types of variance – the question is how much. Empirically, it may be impossible to parcel out variance into these three categories. This impossibility is true, because of the numerous possible sources of extraneous variance, and the numerous sources of error in any measurement, and the associated difficulty in knowing when any particular observation is affected by error. Despite the impossibility of knowing how to attribute all the observed variance, the researcher must still examine his or her methods with this basic question of research design in mind.

Experimental variance is the observed differences or changes in the dependent variable that are a function of the independent variables identified as central to the analysis. For social-scientific analysis, even research of a qualitative nature, there must be a dependent variable – something we are attempting to explain. In some research situations, the dependent variable may be a simple dichotomy – revolutions occur or they do not (Wickham-Crowley, 1991), or people vote or they do not (Butler *et al.*, 1981). In other cases, the dependent variable may be a range of responses of governments to changing economic fortunes (Gourevitch, 1986). In others, it may be a continuous variable, such as per capita expenditures for social welfare in a range of countries (Hicks and Swank, 1992; Castles and Mitchell,

1993) that appears much more like what we usually think of as a variable. For qualitative case studies, the dependent variable may be changes in observed configurations of political power, or the nature of the decisions taken by political élites, with those differences often being very subtle.

Whatever the nature of variable in the research, the investigator is attempting to ensure that two characteristics exist for that dependent variable. One is to be certain that it does vary. Some published political science research does not, in fact, utilise a dependent variable that varies – at least in the data collected for the purposes of the particular research. For example, a number of the recent studies of democratisation have examined only those cases that have democratised successfully, however that success is defined (Bova, 1991). There is always the assumption that the other end of the continuum was different, but that assumption was not really tested. It may be that the variables used to 'explain' successful democratisation may actually have roughly the same values for those countries that did not democratise successfully.

This practice of selecting cases on their values on the dependent variable has been argued to be one of the mortal sins that can afflict comparative research (King *et al.*, 1994), but like most sins it is one which is practised frequently. It appears to make sense to examine cases that satisfy some criterion of relevance, but in fact this simply eliminates crucial variance in the phenomenon to be explained. Even were relationships to be discovered between successful democratisation and any presumed independent variables, we would not know if they were any different from the relationships that might be found for unsuccessful democratisations, or for authoritarian regimes that did not attempt to democratise at all. These may simply be features of systems that have been authoritarian at one particular point in time. About the best result attainable using only cases with the same value on the dependent variable is to demonstrate that *some* independent variable appears to be a necessary condition for the occurrence of the dependent variable (Most and Starr, 1989: 49–51).

As well as varying, it is good to have dependent variables that vary a lot. While this issue may itself be largely a part of the general question of measurement (see Chapter 4), it is also a question for research design and case selection. If we want to develop robust theoretical statements that are meaningful across a range of different types of circumstances (and we certainly do) then it is wise to begin the research with that wide array of cases. Researchers would like to develop, for example, propositions that work not only for the wealthy industrialised world but also for at least the newly industrializing countries (NICs – Singapore, South Korea, Taiwan, and so on), and if possible for the less developed countries as well. Attempting to develop theories with a wide range of applicability is difficult (see pp. 117–26), but we should begin with this as a goal, and therefore be concerned in most research situations with selecting as wide a range of cases as possible. The 'as possible' in that sentence then raises the issue of the judgment of the researcher, and the existing knowledge about variance within the research environment. In the end, there may be no realistic substitute for a researcher's good judgment.

Minimising error variance is less of a problem for case selection. Error variance is that portion of the variance observed in the dependent variable that is a function of random occurrences and errors in measurement. It is the slip of the pen of the data recorder, or by the data entry technician, or sloppy fieldwork on the part of an interviewer, or a host of other occurrences that can produce data points that are just inaccurate. In addition, no measurement of a social phenomenon is a perfect indicator of that underlying characteristic, so a certain amount of measurement error is almost inevitable. For qualitative research, this error variance could result from faulty observations by the researcher, or the misinterpretation of behaviours in different cultural settings, or jet lag, or again a whole range of things that can produce inaccurate observations.

Statistically, error variance is assumed to have a mean of zero, since it is random, and hence is assumed not to bias most statistical manipulations. The comparative researcher cannot afford to be so sanguine about the effects of error. If the cases are selected inappropriately, or the observations made by the researcher are faulty, there is little or no way to recover from the errors. Any results arising from research with such a poor design and execution are likely to be misleading, and therefore in some ways worse than no results at all. This potential for error simply argues for even greater attention to the selection of cases, and a very searching consideration of the comparisons that are planned at the beginning of the research. Further, there needs to be extremely careful weighing of the modes of data collection to ensure that they are indeed compatible in the range of societies within which they are being applied, and that the researcher is capable of doing the research in those countries.

Finally, there is the question of controlling extraneous variance. This is even more a concern for the comparative researcher, because this is systematic rather than random error. With extraneous variance, there are one or more variables that have a systematic relationship with the dependent variable, and perhaps also with the independent variables in an analysis. A researcher may find a relationship (statistically or less quantitatively) between X and Y. The problem is that there is a variable Z, that is systematically related to both X and Y. For example, we may find that democratic political systems spend more money on social welfare than do non-democratic regimes. The problem is that levels of economic development tend to be related to both democracy and welfare spending. Wealthier countries find it easier to maintain democracy and also to spend money for social programmes. Thus, assuming that democracy produces the welfare state may be only partially correct, if at all, but that relationship should rather be tested in the presence of a measure of the level of economic development.

In comparative research, there are an almost infinite number of opportunities for extraneous variance to creep into the analysis. Researchers tend to be focusing upon whole countries or on large subnational governments, all of which come as 'data bundles' containing a huge number of variables and characteristics. John Stuart Mill referred to the nation as a 'permanent cause', which no amount of additional variables would permit one to eliminate. When selecting a country for inclusion in a comparative investigation the researcher will receive all of those factors at once. Attempting to determine, therefore, whether the true 'cause' of the observed state of the dependent variable was the independent variables or not is extremely problematic. Statistically, at least, any variable that differentiates cases at the level of the country (or other geopolitical entity) is as likely to cause the outcome as any other variable having the same effect. In the conduct of comparative political research, minimising and/or detecting extraneous variance is a difficult problem, but not a totally insurmountable one.

One of the first defences against extraneous variance is theory. As Faure (1994: 313) points out, 'comparative method is therefore entirely dependent upon pre-existing criteria of relevance such as concepts, propositions and theories. These can be tested by the method but not discovered by the method.' If there is good theory in the research area then it should help the investigator determine whether the right control variables are being considered for a statistical analysis, or whether the appropriate factors are being considered in selecting the cases in a more strictly comparative design. Faure may have been too pessimistic given that, particularly with statistical research, finding inconsistent or unexpected results may lead to the search for concepts that explain those findings, but, in general, researchers are dependent upon existing conceptions of the political world.

This reliance on theory may be a catch-22 for the research – if the theory is already so good, why do we have to do the additional research? Further, can the theory ever be really tested if we assume that its guidance in the selection of cases and control variables is always reliable? Thus, if the research in question is to remain within the 'normal science' mode (Kuhn, 1970), and assume that there is a reliable body of accepted and verified evidence, then existing theory is a good guide. If the research is more exploratory, or is intended to challenge the existing theories, then the researcher is more alone in the hostile world of extraneous variance. Again, the discovery of 'anomalies' (Kuhn's word) may lead to the questioning and then improvement of the theory.

A second possible defence against the problems of extraneous variance is the use of time-series analysis, or using subnational units from within a single country. Neither of these approaches to analysis is a perfect prophylactic against extraneous variance, but each does provide some limited protection. Using time-series analysis will do two useful things in the detection and potential elimination of extraneous variance. One is to allow for the detection of systematic relationships other than those being tested through the analysis. Suppose, for example, a researcher is using time-series regression and finds a significant correlation between the dependent and independent variables. That is very nice, but it is only the beginning of the research exercise. There are a variety of statistical methods to test whether the residuals (the difference between the actual and the predicted values of each case) of the regression analysis are themselves systematically correlated across time. If there is significant autocorrelation then this systematic error in the relationship can be eliminated, either through removing it by means of statistical manipulations, or by identifying the variables causing the relationship and including them directly in the analysis.

Examining residuals in this manner is most commonly done in time-series analysis, but a similar logic could be used to identify systematic error in other types of regression analysis. If the observations can be ordered by any variable in addition to those included in the analysis, and if the residuals are then examined and are found to have a discernible pattern, then there is an obvious danger of extraneous variance contaminating the findings. For example, assume there were a regression study of German *Länder* that related per capita spending on education to income. The results of that analysis would yield residual errors, and these might be ordered by a potentially confounding factor, for example, the percentage of Roman Catholics in the population (Wilensky, 1974). Of course, a more useful statistical result could be achieved through including the presumed confounding variable as a part of the regression equation, and determining how it performs relative to others explanatory variables. The virtue of examining the residuals directly, however, is that they may present a pattern that can be discerned visually quite easily, but which would be more difficult to detect statistically. For example, a curvilinear pattern might not be as easy to detect statistically as with a simple plot of residuals. Further, noting where in the time-series change in the autocorrelation occurs may suggest the source of the extraneous variance.

Using subnational units from within a single country also may help eliminate some problems of extraneous variance. As has been argued above, these units will tend to be more similar on a number of social and cultural dimensions than will the countries in cross-national research. Therefore, some of the potential sources of extraneous variance will have been eliminated by selection of that locus of research. The problems with this strategy are, among others, its relevance and the potential for a false sense of security. First, many theoretical relationships in which a researcher in comparative politics is interested will not be relevant in a subnational context. For example, legitimacy is largely a question for national governments, not for subnational governments. In many governments, however, subnational units as a group may have more legitimacy than the national government. The increasing disdain for the federal government in the United States may reflect one notable case.

Also, assuming that the problem of extraneous variance is solved by using subnational units within a single country can lull the researcher into a false sense of security. There are often still significant differences among subnational units, even in countries that may appear to the casual observer to be reasonably homogeneous politically, for example, the differences between Sicily and Lombardy in Italy. Therefore, extraneous relationships may well be present in subnational data without the researcher being as sensitive to them as he or she might in a cross-national analysis, and therefore unnecessary error can creep into the analysis.

Research Design and Case Selection

In the best of all worlds, we might be able to do experimental research to test the propositions advanced in comparative politics. This is not however the best of all worlds, and there are a huge number of practical and ethical limitations on the capacity to experiment on people and governments. Therefore, we are left with attempting to find the best possible substitute for the rigourous controls provided by the experimental method. The questions of case selection and research design here are presented as the substitute we have for not being able to manipulate variables and randomise case assignments. Any non-experimental design is subject to a number of threats to validity (see below), and therefore political science researchers are in the position of merely attempting to do the best they can, given the circumstances, to prevent contamination of their research findings.

The above solutions for the problem of controlling extraneous research are ways of skirting the principal issue, which is how to cope with this problem through the more direct means of research design and case selection. We will talk about how many cases and the problem of small *N*s in the following chapter. Here, the principal question is not how many cases but which ones, although these issues cannot be separated entirely. Again, if we return to the fundamental differences between a comparative design and a statistical design, for the comparative design we must deal with the issues of controlling the sources of variance in the *ex ante* selection of the cases, rather than through *ex post* manipulations of data. Comparative design tends to rely upon fewer cases, but ones that are selected purposefully rather than at random.

The most basic question is, What makes cases comparable? (See Lijphart, 1975b). It is difficult to attend any academic meeting on comparative politics without hearing at least once the phrase, 'But those cases really are not comparable.' What does that statement mean, and what criteria should be used for determining if political systems are indeed comparable? Some social scientists (Kalleberg, 1966) have been enamoured of the criteria assumed to apply in the natural sciences, and have argued for very strict standards of comparability. In this view, cases could not compared adequately unless they shared a substantial number of common properties. This argument was an attack on the structural-functionalists, such as Gabriel Almond, who sought to include virtually all national cases beneath their comparative umbrella (Almond and Coleman, 1960; Almond and Powell, 1966). Structural-functionalism used concepts that were so broad that almost any political system could be compared, but sceptics wondered if that truly was comparison, or simply putting essentially incomparable cases into a common, and extremely nebulous, framework.

For the purposes of comparative politics, these criteria from the natural sciences (if indeed they are actually operative there) are almost certainly too restrictive (DeFelice, 1980). First, we may well want to compare cases that display a certain property with those that do not. What factors appear to separate democratic from non-democratic political systems (Lipset, 1959; Przeworski, 1995a, b), or countries that experience revolutions from those that do not (Wickham-Crowley, 1991)? Comparative politics involves the development of theories explaining behaviour within groups of countries that are essentially similar (see pp. 18–19). It is also about contrasting cases that are different in any number of ways. Either focus of comparison – explaining similarities or differences – can tell the researcher a great deal about the way in which governments function.

Most Similar and Most Different Systems

One crucial question in the selection of cases has been advanced by Adam Przeworski and Henry Teune (1970). This is the difference between most similar and most different systems designs. The question here is how to select the cases for comparative analysis, given that most comparative work does involve purposeful, rather than random, selection of the cases. Does one select cases that are apparently the most similar, or should the researcher attempt to select cases that are the most different? Further, like much of the other logic of comparative analysis, this logic can be applied to both quantitative and qualitative work. Theda Skocpol (1979: 40–1), for example, argued in essence for a most different systems design in her historical analysis of revolutions in France, Russia and China. These systems all generated major revolutions, albeit arising within apparently very different political economic and social systems. The question for Skocpol then became: What was sufficiently common among those systems to produce political events that were essentially similar?

Most similar systems design is the usual method that researchers in comparative politics undertake. They take a range of countries that appear to be similar in as many ways as possible in order to control for 'concomitant variation'. Wickham-Crowley (1991: 11) refers to this strategy as the 'parallel demonstration of theory'. Any number of studies have been done of the Anglo–American democracies (Alford, 1963; Aucoin, 1995; Sharman, 1994), for example, or of the Scandinavian countries (Elder *et al.*, 1988), or of the 'little tigers' in Asia (Evans, 1995; Alten, 1995; Clifford, 1994). The assumption is that extraneous variance questions have been dealt with by the selection of the cases. If a relationship between an independent variable *X* and a dependent variable *Y* is discovered, then the factors that are held constant through the selection of cases cannot be said to be alternative sources of that relationship. The most similar systems design has been argued (Faure, 1994) to be *the* comparative design, given that it is the design that attempts to manipulates the independent variables through case selection and to control extraneous variance by the same means.

Another important implication also arises from selection of the most similar systems designs. Any variable that does differentiate the systems is equally likely to be the source of the observed variation among them. There may be a hypothesis being tested, but there can be a large number of other competitors that would be equally plausible. Thus, any set of findings from this research design may be over-determined, with a large number of possible and plausible explanations, none of which can be ruled out. The most similar systems design may eliminate a number of possible explanations, but it also admits and fails to address a large number. Further, as argued above, the major problem in isolating extraneous variance may be that it is not possible to identify all the relevant factors that can produce differences among systems. If we look at the Anglo–American democracies (Table 2.1) – usually taken to constitute a reasonably homogeneous grouping of countries for analytic purposes – we can easily identify a number of social and economic factors that may have political relevance, all of which vary significantly. This does not even begin to get to the political factors (Table 2.2) which also vary in some significant ways.

The alternative strategy identified by Przeworski and Teune is the most different systems design. Here the logic of selecting cases, and indeed the whole logic of research, is exactly opposite that of the most similar systems design. In the first place, the most different design strategy begins with an assumption that the phenomenon being explained resides at a lower, subsystemic level. This means that often this strategy is looking at individual level behaviour, and attempting

TABLE 2.1

Economic characteristics of Anglo–American democracies

	Australia	*Canada*	*New Zealand*	*United Kingdom*	*United States*
Population (millions)	18.3	28.4	3.4	58.9	263.8
GNP per capita ($US)	17 720	18 600	16 320	17 760	25 810
Unemployment rate	8.5	9.5	6.3	8.7	5.5
Inflation rate[a]	1.8	1.6	2.3	2.4	2.9
Labour force in agriculture	6%	3%	10%	2%	3%
Tertiary education[b]	23	40	21	19	31

[a] Increase in consumer price index.
[b] Percentage of adult population with some form of tertiary education.

TABLE 2.2

Political characteristics of Anglo–American democracies

	Australia	*Canada*	*New Zealand*	*United Kingdom*	*United States*
Regime	Federal	Federal	Unitary	Unitary	Federal
Government	Parl	Parl	Parl	Parl	Pres
Party system	3 party	Multi-party	Multi-party	Multi-party	2-party
Turnout (most recent election)	96%	80%	83%	76%	53%
Partison control (February, 1998)	Right	Left	Coalition	Left	Left
Tax as percentage of GNP	29.9	36.1	37.0	34.1	27.6

to explain relationships among variables in samples of individuals. The most different systems design is attempting to determine how robust any relationship among these variables may be – does it hold up in a large number of varied places as if the observations were drawn from the same population of individuals? If it does, then we have some greater confidence that there is a true relationship, not one produced by some unmeasured third or fourth or fifth variables that exists in all relatively similar systems.

Further, the basic logic of the most different systems is falsification, very much in the tradition of Popperian philosophy of science (Popper, 1959). The basic argument is that science progresses by eliminating possible causes for observed phenomena rather than by finding positive relationships. As noted above, there is no shortage of positive correlations in the social sciences; what there is sometimes a shortage of is research that dismisses one or another plausible cause for that phenomenon. By setting up tests in a wide range of settings, the most different systems design attempts to do just that, while the most similar systems design can identify many possible causes but can eliminate none. This problem can be seen in part in a study of the Mediterranean democracies (Lijphart *et al.*, 1988). These systems were thought to be similar, yet once they were analysed differences in their transitions to democracy did emerge. Unfortunately, they were sufficiently similar for it to be impossible to identify effectively the root cause of those differences.

The logic of this approach is therefore fundamentally different from the most similar systems design. Whereas the most similar design dealt with control through careful selection of matched cases, this design deals with the control issue by virtually ignoring it. In the most different case, there may still be unmeasured extraneous sources of variance, but they will have to be very generic in order to survive in the range of social settings in which the research may be conducted. This strategy is, however, also dangerous, given that it can create yet another false sense of security in the strength of the findings. Indeed, the findings may be generalisable to a wide range of political and social systems, but the underlying causal process assumed to exist may not, even though it may appear from Berlin to Bombay to Bogotá.

The most similar and most different designs therefore do very different things. The former deals more directly with countries as a unit of analysis. It attempts to control for extraneous sources of variance by selecting cases in which this is not likely to be a major problem, although the researcher can rarely if ever know how big a problem really does exist. On the other hand, the most different design is not particularly interested in countries; this is more variable-based research, and is many ways closer to a statistical design than to the true comparative design. The principal task in this design is to find relationships among variables that can survive being transported across a range of very different countries. Given the statistical nature of the thinking here, controls for extraneous variance can be imposed by the usual statistical techniques.

The most similar and most different research design strategies appear very reasonable strategies in theory, but perhaps more difficult to implement in practice. Giesele De Meur and Dirk Berg-Schlosser (1996) have demonstrated more clearly how the approach to analysis could be used. They were interested in the success or failure of democratic regimes during the post-war periods in Europe. They first divided the countries into groups of similarity based on the persistence or breakdown of democracy, and then looked at the most different countries in each group, based on distance measures calculated from a large number of social and political variables. Thus, they could look at 'most different, similar outcome' cases to see what variables were in common to explain these outcomes.

Globalisation and Galton's Problem

A special case of the difficulties associated with controlling extraneous variance in research design arises from the increasing globalisation of culture and politics. We can travel around the world and eat the same food, drink the same soft drinks, and watch MTV or CNN (depending upon taste) almost anywhere. We must also be concerned if there are similar globalising trends in politics, so that what we observe in one country may not be the result of any indigenous political process, but rather may be a product of diffusion. Of course, the diffusion does not make the occurrence of a phenomenon any less real, but it does influence any analysis interested in developmental patterns, or the relationship between economic and social conditions and political phenomena. For example, if the familiar argument about the relationship of economic development and democratisation (Lipset, 1959) is advanced, then any contemporary findings may be contaminated by the diffusion of democratic ideals – forcibly through international organisations such as the United Nations and informally through the media and other social processes. This problem may be further confounded by the differential receptivity of some countries to diffused ideas, and the active search by some for alternatives to their existing policies and structures. The Japanese, for example, have been characterised as adept at borrowing constitutional ideas and then adapting them to their own circumstances.

Globalisation is simply a contemporary means of stating a very familiar problem in the social sciences, usually referred to as 'Galton's problem'. This is the methodological problem of sorting out diffusion from other causes of variance in social systems. Galton identified this problem in relationship to similarities among cultures he observed in the work of anthropologists, but it also arises in less exotic research situations. There are some cases in which observed patterns of social behaviour simply could not be the result of natural causes. The prevalence of presidential forms of government in Latin American countries throughout recent history is a clear product of diffusion from the 'Colossus to the North' (Thibaut, 1993), rather than a natural process of institutional selection. Similarly, the prevalence of Westminster-style systems in former British colonies is a product of forced diffusion.

Other observed formats for government and public policy may be less obviously a product of diffusion. Take, for example, the formation of social insurance programmes in the countries of the world. While the concept of social insurance could be invented only once, the pattern by which it spread appeared to follow a natural path of economic and social development rather than one of more forcible diffusion. Several of the wealthier countries in Latin America, for example, adopted social security programmes long before the United States or many countries in Europe (Mesa-Lago, 1978; 1989). Did this pattern result from the simple diffusion of ideas, or were there socio-economic or political factors that made one group of countries more fertile ground for these programmes than were others? Further, even if there were diffusion involved, are societies and governments really just the 'passive receivers of traits' (Smith and Craon, 1977: 145), or is diffusion dependent in part on socio-economic conditions, political traditions, or even cultural affinities that facilitate diffusion? Those conditions may mean that the society is particularly receptive to a programme that has become 'an idea in good currency', or that there may be a greater than average need for adopting the policy in question.

If the former is the case then there is little to say, except to attempt to understand diffusion processes better (Rogers, 1995; Majone, 1991; Dolowitz and Marsh, 1996). If, on the other hand, there does appear to be some systematic relationship of social and political factors to the adoption of social insurance programmes then we may have fodder for the theoretical mill on comparative public policy. The problem for research design is to be able to sort out the possible causes of the observed pattern as a way of addressing the theoretical question. For example, we might begin by looking at diffusion in specific linguistic or cultural areas – do these factors appear to make adoption of similar traits more likely? Or do factors from a more political theory appear to fit the pattern better?

David Klingman (1980) investigated possible means of addressing diffusion issues as they occur across both time and space. The usual comparative strategy is too look only at cases at a single point in time and then infer a process, but Klingman wanted to demonstrate how to cope (statistically at least) with sorting out effects of both temporal and spatial diffusion. His argument is based upon the logic of autocorrelation in regression analysis. As with patterning of residuals produced by systematic relationships with a variable across time, patterning of residuals can be a function of systematic unmeasured relationships across space, and in this instance be a product of diffusion.

Diffusion is a fact of political and social life, but it can confound our comprehension of causation in comparative analysis. It is all to easy to assume that because attribute *X* appears in country *Y* that it developed autonomously. This is especially true if operating from an implicit or explicit functionalist perspective in which any observed trait is presumed to fulfil some function for the society. That need not be the case, and some attributes may represent adoption of foreign traits and values virtually as quasi-experiments or to conform to perceived stereotypes of values such as 'modernity' or 'democracy'. These political 'cargo cults' do show something of the power of ideas in changing behaviour, but also can confuse comparative analysis.

Levels of Analysis

Another fundamental question for the design of comparative analysis is how to link the individual and the collectivity. Comparative politics is concerned about the behaviour of political systems, but it is also concerned about the behaviour of the individuals within those systems (Silverman, 1991). The problem is that it is very easy to slip into fallacious reasoning that attributes the properties discovered at one level of analysis to the other level (see p. 111). On the one hand, researchers are confronted with the 'ecological fallacy', in which the properties of a collectivity are assumed to characterise individuals within them. For example, in his classic explication of the ecological fallacy, Robinson (1950) pointed out that if we identify political units with higher rates of literacy and then find that those same units have high rates of foreign-born residents then it may not be that foreign born citizens are more literate on average.

One more subtle version of this fallacy, which is an all-to-common trap for the comparative researcher in political science, is to assume that something we call a country is a homogeneous unit. We know that the countries in Africa that were carved out by colonial powers for their own purposes are not homogeneous units – the outbreaks of ethnic warfare in Burundi and Rwanda are unfortunate reminders of that. The lack of homogeneity tends to be forgotten for more developed political systems in which variables such as religion may cut across national boundaries. For example, Germany may appear to be a homogeneous country from outside, but the religious cleavage remaining from the seventeenth century still influences the manner in which politics and policy-making function in the two parts of the country today. Other countries such as the Netherlands, Belgium and Switzerland are divided by religion, language, or both (see Lane and Ersson, 1994a).

Furthermore, an entire country may be characterised as an outlier in some distribution, because one part of it (geographically or socially) has very extreme values, while the remainder is quite 'normal', lying within the distribution. For example, the United States has a substantially higher level of infant mortality than might be expected given its level of economic development and expenditure for health care. If, however, that figure is disaggregated by race then the white population has an infant mortality rate equivalent to that found in many European countries, while the non-white population has a mortality rate more similar to transitional or Third World countries. Similarly, the state of New Hampshire has an infant mortality rate of 5.6 deaths per thousand live births, while Mississippi has a rate of 11.3 – more than double that in the lowest state.

On the other hand, researchers also can fall into the individualistic fallacy in which the collectivity is assumed to have the properties of the individuals that comprise it. Perhaps the most important example of this fallacy would be *The Civic Culture* (Almond and Verba, 1967; see Key Text 2.1). This was one of the major pieces of behavioural

Key Text 2.1 Gabriel Almond and Sidney Verba, and the Civic Culture

The Civic Culture has been widely praised and widely damned, but what is certain is that this study has had a profound influence on comparative politics. The study set out to identify the cultural characteristics that made democracy successful in some countries and less successful in others. In the end the argument was that a country such as the United Kingdom with a mixture of participative and deferential components in its political culture would be more successful than would countries that were more participative (the United States) or more 'subject' oriented (Italy or Mexico).

The Civic Culture was one of the first large-scale comparative surveys conducted as comparative politics moved from its earlier institutional focus to a more behavioral focus in conducting research. It was therefore in some ways a model for the (then) newer approaches to the discipline, and demonstrated the potential of mass political surveys as a research tool for comparative politics. It also demonstrated the potential of linking empirical research methods with normative questions (democratic performance) in comparative analysis. Finally, the project developed several interesting concepts about political attitudes and behavior that have informed subsequent research in the field.

Although extremely influential in comparative politics, and the source of numerous dissertations and secondary analyses, this project was also roundly criticised. In the first place, although it purported to be objective and 'scientific' there was a clear prescriptive element in the work, pointing out what a good democracy was, and also what political development entailed. Further, there were methodological questions about how to link individual attitudes with the political culture of a country. Finally, *The Civic Culture* apparently was not as careful about questions of the comparability and meaning of political terms within different cultures as it might have been, so that some of the findings are suspect.

The above having been said, it is hard to diminish the importance of *The Civic Culture*. It was a major source of encouragement for comparative political scientists who wanted to use the methods usually confined to national elections or national public opinion polling. It also demonstrated that empirical comparison was really possible using those methods, even given the problems that inevitably arose.

comparative research, studying a set of cultural attributes assumed to make democracy more or less viable in a country. It found that several of the countries included (West Germany, Mexico and Italy) did not have the attitudinal support for democracy that others did, the inference being that democracy would not survive there. Thus, the characteristics of the system as a whole were being derived from the attributes if individuals – inaccurately as it turns out.

Depending upon the purposes of the researcher, any level of analysis will do well. The problem is simply not to mix the levels, or, if one does mix them, to pay careful attention to the possible misinterpretations that may arise. Cross-level inference should be regarded as a crucial question in comparative politics. As Heinz Eulau (1963: 47) argued, perhaps the most important task in the discipline is:

> to build, by patiently linking one unit to another, the total chain of interrelationships which link individuals to other individuals, individual to primary group, primary group to secondary group, secondary group to secondary group, secondary group to organization, organization to organization, and so on.

If such a sequence can be established then we will have a much better idea of how politics works, whether at the individual, the group or the state level.

Further, this statement by Eulau points out that whenever we begin an analysis we are cutting into a complex chain of causation. Simply focusing on the individual voter, for example, may appear to be the right level of analysis for understanding electoral behaviour, but we also know that there are important effects of community and neighbourhood on voting. Indeed, much of the analysis of voting behaviour has depended upon class as the explanatory variable (Nieuwbeerta, 1995). On the other hand, we can obtain reasonably good ideas about how civil service systems behave by looking at patterns of individual recruitment and the training and ideas of the individual members of the service (Aberbach *et al.*, 1981; Suleiman and Mendras, 1995).

Threats to Validity in Non-Experimental Research

The litany we have been discussing for coping with variance is another way of expressing the problem of validity in social research. Validity is the simple question of whether we are measuring what we think we are measuring, or whether the observations we make (especially on our dependent variables) are a function of other factors not included in the analysis. The experimental design characteristic

Key Text 2.2 Phillipe Schmitter and the Politics of Interest Intermediation

The study of interest groups during the 1950s and 1960s in comparative politics was heavily nifluenced by American political science and its pluralist assumptions. Although it was clear that in many countries interest groups were organised very differently and played a different role in politics, those differences were not adequately conceptualised. Phillipe Schmitter's 1974 article describing corporatism and positing different types (state and societal) of corporatism was a landmark in the understanding of both interest-group politics and the politics of continental European countries (see also Heilser, 1974).

Schmitter argued that rather than being the open universe of pressure groups that was the heart of pluralist theory the consteallation of interest groups in many countries was actually more tightly organised and restricted. In particular, government played a central role in selecting the interest groups with which they wished to interact in makign policy. In this model, a limited number of peak organisations would be granted direct access to decision-making in exchange for some acquiescence to the decisions once they are made.

This basic model of corporatism focussed on macro-economic policy through tri-partite bargaining, although the corporatist notion appeared in principle applicable to a broader range of issues.

The original Schmitter article spawned a number of extensions and elaborations of the basic corporatist argument. For example, there were a number of discussions of the boundary conditions for a corporatist system to exist and why countries such as the United States and Japan had little or no formalised corporatism. There was also a discussion of 'meso-corporatism' for issues other than macro-economic policy . Similarly, the revival of Rokkan's ideas about 'croporate pluralism' (see Key Text 3.1) in which a large number of interest groups are granted direct access to policy-making extended the concept of corporatism.

Despite the impact of the concept and the associated research there have been a number of critiques. One of these has centered on the generalisability of the concept; just as pluralism was used excessively, so too has corporatism. A similar critique is that the concept has been stretched to ocover situations in which it is probably inappropriate. That stretching has been argued to be true in both geographical and policy terms.

of the natural sciences is supposed to solve those problems for those disciplines, and some disciplines that bridge the gap between social and natural science – for example, psychology. As already explained, most social scientists rarely have the luxury of conducting true experiments, and therefore must find ways to make non-experimental designs as valid as possible.

When we speak of validity, we must be careful to separate two different forms of the concept. One type is internal validity. This is the capacity to be sure that, if the independent and dependent variables do co-vary, then indeed the changes in X did cause the observed changes in Y. This question is a manifestation of the problem of extraneous variance, which we have been talking about throughout much of this chapter. Internal validity is generally not a problem for experimental research, since every effort is made to hold as many factors as possible constant through random assignment, and the use of control groups permits checking whether that effort has been successful. In non-experimental research, however, other mechanisms must be developed to cope with the threats to internal validity and the possible influence of extraneous factors on observed findings.

External validity is a very different issue in research. It refers to the question of whether any relationship observed among a set of variables in the research setting is generalisable to the 'real world'. For survey research and statistical analysis, this amounts to whether or not the investigator is justified in generalising from the sample to the population, while for strictly comparative analysis the issue is whether the cases selected do reflect adequately the dimensions of different variables assumed by the researcher. Experimental design actually performs very poorly for this type of validity problem. The artificiality of the laboratory setting for social research that provides it with the ability to control extraneous influences also divorces those findings from the social context within which they have meaning. If we find that people behave in a certain way in a psychological or economic experiment can we have any confidence that they will behave in the same way in their everyday lives? The answer is probably not.

Internal versus external validity is therefore yet another trade-off in comparative research. Experimental designs are generally the gold standard for internal validity, but are of little use for proving the external validity of a finding. Indeed, many people would consider the findings of laboratory experiments about important political issues to be more misleading than valuable. On the other hand, the type of research more common in political science tends to have a good deal of external validity – it is based on observing the real world – but can have a number of serious deficiencies in internal validity.

The use of experiments for many of the important questions of political science may not be practical, so we are then left with attempting to cope with the internal validity problems that arise from non-experimental designs.

The obvious answer is to attempt to do both, and to test the findings of the laboratory in a more natural setting, or to attempt to replicate observed findings in a more controlled environment. One interesting example of this strategy is the attempt to match experimental findings in international relations theory with real cases of foreign policy decision-making. Kaufmann (1994) derived a series of propositions from rational and psychological theories of foreign policy, then tested them by examining evidence in the Imperial German archives. While such testing involves introducing another potential source of error – the coding of the researcher – it still constitutes an interesting way to address the internal and external validity dilemma.

Sources of Invalidity

The principal approach to coping with the numerous threats to internal validity in social research is to be cognizant of their existence, and to use that knowledge to implement strategies to avoid as many pitfalls as possible. When the pitfalls cannot be avoided entirely then conservative interpretations of the findings can save the researcher and colleagues most future difficulties. Donald Campbell and Julian Stanley (1967) have enumerated these potential problems in an extremely useful manner. Some of the threats they mention have little relevance for most comparative research, exerting their major influence on individual level research, but some are endemic in comparative research. These should be discussed at some greater length as means of arming the prospective researcher.

History

One very common threat to the validity of comparative research is what Campbell and Stanley refer to as history. This is the simple fact that, while researchers are observing a case and the presumed interaction between an independent and a dependent variable, there may be a number of other changes going on around them that are impacting the observations being made. For example, any attempt to understand the political behaviour of trade unions in the 1990s must take into account the possibly confounding effects of economic

Key Text 2.3 George Tsebelis and Game Theory

In addition to institutional theory (see Key Texts 5.3 and 6.2), there has been some growth in rational choice accounts of comparative politics. The assumption of this theoretical approach is that the best way to understand the behaviour of individuals in politics is to think of them as rational utility maximisers, much as an economist would assume about their economic activities. In particular, Tsebelis applies concepts of game theory to comparative politics, demonstrating that many common political problems can be conceptualised as 'games' in which individual players choose strategies, with the outcomes being determined by the structure of the payoffs available and the strategies adopted by the competitors in the game.

Tsebelis was particularly interested in 'nested games', that is games that occur are played within multiple arenas simultaneously. These games often generate suboptimal outcomes even when the individual players are acting rationally. As well as describing these games and their dynamics, Tsebelis also points to their implications for institutional design. The utility of the approach is illustrated with several examples drawn from comparative politics, including consociationalism and coalition formation.

Rational choice analysis has a number of critics in political science. The critics argue that political actors are not (necessarily) the rational utility maximisers presented in these models but rather operate from a number of motives, personal utility being only one of many. Further, the critics contend that these models oversimplify complex realities found in politics, especially the behaviour of political institutions. The result of that oversimplification is argued to be results that are either trivial or misleading. Further, it is argued that rational choice approaches place too much emphasis on individual actors and not enough on the role of collective actors in politics, largely because of the problems of aggregating preferences and rationalities in institutions.

Tsebelis acknowledges the criticisms and provides a vigorous defence for the approach. The defence may not be entirely convincing to the more committed opponents of rational choice, but it will give even them reason to reflect on their assumptions about politics. This book is a crucial starting point for anyone attempting to understand rational choice approaches in political science and their applicability to comparative politics.

insecurity in a globalising economy. So, while trade unions may appear much less activist than in the past, that may have nothing to do with factors such as changes in leadership or changes in management practices but a great deal more to do with the changes in the economy.

Observing a single case may make research particularly prone to the effects of history, but using multiple cases may be no guaranteed way to avoid the confounding effects of that problem. For example, different countries may react very differently to changing economic circumstances as a result of historical experiences. There is some (Schmolders, 1960) evidence, for example, that the British public is extremely concerned about any threat of unemployment, while the German public is more concerned about inflation. These concerns can be seen as a function of the economic histories of the two countries. Britain was plagued by mass unemployment between the two wars, while Germany suffered two massive inflations that wrecked the economy. Younger generations may be less affected by these fears, but there is some sense that they do persist. Thus, a change in economic variables would have a differential impact in these two systems that might confound the findings of research attempting to assess the effects of economics on political behaviour (Lewis-Beck, 1988; Anderson, 1995).

Selection Bias

We have been discussing the selection of cases in much of this chapter, so that it may appear that there is little else to say on the subject. One point still to be mentioned, however, is that there is a natural bias in comparative research arising from the tendency to select the cases that the researcher knows best, and to attempt to make the theory fit the cases rather than vice versa. This bias is very natural, and in some ways logical, given that it prevents other types of errors of interpretation and the barriers of foreign language to meaning research. The same logic also creeps into the recruitment of multi-person research teams on different countries, in which the tendency is always to 'round up the usual suspects', for example, researchers with whom the organiser is familiar and who have shown themselves to be reliable contributors in the past. A case may be selected because of the availability of scholars rather than its intrinsic merit. Again, that can be an antidote to other types of practical problems arising later in the research.

The above said, however, the preference for familiar cases can present severe problems in testing theory with the data collected. The cases with which we are most familiar are not necessarily the best for testing theories that are intended to have general applicability.

Further, almost by definition, if we want to think about theory testing through difficult cases, then the less familiar countries and the places with perhaps the least well-known scholars on the international 'circuit' will probably be the most interesting. Comparative politics is sometimes described by its critics as the search for the most exotic locales and for academic adventure, but in practice researchers sometimes are wedded to the least exotic and the excessively familiar, and that may be detrimental to theory development.

In looking at instances of selection bias in comparative analysis it is easy to assume that this is a problem for small-*n*, qualitative studies. Unfortunately, elegant quantitative analysis can be used to mask some fundamental problems in case selection. All the analysis in the world, however, cannot make up for a 'sample' that contains some systematic bias. Take, for example, Hahm *et al.*'s (1996) study of fiscal policy. This study used a high selective sample of nine countries to test the influence of the nature of fiscal institutions on deficits. That sample excluded Sweden and Norway, however, which have quite similar administrative systems, but have had wildly different fiscal policy fortunes in recent years. It also excluded Ireland, which has an administrative system not dissimilar from that of the United Kingdom, but which again had had very different policy outcomes. One can only wonder at the utility of these findings. Similarly, much of the research arguing for the negative impact of presidentialism on democratic stability appears to be beset by some selection bias (see Power and Gasiorowski, 1997).

Instrument Bias

Instrument bias in comparative politics may be closely related to selection bias, in that our selections are sometimes made on the basis of available 'instruments'. The crucial instrument for comparative political analysis is the individual scholar. That scholar may employ a variety of other instruments, such as questionnaires or interview protocols, in his or her work, but scholarly judgment and knowledge are the crucial factors. The problem is that scholars all come with some built-in biases. These biases may be theoretical, national or temperamental, among others, but they will be present. Further, given that comparative analysis is often interpretative, those biases are likely to influence the conclusions of the work. Even if the research is quantitative, the selection of the research question and the particular quantitative measures may be influenced by theoretical and methodological biases that exclude other possible explanations.

One common strategy in comparative research projects is to have one national expert write a chapter on his or her country about what ever the issue at hand may be. This practice often produces a published collection in which, as Christopher Hood once commented, the major independent variable is the author. Such a strategy may be especially problematic when the experts are recruited from the nations themselves, and therefore tend to replicate the prevailing national analysis of their own system. In such a case, any implicit comparison with other systems may be lost, and it is only the compiler of the volume who can attempt to make any comparative sense out of the national studies. Many editors have done this successfully, but just as many appear to have failed rather badly.

Maturation

As well as the external circumstances changing around a research site, the internal circumstances can change as well. For example, take the case of a scholar who is interested in decision-making in cabinets, and spends time following the deliberations of a particular cabinet, even if from afar, and through interviews with participants after the fact. Let us now assume that there is a reshuffle (a very frequent occurrence in parliamentary governments – Italy has had over 40 since 1945). In this case, the research site has changed in a fundamental way, particularly if a key figure is shuffled out, or a particularly effective new minister is shuffled in. Depending upon the particular focus of the research, the project could well be ruined, and have to start again with the new cabinet.

The change in a cabinet is a very visible change in the research site, and that is probably fortunate. In that instance, the researcher can easily notice that something has happened in the research setting, and then can make a decision as to whether that change really impacts his or her investigation. On the other hand, subtle and gradual changes in individuals or organisations present a more difficult collection of threats to the external validity of findings, simply because they are likely to occur unnoticed. For example, after lengthy bargaining over an amendment to a piece of legislation, the legislators involved finally reach agreement. Is this because the demands of all the participants were satisfied in the final proposals, or did they simply become tired? In short, individuals and groups do change over time, and those changes can affect the validity of findings. The only real defence against these threats appears to be awareness of the problems.

Regression Towards the Mean
Another source of potential invalidity in research is referred to as 'regression towards the mean'. This defect will result when the cases for research are selected on the basis of extreme values on the dependent variable. Given the errors inherent in any social measurement, all subsequent tests are likely to be less extreme. Further, given the extreme values in the initial measurement, there is nowhere else for the observations to go, except back towards the mean, when there has been any error and extraneous variance in the initial measurement. For example, suppose students are selected for an investigation on the basis of poor scores on a test of educational skills, and are then given a special class and then tested again. The second measurement is likely to show that they have improved, and that the class was a success. This observation could, however, be totally an artefact of regression towards the mean, rather than revealing any real impact of the educational programme.

Such a source of invalidity represents a more individual-level version of the problem in comparative politics of selecting cases on the dependent variable. If we select cases of successful democratisation, for example, then examine them across time, there is likely to be a significant failure rate of democracy. The 'sample' will, in essence, have regressed towards the mean of the distribution of democratic political behaviour in the world. Thus, any 'treatment' we are inferring from the environment of these political systems – for example, changing economic fortunes or increased ethnic tensions – is suspect as a cause of the declining rate of democracy. Similarly, the 'breakdown' of institutionalised party systems in democratic countries (Dalton *et al.*, 1984; Lawson and Merkl, 1988) may merely represent a regression, of an aberrant form of party system observed for only a short period of time, towards the mean of party systems in the generally more fractious political world. We have cautioned against this practice in a number of places in this volume, but the above discussion provides a somewhat more formal justification for those admonitions. We should, however, also point out that selecting cases on the dependent variable may be acceptable and desirable as a means of generating hypotheses, just not for testing them.

Regression towards the mean can occur when the 'sample' used in the research has been selected on the basis of its extreme values on the dependent variable. While King *et al.* (1994), among others, have argued against selecting on the basis of values on the dependent variable, there are some instances in which this practice may be

Key Text 2.4 Vincent Wright and the Reform of the State

Most of the attention on transformation of political systems has been directed toward the spread of democratic politics and market economics in the former Communist countries of Central and Eastern Europe (see Key Text 7.1). To the West of those countries there also has been a major process of transformation and reform, less dramatic but nonetheless significant. This article, along with the others in the same special issue of *West European Politics* (1994) describe and analyze those changes very well. A thorough reading of these articles will provide an enhanced understanding of the intellectual debate over reform in West Europe and the other developed democracies.

Vincent Wright and the other authors in this special edition demonstrated that the state in Western Europe is becoming fundamentally different from what it had been in the past. The numerous political and economic pressures for reform have required some rethinking of just what government can and should do in these countries. Further. the availability of ideas for changing the State, especially the important of the market as an alternative to the hierarchy of State bureaucracies, has facilitated the process of change. Finally, the different policy challenges to government, many arising from globalisation and Europeanisation, appear to require a different set of structures and practices in order for government to be effective.

What is perhaps most important in this discussion is that although these states are changing in some important ways they remain in many ways unchanged. The basic Rechtstaat character of most European states is still in place and, despite the numerous 'marketising' and other reforms bureaucracies remain a central part of the apparatus for making and delivering services.

Further, despite privatisation of many public firms the State remains a major socio-economic actor and continues to influence the economy in many ways. These articles help the reader to see that despite the change government remains the principle source of guidance and control in most Western countries.

acceptable or even desirable. The regression argument makes it manifest that one condition is clearly that there should be no inference based on the retest of the same 'sample', especially if that sample is extreme in its values. This is rarely a problem for comparative politics, other than for some cross-national studies of public policies, in large part because of the inability to have a clearly defined intervention that would make a retest meaningful.

Summary

Conducting valid political research is never an easy task. There are a large number of threats to that research lurking in practices that appear normal, and even desirable (for example, looking only at cases that illustrate a particular trait). Other threats to the validity of comparative research, for example, maturation, occur as very normal parts of the political process, but still constitute significant threats to good research. Again, these threats are almost inevitable in non-experimental research, so that the major benefit to be gained from this description of those threats is simply to be aware of the threats, in order to be able to discount their possible impact on results, if not always avoid them. Thus, if a researcher knows that a particular threat to validity is present, and can estimate the direction in which that threat is likely to have operated, then he or she can make more conservative interpretations of the results.

Conclusion

Comparative political analysis is heavily dependent upon the cases selected for analysis. This selection is often done in a haphazard manner, or on the basis of familiarity; as in *Casablanca*, we tend to round up the usual suspects when starting on a project. These may well be the right cases, but often they are not! Any project on European politics appears to have to have the big three or four countries, although the smaller ones are much more relevant theoretically. A researcher should be able to justify the choice of cases on theoretical grounds rather than on convenience grounds, but there are few consumer warning labels on comparative research projects.

There are several views on how to select cases for analysis, the dominant being the 'most similar' and the 'most different' systems designs. These two designs enable the researcher to examine different form of relationship between independent and dependent variables, and therefore are suitable for different types of enquiry. Again, however, one design or the other often is selected on the basis of ease or familiarity with cases, rather than through thinking about the nature of the type of comparative results to be sought. Without attention to the projected outcomes of analysis, the choice of designs and of cases is unlikely to be the best one.

There is no single answer to all these questions. Although Przeworski and Teune (1970) have rather strong opinions about the best way to design analysis, other scholars appear to have diametrically opposed views. What appears to be most important is that the researcher consider his or her options carefully before selecting a research design and the cases that will be fitted into that design. It may be that the purpose of the research is not so much to find *the* cause of a particular phenomenon, but rather is more exploratory, looking at an interesting phenomenon and attempting to understand better something of its nature. In that case, selecting 'most similar systems', and selecting on the dependent variable, might be a very reasonable thing to do. We tend to focus attention on the uses of comparative research for theory testing and falsification, and often forget that there are more exploratory uses that are equally valid.

3

The Number of Cases

Comparative politics often appears afflicted with a variety of analytic greed, in which 'more is better'. This greed is driven in part by the dominance of statistical analysis in contemporary political science, with the consequent need to have relatively large 'samples' of countries in order to be able to meet the assumptions and requirements of statistical analyses. In some ways, however, this concentration on the demands of particular statistical techniques reverses the appropriate logic of research design. The statistical techniques, or other methodological tools, that researchers select for use should be employed in the service of the analytic and theoretical questions we are pursuing, not vice versa. Certainly, there are some research questions that can only be addressed with large and almost comprehensive data-sets, but they are also some questions that are best addressed with small and focused selections of cases, or even a single case. Indeed, the use of larger 'samples' of cases may make some styles of research less useful rather than more.

In addition to meeting the requirements of formal explanation of phenomena, the statistical method is also attempting to achieve another of the fundamental goals of scientific enquiry – parsimony. One problem with cross-national research based on a limited number of cases is that it is difficult to exclude many of the extremely numerous possible causes for the observed differences in the dependent variable. Each case brings with it so many interrelated variables that it is impossible to exclude very many independent variables with such a limited number of cases. As the size of the *N* in the sample increases, the possibility of reliably excluding possible causes increases with it, and greater parsimony of explanation is also achievable.

Even more fundamentally, the statistical and comparative methods are fundamentally different orientations to social science research (Frenderis, 1983; Ragin, 1987). The comparative depends upon the careful *a priori* selection of the cases. If we return to the fundamental litany of research design – maximise experimental variance, minimise error variance and control extraneous variance – then the comparative method depends upon the initial selection of cases to achieve those goals of research design. The cases must be selected in such a way as to control known sources of extraneous variance. This research method is therefore often inaccurate and incomplete; if we knew all the sources of extraneous variance in advance then there might be little need to do the research. Still, if care is taken in the selection of cases then there is some greater hope of achieving control.

Statistical analysis, on the other hand, generally is willing and even anxious to include all available cases, and then use a variety of *ex-post* statistical techniques to attempt to determine the impact of extraneous variables. This is a slight overstatement, but not by much. The canons of statistical methods seem to always push for more cases, given that they can be seen as part of the same population of cases. Statistical techniques have the virtue of being more independent of the selection of the cases, but even so, if the appropriate data are not collected then there is no way in which to determine the sources of the extraneous variance. Further, if some countries are systematically excluded because of poor quality of data then another source of extraneous variance may be introduced. Looking at the outliers in a regression analysis may enable the identification of the geographical source of the variance, but often not the variables producing the deviations from the neatly devised theory of the researcher. This potential problem also points to the need for substantial descriptive knowledge of the cases being studied, even in a statistical analysis. Without that sort of substantive knowledge, identifying why country *X* is an outlier, and choosing variables to use for a subsequent test for the fundamental source of extraneous variance, can become little more than an academic fishing expedition. Of course, no researcher can know about all relevant countries, but as comparativists we abandon our descriptive studies in favour of being 'high tech' at great peril to any real understanding of countries and political dynamics.

Both the comparative method and the statistical method depend upon the ability to identify, *ex ante*, the potential sources of extraneous variance in the research question. If a comparative analysis does not identify those potential sources of confounding variance when making the initial selection of the cases the researcher will not likely be able to recover and create adequate research later. The consequences will be results that are confounded by the unmeasured characteristics of the cases selected for the 'sample'. The statistical method, likewise, may have its results confounded in an almost irretrievable manner by the failure to identify, and measure, important correlated variables. A statistical researcher does have the slight advantage of being able to rerun the analysis with the previously unidentified variable included. The identification of the crucial unmeasured factors may, however, require waiting for new theoretical development and a substantial passage of time. This delay may not be as serious in the social sciences as it might be in medicine or the natural sciences, but it may still lead researchers and even practitioners down false and/or unproductive lines of enquiry.

In addition to the theoretical considerations that may argue for a smaller and more focused analysis, there are always practical research questions. Unless there is aggregate data – for example, budgets or voting data – readily at hand, relatively few social scientists can afford to collect extensive data over a large range of political systems. There have been a number of studies of this type historically, but fewer have been completed recently. There are some exceptions to that generalisation, for example, the huge and detailed data-sets compiled by Barry Ames, first on Latin American budgets (1987) and then on Brazilian public expenditures (1996), and the massive study of public opinion in Western countries titled *Beliefs in Government* (Kaase and Newton, 1995), but they have been few. Further, even if extensive data collection in a number of countries is feasible economically, it may still not be the best use of scarce resources – temporal as well as financial – for the researchers. The fundamental questions must always be, What does a researcher gain from adding another dozen cases, or even adding a single case, to the sample? And, Does that case add anything to the argument and the ability to reject theoretical propositions, or is it simply just another data point for the analysis?

This chapter addresses the important 'Goldilocks question' of just how many cases are sufficient for effective comparative analysis. The previous chapter addressed one aspect of the case selection question by asking whether the cases selected should be most similar or most different, and further, on what dimension(s) they should be most similar or different. This chapter will extend that set of questions by looking at the quantitative dimension. It may appear excessive to have two chapters concerned with the selection of cases, but in some ways case selection is the crucial question in the design of comparative research design – first, how many cases, and then which ones? It may be that more cases are, on average, better, but more cases may merely be a compensatory mechanism for the poor selection of a smaller number of cases. As with so many things in this field, there is no single correct answer as to what is the right number of cases – the only real answer is that 'It depends.'

Strategies with Different Numbers of Cases

The remainder of this chapter is an examination of strategies available to the researcher who is faced with the possibility of using different numbers of cases. This choice could also be expressed in other ways, given that we have been arguing throughout that theoretical questions should guide the selection of cases, including both the number and the particular cases. The theoretical issues can lead to a choice of the appropriate number of cases, but there remain questions of just how those cases are to be investigated, and what can be done to maximise the theoretical utility of the research. Further, there are some instances in which there is simply a possibility of only using a very small number of cases. If, for example, a scholar wants to examine successful democratic governments in Africa, the range of possibilities is unfortunately very limited at present (Picard and Garrity, 1994; Molutsi and Holm, 1990).

One Case

It is indeed possible to do comparative research of a sort with a single case. This statement appears to be almost a contradiction in terms, but the seemingly impossible can be done successfully in several ways, and for several reasons. The reasons for choosing this particular route for comparative research are more important than the particular manner in which the research will be done, although the two issues may be closely related in practice. We should also be cognizant that another of the social sciences, anthropology, has developed primarily through the accretion of case after individual case, each one developed and considered individually. Although perhaps less directly concerned with the process of comparison than either political science or sociology (but see Naroll and Cohen, 1973), anthropology is certainly a comparative social science and has developed most of its theory through the accumulation of case evidence. Although often seen as atheoretical and purely descriptive, if it is well done then case-analysis can, paradoxically be one of the more theory-driven forms of comparative analysis.

One primary reason for attempting to do comparative research with only a single case is to utilise a very particular case to characterise a phenomenon that appears to be especially apparent in that one case. The single case therefore becomes a pre-theoretical exercise, leading, it is hoped, to a general statement about the phenomenon; this strategy is what Richard Rose (1991: 454) calls the 'extroverted case-study'. The researcher has identified, or believes that he or she has identified, an important exception to the prevailing theory, or a case which demonstrates a phenomenon that previously had been excluded from the literature. Tocqueville was following this strategy quite explicitly when he did his research on the USA. Tocqueville states: 'It is not, then, merely to satisfy a curiosity, however legitimate that I have examined America . . . I confess than in America I saw more that America; I sought there the image of democracy itself, in order to learn what we have to fear or hope from its progress' (1946: 14).

The purpose of the extroverted case-study then becomes to explore fully this one case with the existing theory in mind, with the expectation of elaborating or expanding that body of theory with the resulting data.

Take, for example, Stein Rokkan's investigations of corporate pluralism in Norway (1966; see Key Text 3.1 and also Olsen, 1987). These studies were being developed at, or even before, the time in which there was a great deal of theoretical attention directed at the development of corporatism as a more general concept describing state–society interactions (Schmitter, 1974; 1989; Wiarda, 1997). This work can also be seen as a reaction to the prevailing pluralist model of American political science. Indeed, one of Rokkan's most important articles on the subject appears in a volume edited by Robert Dahl (1966), the leading figure in pluralist political science. The more general corporatist model implies a formalised and structured relationship between interest groups and the state. The standard corporatist model further implies a singular relationship between the state and each interest group, with government choosing a single group (or peak association) to represent each sector of the economy.

Key Text 3.1 Stein Rokkan and the Study of Centre–Periphery Politics

The Norwegian Stein Rokkan was one of the founders of contemporary comparative politics. He made a number of significant contributions to the discipline, including developing the idea of 'corporate pluralism' (1966) that bridged the gap between corporatism and pluralism (see Key Text 2.2). He also developed some of the earliest concepts of data archives for the social sciences, and was instrumental in compiling such an archive at the University of Bergen.

One of the most important of his contributions was the construction of a model derived from historical sociology to explain the development of centre–periphery politics in Western Europe (and see Lipset, 1967). This model argued that contemporary structures of political cleavage in Europe developed through successive overlays of three sources of cleavage. The first was the national revolution, as feudal decentralisation is threatened by centralising élites. The second was the Protestant reformation, and the continuing divisions between religions in countries such as Switzerland, Germany and especially Northern Ireland. Finally there was the industrial revolution with the separation between labour and capital that has been the dominant source of political conflict in European countries for most of the twentieth century.

Despite the significance of economic cleavages in Europe Rokkan pointed to continuing importance of the other sources of cleavage. This was to some extent a function of his observations of politics in Norway, with the political importance of peripheral groups such as fishermen and farmers. Further, he could not help but notice the importance of religious cleavages in other small democracies in Europe. Rokkan's background as a sociologist led him to emphasise these social bases of politics.

It might be argued that Rokkan's theories were to some extent an attempt to generalise from Norway to the rest of Europe. Further, political developments since the time of his book have pointed to some of the ways in which economic cleavages can be overcome in the management of states. Still, Rokkan's contributions remain one of the foundations for the understanding of contemporary politics in Western Europe, and to some extent in the rest of the world.

The model developed by Rokkan identifies a somewhat different relationship between state and society, in which the state consults a wide variety of societal actors over policies, and expects them to bargain among themselves, as well as with the public sector actor or actors involved, until a consensus is attained. This concept is similar to corporatism, in that it requires the state to accord a legitimate status to interest groups, but differs in the number of groups involved and their relationship among themselves. This fundamental observation and conceptualisation of the nature of government in Norway was then expanded into a much longer treatment (Olsen, 1987). Corporate pluralism has also been the subject of critiques arguing that even if the model did succeed in building a theoretical basis for understanding politics in Norway, that model could not be extended to analyse other systems (Heisler, 1979).

The second reason for using a single case is that the case may be the hardest one, so that if the theory appears to work in this setting it should work in all others. This strategy can be seen at work in many contemporary analyses of Japan. The mystique of Japan as a distinctive political system has grown to the point that it is being used as the most difficult test case for a variety of political theories, with the assumption that they will not work in that setting. For example, McCubbins and Noble (1995) undertook a study of budgetary behaviour in Japan, testing the common assumption that this political system was dominated by bureaucracy and that there would be minimal political influence. Even in this case, however, they found that there was a pronounced influence of political parties over budgetary choices, thus putting the usual characterisation of Japanese politics into question.

Finally, there is the 'Mount Everest' reason for doing studies with just a single case – it is there. That having been said, a careful and insightful examination of a single case, even one already very well known, may be proto-theoretical. For example, it is not at all clear that Samuel Beer set out to develop general social science theory when he wrote his second major study of British politics – *Britain Against Itself* (1982). That may not have been the intention, but his analysis of the blockages produced by the seemingly excessively pluralistic nature of British politics parallels closely Mancur Olson's more theoretical analysis of the *Rise and Decline of Nations* (1982), as well as some discussions of hyper-pluralism in the United States (see Peters, 1995b). In short, although it is not the usually recommended strategy for comparative research, an insightful analysis of a single country can produce large dividends, even if the benefits are unanticipated, or not even recognised, at the time.

Whether or not it is the best strategy for theory development for comparative politics, the single country study is likely to remain a central feature of comparative politics for a very long time. Language and geographical restrictions are likely to persuade individual scholars to focus their attention on single cases, or at most a limited range of cases. Furthermore, we might well think that, given the continuing dearth of resources available for extensive multi-country research, there will be more rather than less attention paid to monographic studies of single countries. The real task for comparativists, consequently, becomes to develop those individual case studies (see below, pp. 139–54) so that they have as much theoretical content as possible, while still retaining their descriptive richness. The second part of that challenge is to work to compile the individual case studies into theoretically meaningful groupings and to attempt to draw some conclusions from them.

Two, or a Few, Cases

We will now double the number of instances to be considered and think about the logic of doing comparative analysis with only two cases. Using two cases appears to be a more sensible way to do comparative politics – there is now something to compare. With properly selected 'focused comparisons' (Hague *et al.*, 1992: 39–40) some comparative understanding can be generated from two cases. Despite that, this strategy is fraught with many of the same dangers encountered with single country analyses. Therefore, using two cases requires the same caution in design and execution as do single country studies. Indeed, the two country comparison may be even more dangerous, simply because it appears that a genuine comparison is being done, and therefore the logic of analysis must surely be acceptable. That may not be the situation, however, and absence of care in the selection and analysis of the two cases may produce misleading results (De Winter *et al.*, 1996).

The problem with this mode of analysis is not small *N per se*, but the mismatch between a rather small number of cases and a large number of variables (Lijphart, 1971: 686). When a country is selected for a comparative analysis, it brings with it a large bundle of variables. The history, culture, economy and society all come along with the particular political dimensions in which the researcher is interested primarily. Therefore, there are a huge number of sources of extraneous variance, but only a few cases in which to attempt to discover the manner in which all those variables operate. In statistical language, the dependent variable is over-determined, with too many possible explanations, so that no real choice can be made (Lopez,

1992). The researcher may focus on a few variables he or she thinks are particularly important, but unless the cases are selected carefully to falsify a hypothesis, any number of explanations will still be acceptable.

We must return to some of the logic of Teune and Przeworski in thinking about this form of comparison. Which two cases, and why? – these are the dominant questions. In some instances, the logic of most different systems will direct us to attempt to find two systems that are as different as possible on a number of variables, thereby maximising the variance with which to explore the differences among countries. The trouble may be that with only the two cases there are so many variables that it is difficult to determine how to explain the differences. As Sartori (1991: 244) argues, the fundamental aspect of comparison is control, and the capacity to remove as many alternative explanations as possible from the 'equation', i.e. the implicit regression equation explaining the dependent variable.

Any two cases are in some ways comparable. Any two countries (or provinces, or whatever) that we select for analysis will have some features that are comparable – they all have politics, they all have political institutions of some sort, they all make policies of some sort – but the question is whether the comparison is the best one for the particular item of research under consideration. The problem for comparison is that cases often are selected for reasons that are not scientific, but rather are based on familiarity, funding, convenience, or even commercial considerations (most two country studies seek to include the USA, given the size of the US market for books). If there is to be only a pair of cases then those cases should be as similar as possible on as many variables as possible, but the dominance of familiarity and convenience usually prevent that from occurring.

One way to understand the logic of comparison for two cases is that this is inherently a 'most different systems' design, and the two cases must be conceptualised as almost totally different. Given that a researcher has no other information available when looking at the two cases, he or she must assume that the cases are substantially different. The logic of comparative analysis, therefore, becomes to attempt to identify similarities between the cases (see Chapter 2) that can then be used to explore common themes, rather than looking at their all-too-apparent differences.

The dangers of binary research in comparative politics can be illustrated by Seymour Martin Lipset's (1994) interesting, but basically flawed, example of the comparison of the United States and Japan as two 'exceptional' political economies. The model he uses is, in effect, a version of the Teune and Przeworski 'most different system design'. The question Lipset poses is, What, if anything, can explain the economic success of these two very disparate countries? Lipset examines both on a variety of variables, and finds they differ fundamentally on virtually all of them, yet have both been very successful. Fukuyama (1995) provides a more extensive examination of the economic success of systems, using some of the same variables used by Lipset, but focusing on the existence of trust in the commercial system rather than on the social and political variables that are more central to Lipset's analysis. In particular, he points to the differences in the roots of economic success in Japan and Korea.

The research design flaw here is selecting cases on the dependent variable, combined with the extreme differences in the systems, with the consequence that every difference appears equally invalid as an explanation. If, however, the cases had been selected with some variance on the dependent variable then there might have been some better chance of generating more useful results. As we pointed out above, however, there are disputes over the appropriateness of selecting cases on the dependent variable, with qualitative researchers arguing that this is essential, and quantitative researchers arguing that it invalidates most findings.

The problems with binary comparison can be reduced by focusing on a single institution, policy or process. For example, a researcher may want to compare the British prime minister and the German chancellor (Helms, 1996). Given that these two offices perform many of the same functions in government, some of the potential for extraneous variance is reduced. Further, because for most of recent history both of these offices have been dominated by a single, conservative party, the extraneous variance may be reduced further. These factors are still however no a guarantee that the research will make the contribution a scholar might like. Why these two countries? Is there anything theoretically interesting about the pairing of two cases, or have they been selected merely for convenience? Roy Pierce (1995), for example, focuses on the presidency in France and the USA as the two major examples of this office in developed democracies, as a means of understanding how electing the chief executive affects voting, but is still able to make interesting theoretical arguments about the differences between the two systems.

Small N Research in General

The same logic of comparability discussed above is applicable if researchers extend the analysis to a number of cases greater than two, albeit still a small number. If the units are very disparate, then the comparison may have to be at such a high level of generality that the results are not very meaningful or useful for theory development. Of course, the strategy of most different systems designs (pp. 37–41) argues for a great deal of diversity of cases, but that argument is more readily applicable to the tradition of statistical analysis rather than to the more constrained number of cases used for comparative analysis. With only a limited number of cases, the most different systems design usually generates comparisons of the type common when systems analysis and structural-functionalism were the dominant approaches to the comparative politics (Wiseman, 1966; Almond and Coleman, 1960; Jones, 1967). These functionalist studies managed to compare extremely disparate systems, but also managed to do so in such an equivocal manner that the results actually could say very little about what happened in those varied systems. In such a research outcome, there are simply too many factors that differentiate the systems to be able to say what the more important independent variable or variables might be.

For a strictly comparative analysis, careful selection of cases is essential. Even then, it is not clear how much leverage the researcher can get for isolating cause and effect in the analysis. Lieberson (1991) argues that, for small *N* studies to be able to make causal claims, a number of stringent conditions must be met, most of which simply do not exist in the social sciences. For example, he argues (pp. 309–12) that the cause must be deterministic rather than probabilistic. That is, for a study with only a few cases, to say that *X* causes *Y*, the linkage must be necessary and sufficient, and *Y* will not occur without *X*. Very few relationships in political science would meet that criterion, and even more 'advanced' social sciences depend heavily upon the *ceteris paribus* disclaimer. Most of the relationships with which we work are probabilistic, and with a small sample it is not possible to rule out a chance finding.

Further, Lieberson also argues that for small-*N* studies to demonstrate causation, there can only be a single cause, and no interaction among independent variables. This statement assumes that the methods for determining causation developed by Mill (see above, pp. 29–30) are being applied, but the argument would hold even without that assumption. With a small number of cases there are rarely sufficient cases to have all possible combinations of several independent variables, so that the research runs the risk of falsely imputing causation when changes in the dependent variable may well be a function of interactions among variables. Given the complexity of most social processes, those interactions are almost inevitable. Lieberson also argues that for these methods to work there must be no measurement errors. In other words, for small-*N* studies to produce valid causal results, there is no room for either extraneous or error variance, both of which are almost unavoidable in the social sciences.

There have been several critiques of the rather rigid claims made by Lieberson. For example, Savolainen (1994) argues that Lieberson has confused comparative methods used to *prove* causal assumptions with those intended to *eliminate* possible causes. Establishing that *X* causes *Y* is difficult; it is much easier to argue that *X* does *not* cause *Y* (see also Skocpol, 1984). Eliminating possible causes is in itself a valuable service to comparative politics, however, given the number of contending theories of cause available. Similarly, Savolainen argues that probabilistic explanations can be used with small-*N* studies, assuming that the researcher is conservative in the claims made for the findings. The same would be true for the presence of interaction effects in the explanation. Even if we grant the critics their points, imputing causality with a small *N* is difficult, however carefully the cases are selected in advance. The complexity of the social and political world is such that eliminating other possible causes is difficult. The Boolean approach (see below, pp. 162–73) begins to address these problems, but the findings then still depend upon the nature and size of the sample used.

Thus, very much like the single country case studies, small *N* studies appear more useful for generating hypotheses than for testing them. The only viable exception to this statement appears to be in carefully crafted, most similar systems designs, when the similarity of the countries selected can be demonstrated very clearly and convincingly. Without that knowledge of the countries, the capacity of small-*N* studies for making statements about causation appears a very limited indeed. Even in 'comparable' cases, however, Przeworski and Teune (1970) would argue that the dependent variable would most likely be over-determined because of the number of rival hypotheses that could not be rejected on the basis of any small number of cases.

Reducing Variables

An alternative method for coping with the small-*N*, many variables' problem is to reduce the number of variables included in the analysis (Collier, 1993). This reduction can be done in one of two manners. The first way is to employ a more elegant theory, with fewer presumed explanatory variables than other contending approaches. The argument here is that if the researcher goes into the field with a loosely constructed theory, then the data from a small number of cases can support any number of possible theoretical explanations. If, on the other hand, the researcher works with a clearer and more parsimonious theory, then that theory can be tested with the limited number of cases. This is especially true if the cases are selected to make falsification more likely, for example, if the researcher looks for the hardest cases. Collier, for instance, uses the example of rational choice theory, with a very few variables and relatively simple hypotheses.

The danger of the variable reduction strategy is that the researcher imposes a premature closure on the possible explanations for the phenomenon. Just because a single hypothesis can be tested with a limited number of cases does not mean that there are not other possible explanations. Further, a strong theory such as rational choice may contain a number of untested assumptions that are, in many ways, also hypotheses. Failure to test the assumptions empirically may lead the researcher to accept what is in essence a spurious relationship. For example, in the case used an example by Collier (Geddes, 1991), a game theoretic analysis was applied to explain administrative reforms in Latin America. This appears to be an elegant treatment of those reforms with few variables, but also appears to avoid a number of factors that scholars coming from other traditions might consider crucial components of any investigation of administrative reforms. Most scholars of public administration, for example, might consider the exclusive focus on legislative decision-making for studying administration risible.

The alternative means of reducing the number of variables is to perform that task empirically rather than theoretically. Many of the variables that researchers use in comparative research are closely allied to other variables, so that not only are there statistical problems in using them together, but there may also be conceptual and theoretical confusion. The statistical problem is multicollinearity, or the confounding effects of highly intercorrelated independent variables in regression equations. This tends both to reduce the reliability of the estimates and also to reverse signs for the variables that are not the mostly strongly correlated with the dependent variable. The theoretical problems are more difficult to solve.

A variety of statistical techniques such as factor analysis can be used to combine possible independent variables, and, even without these statistical techniques, indexes can be created to combine variables that are conceptually related. These aggregation strategies do not permit the researcher to answer questions about the relative effects of the closely related components of these 'syndromes' of variables, but they do permit the testing of theories in rather broad ways, with the possibility of later refinements of the analysis with the individual variables.

For example, a number of micro-level comparative research projects have used various data aggregation techniques to produce more parsimonious explanations. The typical method is to collapse a number of separate independent variables into composite explanations using methods such as factor analysis (Lewis-Beck, 1994). These aggregation techniques select a number of candidate independent variables, and identify underlying dimensions that link those variables. Thus, one variable can be used to represent a number. Further, these techniques produce dimensions that are themselves uncorrelated, so eliminating any further statistical difficulties.

One potential pitfall in doing small-*N* research is to select cases on the basis of values of the dependent variable rather than on those of the independent variables. This is an all too human tendency. Researchers identify several cases that are interesting because of their success or failure, and then proceed to study them alone, for example, cases of successful democratisation. The problem is that even if there are independent variables that are highly correlated with those dependent variables, there is no real variance to explain. How do we know that the same pattern would not emerge for cases that were unsuccessful, or that did not attempt to democratise at all?

Research based on a common value of the dependent 'variable' can effectively eliminate viable hypotheses – if none of the cases in the sample exhibit a certain trait then it is rather certain that this variable is not a concomitant of that dependent variable. This statement again points to the essential role of theory in the selection and analysis of comparative cases, and in guiding the collection of data. If we do not initiate research with some theoretical guidance then we will not know which hypotheses to consider and which to reject. Further, without the theory we will not even recognise what data to look for to be able to reject relevant hypotheses. There is no shortage of interesting research questions, but the real consideration is how to relate those specific questions to more general theories.

Counterfactuals

If nature supplies the researcher with too few usable cases, or if funding agencies supply the researcher with too little money to investigate all the potentially usable cases, there may still be a way to increase the *N* of the study, and thus satisfy the usual scientific canons. One of the more interesting ways is to develop counterfactual arguments that are, in effect, additional cases. Max Weber (1949; see also Polsby, 1982) actually discussed this as one strategy for dealing with the problem of too few relevant cases for many issues in social research. Fearon (1990) also has argued for using this methodology for comparative research, and its logic has been examined relatively thoroughly in several recent methodological studies (Tetlock and Belkin, 1996; Kahneman, 1995). Fearon argues that this style of analysis is at least a partial antidote to the research problem already mentioned several times – having a collection of cases without variance on the dependent variable. With counterfactuals, researchers can always generate such variance, even if it does not occur in the 'real' world.

Arguably, any small-*N* study is based on counterfactual arguments. If causation is imputed to a cause in the case-study, or in a study with only a few cases, the assumption is that were there cases that had the other values on a variable present then the outcomes would have been different. A case researcher tells a causal story, and must attempt thereby to dismiss other causes and to show that had things been different then the outcome would have been different. In the example that Fearon uses, Alfred Stepan (1988) argues why a military coup in Brazil was not inevitable but, given particular events and decisions by the government, did eventually occur. In the criteria for counterfactual arguments advanced by Tetlock and Belkin (1996: 19–22), one of the guiding principles is that arguments that require fewer deviations from the 'real world' and the specification of fewer steps are more realistic than more elaborate departures from observations.

Przeworski (1995) argues that counterfactual argument is essential to comparative political analysis. The limited number of cases available for any interesting research questions means that the researcher inevitably must use counterfactuals, especially to fill in the cases that are more extreme. Nature rarely provides the researcher with the full range of cases that might be needed to test some hypotheses, so that the only option is to ask 'What if . . .?', and attempt to fill in those missing cases in as unbiased a manner as possible. These 'thought experiments' are not substitutes for field research, in Przeworski's view, but they are crucial for developing theories after the range of real, available cases has been exhausted.

Analogies

It is also easy to move from 'what if' to 'as if'. That is, analogies can be an important source of comparative case material and counterfactuals. The use of analogies has been developed more in the study of international relations than in comparative politics, but the logical basis of their use is very much the same in the two fields. Khong (1992; see also Houghton, 1996), for example, examined the extent to which various analogies were used to justify decisions in foreign policy debates, and the extent to which the analogies selected could explain decisions. One way to employ analogical reasoning for comparative politics is to think about time more creatively and to utilise historical cases that are functional analogies of more contemporary events (see Bartolini, 1993: 139ff.). This style of analysis may be especially important for studying political development as countries today go through processes that are not dissimilar from processes that others went through decades ago.

For example, Halperin (1997) discusses asynchronic comparisons of weak states in contemporary mid-East and medieval Europe. The logic of this analysis is clear. In each case, there were states that, by contemporary standards, were weak and had difficulty in enforcing their authority throughout their territory and dominated by informal politics. By using the two sets of countries, the researcher had increased her *N* significantly. If the processes in the two sets of systems appear similar, despite their separation in time and space, then there is greater hope that a general explanation of development can result from the analysis. This strategy of asynchronous comparison appears potentially extremely fruitful, but also raises questions, most notably just what sort of evidence would be needed to establish the functional equivalence of different eras and political events. There appear to be no clear rules yet for this strategy, the test being what survives when it is exposed to the scrutiny of the remainder of the scholarly community.

In summary, the counterfactual strategy of coping with confirmation of hypotheses is the antithesis of the statistical method (see below). Fearon argues that this strategy is to be preferred in many ways, because it does not give the researcher a false sense of security. The large-*N* study assumes that all the threats to validity are taken care of by the size of the sample, but in social science that may not be the case. That assumption may be especially problematic in comparative politics, given the lack of independence of the units of measurement and the problems of diffusion and compensatory effects in the dependent variable. There may well be a number of systematic relationships and a systematic dispersion of political practice, which make the independence of observations very suspect.

Comparisons of 'Natural Groups'

Another strategy for comparison is to begin with relatively small groups for comparison, with those groups being defined as composed of relatively homogeneous 'families of nations' (Castles, 1993; Esping-Anderson, 1990 – see Key Text 10.1). For example, there has been a great deal of interesting and useful research done comparing the Scandinavian countries (Elder *et al.*, 1988; Lundquist and Ståhlberg, 1983; Laegreid and Pedersen, 1994). These countries (three to five, depending upon how one counts) have a number of political, economic and social characteristics in common. Further, they countries are in almost constant contact with one another on issues of policy and administration, so the researcher can determine relatively clearly how ideas filtered through national political settings can be implemented. Thus, while this research may have the advantage of holding constant a number of socio-economic and even political factors, it has the disadvantage of a severe case of Galton's problem, that is, sorting out the effects of diffusion from the effects of indigenous developments (see pp. 41–3).

Another of these natural groups of countries for comparative analysis is the 'Old Commonwealth', or the Westminster democracies, meaning those industrialised democracies derivative of the British tradition, including Britain, and sometimes the United States to make the 'Anglo–American democracies' (Lijphart, 1984; 1990; see also Aucoin, 1995). It is assumed that this common heritage makes these countries readily 'comparable'. Yet, if we look at some relevant data on this group of countries (Tables 2.1 and 2.2), we find that in many ways they are quite heterogeneous socially, economically and politically. Therefore, any comparison among these countries tends to be arguing implicitly that political heritage and political culture are more important features than are the social and economic fabric of a country. Further, it tends to be arguing that for comparison the constitutional heritage is more significant than even some important structural features of constitutions such as federalism.

That argument would be particularly interesting were the comparison extended to cover the members of the 'New Commomnwealth' (see Braibanti, 1966). In these countries, there was also a long period of British rule, and a direct implementation of British governmental institutions before and after independence. That connection was substantially longer in some cases (India, Pakistan) than it was in the United States, and more recent than in most of the Old Commonwealth countries. The failure to include these countries in most comparative analyses looking at the impact of the Westminster model therefore seems to argue that cultural and social factors are more important than constitutional inheritance. So these two implicit arguments are inconsistent, but the contradiction does point to the way in which conventions and indeed prejudices can creep into comparative analysis.

Although the comparison of these families of nations may face some apparent or not so apparent problems, there are also some potential benefits. Joseph LaPalombara (1968), for example, argued in favour of developing 'middle-range theories' of comparative politics, rather than the grand theories such as systems analysis or structural-functionalism that tended to dominate comparative analysis when LaPalombara was most concerned with theory development. These middle-range theories would address the politics of a geographical region, or perhaps a government institution, rather than providing the global explanations sometimes thought necessary to qualify as a theory. By using this mid-range strategy, LaPalombara argued, the discipline could develop building blocks for the more comprehensive theories while at the same time providing more useful and convincing explanations for politics within those more limited domains. Roy Macridis (1986: 22) supported that view, and argued that 'clustering [geographically], as opposed to the search for grand theory, has given to the field a new vitality, and may ultimately pave the way to the development of some unifying models and priorities'. We will point out (see Chapter 5) some problems in defining the clusters, but this does appear to be the current direction of theory development.

Sometimes, without explicitly acknowledging the strategy, comparative politics has been proceeding in this direction. Any number of books and articles have been published offering theories for some parts of the world, or for particular institutions. Take for example, Hydén and Bratton's (1992) work on governance in Africa. The theoretical chapters of this book address primarily questions of African politics and the breakdown of governance in that continent, but the general considerations about governance raised there could be applied anywhere. Thus, by developing a theory about governance in Africa, the authors have actually made a good beginning on a more general theory about governing, and especially about governing in less-developed political systems.

One subsidiary question that arises is how to determine the appropriate focus for these middle-range theories. As pointed out above, the natural groups that we might begin with do not always have the degree of homogeneity assumed. Although Hydén and Bratton's analysis of African states is interesting, the degree of variance in political form, political tradition, social structure and the like among those nearly fifty sub-Saharan states may make attempting to piece together one approach to fit them virtually hopeless. Indeed, such an approach may have to be so general that it would become capable of being applied almost anywhere, regardless of the geographical location. On the other hand, schemes that have been put forth as theories of European politics tend to do better at describing and explaining a part of Europe rather than the diverse politics in that continent.

One approach to the problem of identifying an appropriate focus for a middle-range theory is to make that determination empirically. As discussed above, some approaches to comparative politics (perhaps more appropriately referred to as statistical analyses of sets of countries) have employed factor analysis and other dimensional techniques to identify meaningful clusters of countries (Rummel, 1972; Castles and Mitchell, 1993; Peters, 1993). This body of research has the virtue of being able to demonstrate that the countries in question do constitute a statistically meaningful group, but is potentially suspect on other grounds. In particular, the clusters of countries that emerge are a function of the data that are put into the clustering programme. If there was inadequate theory guiding selection of the concepts, or even inadequate measurement of the concepts used, then the results will not necessarily reflect the groupings of countries that actually exist.

Further, having grouped countries in this way, it may be difficult to employ the groupings to test comparative propositions anyhow other than through the most similar systems design. If anything further is done with the data within a grouping, the results may be almost predetermined. As Teune (1990: 43–4) points out, 'Selecting a type to reduce variance made it impossible to find out what difference the category of inclusion made. Thus, if being wealthy and democratic has consequences, it is necessary to look at some cases of being non-democratic and poor.' What therefore may be most interesting approach to comparison is a two-stage process. At the first stage, some dimensional technique can be used to identify groups of countries, while in the second stage comparisons are made across the groups, rather than within them. This strategy does not meet all the stipulations of LaPalombara's mid-range theories, but it does enable the creation of theories that differentiate among groups of cases.

Global Comparisons

Finally, we come to what might be considered to be the dream of the statistical version of comparative analysis – global comparisons of virtually all political systems. We have noted already that there have been several major research studies of this type, attempting to develop measures and concepts that would travel, and then to classify the countries of the world on those variables. In many ways, these global studies represented the early, euphoric days of the behavioural revolution in political science theory and the computer revolution in the managing of data. The assumption was that if we could just get enough data from enough political systems then we could answer all the relevant questions of political science.

The euphoria concerning this style of research quickly wore off, and has been replaced with some healthy scepticism. First, as we point out below in Chapter 4 on measurement, developing measures that can travel from the United Kingdom to South Korea to Vanutu often implies that they become so general that they mean very little, and actually are able to contribute very little to the development of social science theory. For example, Jean Blondel's study (1980) of political leaders and institutions around the world has been criticised for its generality and its failure to make useful interpretative statements (see also Key Text 6.2). For Blondel, there were so few indicators that could 'travel' across this range of systems that there was relatively little that could be said to compare the systems, despite the importance simply of amassing comparative information on political executives that was not previously available.

Similarly, the idea of the country as a unit of analysis and as a meaningful entity tends to become lost in studies of this nature. A country simply becomes a data point, and the possibilities of understanding why and how Vanutu or Bulgaria functions the way it does may be sacrificed on a statistical altar. This research may be comprehensive statistical analysis, but often it is not really comparative politics. Comparative politics is constantly forced to trade off the particular for the general. Individual scholars must decide if they are experts in one country, or even one region of one country, or in one region of the world, or in comparative political theory that spans the globe – it is difficult to do all those things. Also, we must decide whether the real questions to be answered are about real countries or about distributions of data.

Summary and Conclusion

Comparative politics requires the selection of particular cases in the pursuit of general theory. At the extreme, a wide range of cases should be used, but that is a luxury available only for aggregate data analysis or a few extremely well-funded studies. Further, involving a large number of cases may mean that each one is not addressed carefully. If there is to be any primary data collection then there must be some selection of cases, and with that the development of criteria for how many are sufficient. This chapter should have demonstrated that there is no single answer to questions about the appropriate size or composition of samples for comparative research.

What is crucial in this discussion is that the size and nature of the sample be determined by the questions that are being addressed, rather than some predetermined idea of how research should be done. In some instances a single case is all that is required, and indeed in some instances more than one case might muddy the water rather than clarify the issues at hand. If a single case is selected wisely, and the research is done thoroughly, it may say a good deal more than any statistical study. On the other hand, there are some questions that may require a large sample and call for including as many cases as possible.

This chapter has pointed out that an intermediate strategy is often a good option for comparative research. Developing approaches that capture some of the complexity of individual cases in a geographical region, but still permit covering some portion of the possible cases, may provide something approaching the best of both worlds. Despite its potential virtues, however, this approach can be taken too far. It can produce research that takes as given what may be important hypotheses, for example, that the countries within the regional classification are similar in theoretically relevant ways. Further, this strategy can virtually eliminate the testing of some hypotheses by limiting the range of variance available. Like almost everything else about comparative politics that we have discussed here there is a trade-off, and there is no magic solution to substitute for the good judgment of the scholar in making decisions.

4

Measurement and Bias

Perhaps the most fundamental barriers to good comparative research are measurement and the problems of comparability of measures. If comparative analysis is to be at all meaningful then we must be sure that the same terms mean the same things in the different contexts within which the research is conducted. In particular, the comparative analyst must be concerned with the problem of establishing equivalent meaning for concepts within different social and cultural contexts. Words that we use to describe political life in one country, or that have theoretical meaning in one context, may elsewhere have very a different meaning, or indeed be meaningless. Europeans conceptualise the 'state' (Dyson, 1980) as a real, yet also metaphysical, entity while for most Americans the term has little meaning beyond a component of the federal system. Similarly, for Europeans outside Germany, Austria, Belgium and Switzerland, the concept of federalism means little, or is simply misunderstood; while for Canadians or Americans (as well as the four European systems mentioned above) there is a rich conceptual and empirical literature on the subject (Wright, 1988; Fitzmaurice, 1996; McKenna, 1993; Gauger and Weigelt, 1993). Even in the four European cases the idea of federalism may be very different from that encountered in North America, Brazil, Nigeria or India (Tushnet, 1990; Mahler, 1987; Mukarji and Arora, 1992). The misconceptions around federalism begin to have a practical effect, as well as an academic one, because the European Union may have a federal future, but the nature of that potential is completely misunderstood in some unitary regimes.

This measurement problem is crucial for comparative research, whether that research uses quantitative or qualitative measures, although measurement issues become more evident in quantitative research. Measurement is more crucial for quantitative research, because it requires much tighter specification of the instruments through which that measurement is to be conducted. For example, survey researchers conducting their investigations in a number of countries must be sure that the items on questionnaires are indeed comparable stimuli to which the respondents will give their answers. However comparable the stimuli, there will be no guarantee that the underlying dimensions of attitudes and values being tapped are identical across cultures. That common meaning may be problematic, even within a single countries, for example being the differences that may exist between sub-populations in culturally divided countries such as Belgium (Fitzmaurice, 1988), Canada (Laponce and Safran, 1996), Sri Lanka or Nigeria.

Although the measurement problems are more obvious in quantitative research, they are also very real for more qualitative empirical work. In qualitative analysis, the researcher is still looking at evidence of some sort and using that evidence to characterise a political reality and to make judgments about the behaviour of actors. Even seemingly simple issues in case research, for example, when a decision was reached and what it was, are often not obvious even for those who took it. For example, March and Olsen (1976) point out that choice in most organisational settings is extremely ambiguous and at times almost unconscious. Further, if a researcher is interested in policies, as opposed to discrete choices, then this may be the product of a large number of individual decisions. How then does he or she identify the crucial stages of choice?

Measurement problems for comparative research are to some degree merely an extension of the issues of measurement that are encountered in all the social sciences. For example, there are choices that must be made about the appropriate level of measurement. In general, researchers attempt to move up a scale of measurement from nominal categories to interval and ratio measures. Nominal measures are the lowest order, being simple naming of categories without any presumed ordering of those categories, for example, 'democratic' and 'authoritarian' political systems. A great deal of comparative political analysis is built on simple nominal categories, and is closely related to the configurative approach to comparison described above (see Key Text 3.1). More formal analysis through nominal categories does go somewhat beyond the simple description generally characteristic of case studies and configurative analysis. That is, even nominal measures assume the existence of an underlying concept to which the variable name being used can be related. In contrast, simple descriptive studies describe only by using more common-sense language, although concepts may later develop out of those descriptions.

Perhaps the most fundamental point about measurement in the social sciences, and indeed in science in general, is that there is a gap between the concepts researchers utilise and the measurements they use to provide an indication of the level of that concept in an observation. Even for measurements that are well established and appear 'hard', there is a discrepancy between the concept in the world of ideas and the operational measures used in the empirical world. For example, gross national product is used as a composite measure of economic performance, and as a major guide for economic policy-making in most countries, but the measurement of this concept poses a number of questions and problems (Beckerman, 1968; Zelditch, 1971; Shaikh and Tonah, 1994) that are often forgotten when it is being used. These measurement deficiencies are especially evident in a comparative context, when terms such as 'income' may have a different meaning in different national contexts (Kravis *et al.*, 1975). In particular, gross national product appears to be systematically under-measured in less developed economies, because of the larger proportion of non-marketed goods and services (Morris, 1979: 13). This is but one example of the general statement that every attempt to relate empirical observations to concepts and theory will be only a partial measure of the concept, and there will always be some discrepancy.

If the gap between concept and measurement is present for a entity such as gross national product, it is much greater for the terms that political scientists use (Somers, 1995). For example, we often talk about 'political culture' as a means of explaining differences among political systems. Culture may be a residual explanation that is used when the other variables in which a scholar is interested fail (Elkins and Simeon, 1979), but some studies are explicitly concerned with culture and its capacity to explain other political phenomena. The *Civic Culture* (Almond and Verba, 1967 – see Key Text 2.1), Ronald Inglehart's work on political culture (1977; 1990; 1997; see also Key Text 6.1) and the Kaase and Newton (1995) collection of books on political values are the most notable examples, but by no means the only ones.

Conceptually, political culture (see Welch, 1993) means something on the order of a 'particular pattern of orientations to political action in which . . . every political system is embedded' (Almond, 1956:

396), or perhaps 'The attitudinal and behavioural matrix within which the political system is located' (White, 1979: 1). These are relatively clear conceptual definitions, but they are also extremely difficult to operationalise; it is not entirely clear they would be operationalised in the same way. Inglehart's work, and that of Almond and Verba, taps some aspects of this concept, but certainly not all. More ideographic studies of individual political cultures may explain a great deal about the particular country, but in most instances the findings and the components of cultures do not travel well at all (Berg-Schlosser and Rytlewski, 1993).

Finally, there are some attempts to provide conceptual schemes for culture (Pye, 1965; Douglas, 1982) that go further in providing a general approach to political culture, but these also are more powerful conceptually than empirically, and tend to demand a number of qualitative judgment by researchers.

In its simplest form, this discrepancy is simply a problem of language, and of translating survey instruments into other languages so that a respondent in one country will be replying to a stimulus that is as near as possible to that presented to respondents in other countries. Given that the social sciences deal with many concepts and words that have meanings deeply influenced by culture, solving this translation problem is far from easy. A word that has a rather straightforward meaning in English may imply a host of complexities in other societies and language groups, and terms like 'authority', 'class', and 'community' may have different denotative meanings elsewhere. One of the more common examples of these linguistic problems is that German and some other European languages do not have different words for 'policy' and 'politics' as are found in English. Even operating in the same language may be no proof against misunderstanding, especially if the interviewing process requires coding of open-ended questions; American and British respondents may seemingly report different degrees of intensity of feeling because of differing degrees of volubility.

The linguistic problem is, however, by no means the only problem, or even the most serious one, facing comparative researchers in establishing the conceptual equivalence of their work. The most important problem is conceptual. The primary task of comparative politics remains that of developing concepts that are usable across national boundaries and across cultural boundaries. Terms that have one meaning (or even some meaning) in one context may be very different in others, so that research constructed on one set of assumptions will simply not work in another. The researcher may collect data, but how does she or he know that they are on the same dimension in different countries, or in different time periods? As Max Weber (1988: 278–9) argued, the basic quest for the social scientist is for good concepts.

There is no easy answer to this question, but there are some means of validating measures that can be employed to avert the worst pitfalls of comparative research. We should think of all our measurement instruments as having a variety of forms of validity: face validity, construct validity, predictive validity, and internal and external validity. Face validity is the simplest test. If the researcher is interested in voting behaviour then the instruments used for research should be related to voting and political participation. If politics in a particular country is a sensitive matter then the researcher may think about using indirect measures, but the further those measures stray from the issue of voting the less face validity they have, and the more suspect are the findings. For example, some studies (Laurin, 1986) of tax evasion – a ticklish matter anywhere – do not ask respondents if they evade taxes, but instead ask if they believe their neighbours evade. This question is clearly about taxes, but avoids asking respondents to make overt confessions of possible illegal behaviour.

Predictive validity is assessed by determining just what other variables the measurement instrument in question is related to statistically – can it predict the values on another variable as it should? For example, if we want to determine if a measurement of political efficacy were valid then we would want to determine if it were positively related to voting and other forms of participation. Also, we would not want it to be related to other measurements that are peripheral to this area of political behaviour, for example, political liberalism. Campbell and Fiske (1959) talked on validation using a matrix of variables, some presumably related to the new measure in question and others presumably not. If the measure in question is highly correlated with measures thought to be related and uncorrelated with the others, then there is some sense that the measure is tapping the attributes desired.

In comparative analysis, this form of testing could be applied when an measurement instrument is imported from another setting. For example, in the early days of the analysis of voting behaviour, much of the methodology was exported from the United States to other countries.

Cook and Campbell (1979) have discussed several additional conceptions of validity that are particularly important for non-experimental research, such as that commonly used in political science. For comparative politics in particular, inadequate attention to construct validity has the potential to undermine the utility of research. Construct validity is the basic measurement question, of whether the instruments used to tap the construct actually do so. This requires ignoring the fundamental gap existing between concepts and measures, and determining if there is a reasonable relationship between the two levels of abstraction. There may be no way of guaranteeing that a particular measure is an adequate reflection of the concept to which it is directed, but experience with similar measures and the face validity of the measurement can provide some assurances.

In comparative politics the problem of equivalence is a major problem for construct validity and measurement. As Henry Teune (1990: 53–4) has argued:

> Encounters with diversity in comparing countries heightened awareness of the problem of equivalence across systems. In order to compare something across systems it is necessary to have confidence that the components and their properties that are being compared are the 'same' or indicate something equivalent.

In other words, in comparative politics there is the danger of engaging in a wonderful, creative exercise of comparison that ultimately is meaningless because the systems or institutions being compared are not equivalent. The problem is often however that it is difficult or impossible to establish equivalence, or the lack of it, without actually doing the research. Further, even if there is no direct equivalence, the research establishing that lack of similarity may be extremely informative about the differences between the political systems in question.

Campbell and Cook also discuss threats to 'statistical conclusion' validity that exist in social research. As we will discuss in greater detail in Chapter 8, statistical techniques for explanation are based on principles such as random selection and the independence of observations. Those assumptions are sometimes difficult to maintain in social science research, given the numerous ways that error can creep into the analysis. For example, almost all statistical techniques assume that observations are independent, but, given the diffusion of political forms and practices, that assumption is difficult to maintain as valid for the real world, especially for proximate groups – for example, European countries – that are often compared (Frenderis, 1983). Similarly, given that comparative politics often examines the universe of countries, the fundamental assumptions of randomness and measures of statistical significance have relatively little meaning. All of these problems mean that the statistical analysis on which so much of contemporary political analysis depends may not be as valid as is usually assumed.

The Travelling Problem

Perhaps the most fundamental problem in comparative research is the 'travelling problem' confronting measurement (Sartori, 1970; 1991). The basic question raised here is whether measures that are constructed for use in one political setting, and that are based upon the experience of one society or culture, are necessarily meaningful or useful in another setting. This problem has been manifested in a number of different forms of comparison. It is clear that this problem can exist in cross-national comparisons, especially when the concepts travel a very long distance, for example, from Anglo-Saxon North America to French Central Africa. It can however also occur when the distance (geographical and cultural) are less extreme, for example, in assuming that French and German politics are in essence undergirded by similar cultural principles, since the two countries happen to be neighbours. Even within a single country, the differences between cultures – for example, between French and English Canadian political cultures – are perhaps sufficient (Laponce and Safran, 1996) to make direct comparisons of research findings difficult.

The travelling problem actually has two levels at which it must be considered, and then addressed, by comparative scholars in their research. The first is the conceptual level of analysis. At this level, the question is whether the concept to which an empirical measure is related is meaningful in the different settings in which it is being used. We have already pointed out that some conceptual terms that appear widely in the literature on government and politics may mean very dissimilar things in different political cultures. Even if the denotative, 'textbook', meaning of the concept is the same in the various settings the connotations of the term may be very different. Therefore, if the public is to be involved directly in the research, the comparative applicability of the concept is limited.

The example of the familiar term 'bureaucracy' points to the problem of differential interpretations of a concept. In almost all political cultures, this word would have the same textbook meaning based largely upon Weber (Gerth and Mills, 1958), that is, a structure of hierarchical authority used to administer policy, whether in the public or the private sector. The significance assigned to it would, vary considerably however. In the Germanic countries it often has a neutral, or even positive, denotation, and 'bureaucrats' are respected figures in society. In the Anglo–American tradition, though, bureaucracy has a very different, and largely negative, connotation. Any attempt to do research on this concept in these different cultures will be conditioned by those differences of cultural interpretation. If this problem arises for a concept with a very clear denotative meaning as bureaucracy, then the range of variation in interpretation for more recondite concepts such as 'democracy' (Sartori, 1995; Dahl, 1982) or 'power' is very wide indeed.

One way to address these more difficult concepts is illustrated by Schmitter and Karl's attempt to develop a conception of democracy that is useful across a range of countries. They follow one of the paths suggested by Collier and Mahon (1993: 850–1) by treating democracy as a set of 'radial' categories. That is, each of the types of democracy they discuss has some basic features of a democracy, but also has some other features that distinguish it. In particular, Schmitter and Karl develop the categories (see Figure 4.1 and Key Text 4.1) of corporatist, populist, consociational and electoralist democracy. The categories are based upon the relative strength of state and society, and on the relative importance of electoral and interest group participation. They argue that these categories enable them to capture the varieties of systems that all fit into the broader category of democracy.

Operational Travelling Problems

This problem also arises at the more operational level of developing measures of the concepts we use for comparative analysis. As noted above, these differences are especially important for quantitative research when a concept must be transformed into a series of questions, or into a series of items on a checklist of measurement. Sartori (1970: 1041; 1984: 24) described measures as having the properties of extension and intension. *Extension* is the question of how many cases the measure is meant to apply. The term 'corporate

FIGURE 4.1
Typologies of democracy

A. Lijphart typology

		Political culture	
		Homogeneous	*Fragmented*
Elite behaviour	*Coalescent*	Depoliticised democracy	Consociational democracy
	Competitive	Centripetal democracy	Centrifugal democracy

B. Karl typology

		Strategies of transition	
		Compromise	*Force*
Relative actor strength	*Elite ascendent*	Pact	Imposition
	Mass ascendent	Reform	Revolution

Sources: Lijphart *et al.* (1968); Karl (1990).

pluralism', for example, was developed within the context of Norwegian politics (Rokkan, 1966; Olsen, 1987), and may apply easily perhaps only there (Heisler, 1979). Rokkan was attempting to differentiate the right of a large number of interest groups to have legitimate interactions with government from the more exclusive and restrictive concept of corporatism. The term has, however, been extended to several other democratic regimes, and advocated as being applicable for still others. Other similar conceptualisations of state–society relationships, for example, 'bargained pluralism' in Italy (Hine, 1993), have also been advanced by scholars.

When a term like corporate pluralism is extended to other countries, it may be forced to climb up the 'ladder of abstraction' in order to be used effectively. That is, given that this concept is so closely linked to the character of Norwegian politics, if it is moved outside that setting then it is better treated as one variation on a more general concept if it is to be used for comparison. For example, corporate pluralism can be understood as a having some elements of the more general concept of 'pluralism', or that of 'corporatism', or of both. If those concepts still proved too specific, then the more general concepts of 'state–society relationships' or 'interest intermediation'

Key Text 4.1 Philippe Schmitter and T. L. Karl, and Kinds of Democracy

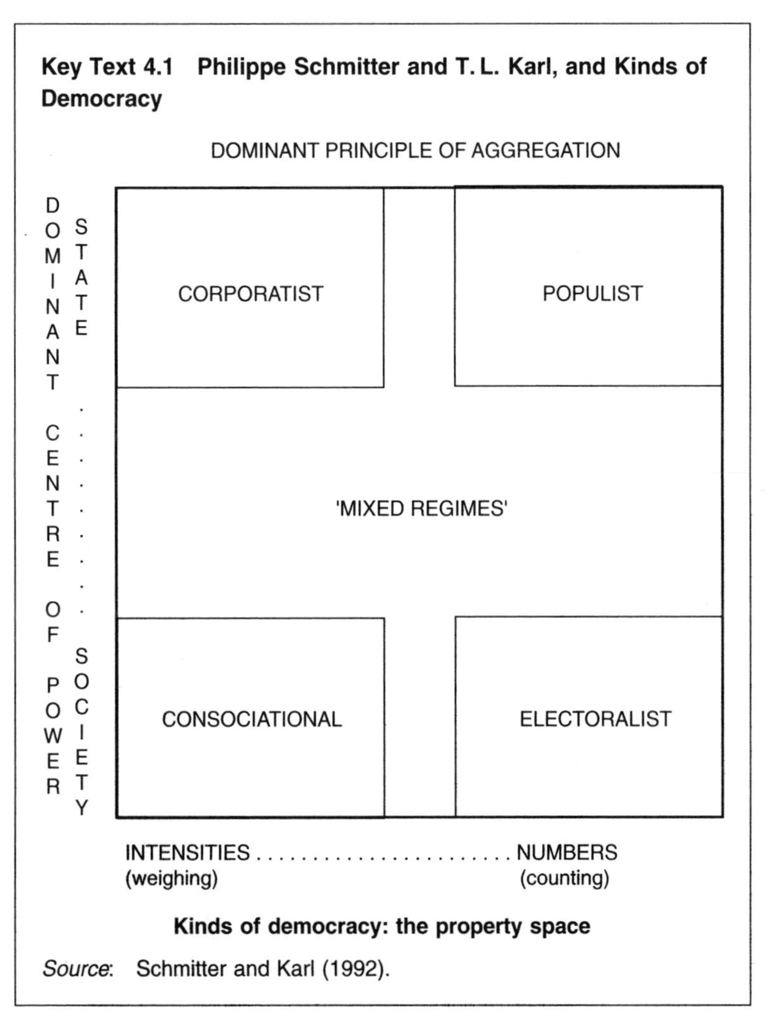

Kinds of democracy: the property space

Source: Schmitter and Karl (1992).

might be invoked (Harbeson *et al.*, 1994; Migdal, 1988; Wiesenthal, 1996). Atkinson and Coleman (1988), for example, have developed a large typology of state–society relationships, built on the characteristics of both the state and interest groups – particularly business groups. This typology categorises much of this variation in the policy networks that emerge from these relationships, and makes them more amenable to comparative analysis.

The use of the more general concept naturally decreases the specificity sharpness of the comparison, so that, as researchers are forced to move further up that ladder, clarity is lost. As concepts become able to encompass the entire world, the extreme vagueness of approaches such as systems analysis, which could compare almost anything but never very precisely (Dogan and Pelassey, 1990: 103 ff.), is in danger of being reached. Much the same analytic logic would be applied if we took Schmitter's (1974) category of corporatism and then added additional attributes to make it either 'state' or 'societal' corporatism. In Europe, the Iberian systems might have been 'state corporatism' at one time, but this term would not be useful for other corporatist systems.

Another way to think about this problem is that concepts can be so reduced in content that there is no opposite logically possible. It often happens that some terms used to describe and evaluate governments – corporatism, clientelism or even democracy – become so popular that analysts want to use the term to use their own favourite country, regardless of its real applicability in that setting, and to loosen the definition of a concept to make it applicable. This academic version of faddism tends to deprive concepts of any real meaning. It is a conceptual version of Popper's (1959) problem of falsification; theories can be designed to be so encompassing that there is no way to exclude any cases and hence the theory is meaningless.

The other characteristic that Sartori (1970) used to describe concepts was *intension*. This is the number of attributes used to define a concept or a variable. The more attributes used in a definition, the less general the category becomes, and hence the fewer cases to which it is applicable. If we return to the 'corporate pluralism' example used above, the 'corporate' element adds another attribute to the term pluralism, and hence restricts the application further – it forces the measurement down the ladder of generality. Thus, extension and intension are values that must be traded off when developing empirical measurements. The more precise a researcher wants his or her measurements to be, the fewer are the cases to which they can be applied fruitfully. Likewise, the larger the geographical scope that research attempts to cover, the fewer are the attributes that should be used to describe concepts. This is, for Sartori at least, a fundamental constraint on the generality of comparative politics. This inverse relationship between intension and extension also reinforces the views of some of the sceptics on social science, who stress more interpretative conceptions of comparison rather than quantification and formal measurement (MacIntyre, 1978; Rabinow and Sullivan, 1979).

David Collier and James Mahon (1993) have sought to identify a way around the constraints imposed by Sartori's formulation. They argue that rather than taking membership in a category in a strict, classical sense – for example, sharing all the attributes in the category – it is sufficient to have a 'family resemblance' or to use 'radial categories'. These loosened requirements would permit inclusion of a case in the broad category if it shared most characteristics (family resemblance) or a dominant characteristic (radial categories) with the concept in question. Collier and Mahon argue, for example, that the term 'corporatism' remains useful even though a number of the Latin American countries to which it has been applied do not share all of its attributes in every time period under study (see also Collier and Collier, 1991; also Hammergren, 1983). This lack of total correspondence between concept and measure might have been even greater had they also chosen to look also at European systems usually described as corporatist (Katzenstein, 1984: 1985).

The basic research question, then, is whether a term such as corporatism should remain as a component within the arsenal of political science. Or should it instead be discarded in favour of a concept that can be applied equally well in all these countries, albeit a concept with less intension? The option would be to struggle through with a category that appears less generic, but yet still can convey a great deal of the meaning, both to scholars and to participants in the policy process, in the full range of countries. Either strategy would have its benefits, as well as some costs, and must be matched with the particular purposes of the research project and the degree of variance in the sample of countries under consideration.

Collier and Mahon are not the only scholars who would relax some of the more stringent criteria of measurement, and thus be willing to stretch a concept or two. Przeworski and Teune (1970: 11–12) argue that comparative research should at times adopt a 'systems-specific' approach to measurement that might permit different measures to define the same category or concept. They argue that the level of intellectual development of the social sciences was (and probably still is) sufficiently low for researchers not to be so purist about the manner in which they address concepts across cultures. Sartori, of course, would argue that if researchers continue to relax these measurement criteria, then the social sciences may never progress any further. If categories are stretched so much, he might argue, then we can never really test theories.

This scholarly debate on measurement points to yet another fundamental trade-off in comparative political research. On the one hand, we need to develop concepts and measurements that are sufficiently general to travel across societies – it is almost impossible to conduct comparative political research without concepts of that type. On the other hand, we also must have concepts that are sufficiently specific to isolate characteristics of a particular political system (national, subnational or even supranational) so that we can understand that system better. How can we conduct comparative research without violating one precept or the other?

As with many apparent dilemmas in this field, the way to resolve this one is to ask what the purpose of each piece of research is. If it is to understand a single system, or a small number of systems, then one strategy is preferable, while the alternative is appropriate for larger-scale research. Further, the measurement question is not a simple dichotomy: it is a continuum, or a 'ladder' with a number of rungs. Therefore, the researcher should be able to choose just where along this continuum to attempt to measure concepts. For example, the notion of 'new social movements' was developed in the industrialised democracies to describe movements such as environmentalism and feminism. When considering whether the concept could be applied to Latin America, Hellman (1992; see also Markoff, 1996) argued that there were some important points of similarity but yet some equally important points of difference. Other scholars have attempted to apply the concept in other settings (see McAdam *et al.*, 1996). Understanding both the similarities and differences that occur in different settings helps to understand both the concept and the particular political systems.

Empirical Travelling Problems

As well as the conceptual travelling problems, there are also some simple empirical travelling problems. Take, for example, the study of the welfare state and social service provision in the industrialised democracies. It is by now axiomatic that the USA is a 'welfare state laggard' (Wilensky, 1974). This is almost certainly true, but it is not so much of a laggard as it is often portrayed when the full range of services provided through employers is considered (Rein and Rainwater, 1986). These are privately provided, but are supported in a very significant manner by government by virtue of being tax-exempt for the recipients and tax-deductible for the businesses. Thus, although the concept of social services, and even that of the welfare state, appear to travel reasonably well, the failure to develop an empirical measure that taps alternative forms of provision (Peters and Heisler, 1983) skews the empirical results.

The point here is that measurements and even concepts that appear very sensible in one setting distort reality in others. Another example using the United States may further illustrate this point. The relatively low level of voter turnout there is taken as a measure of a lack of political participation in that country. If, however, one weights the turnout figure by some measure of the legal difficulties of registering to vote, then the American public, if not the electoral laws themselves, appear substantially more participative; in states with simpler registration laws, for example, those in the upper Midwest, voter turnout approximates that in many European countries. Similarly, when the total number of times Americans must turn out for elections – numerous state and local campaigns, referenda and initiatives, party primaries – is taken into account, then the American political system also appears more participatory. Finally, if additional measures of political participation, for example, volunteering in political campaigns, are employed, then the United States again appears more participative.

Typologies

Some measurement issues in comparative research revolve around how to develop single variables. Others involve the interaction of two or perhaps even more variables, with those interactions producing a new variable, or classification, of political systems. This practice is the formation of *typologies*. It goes back to Aristotle (see Hague *et al.*, 1992: 26), whose classification of political systems depended upon interrelating the number of rulers with the 'form' of the system (genuine or perverted). More recently, one of the more notable attempts at typology formation is the classification of democratic political systems developed by Arend Lijphart (1968), as presented in Figure 4.1 and Key Text 4.2. The two variables in this case were the nature of the élite political culture and mass political culture; in each case, the culture could be fragmented or integrated. The interaction of these two dichotomous variables generated four types of political systems. Lijphart argued that these four types were fundamental forms of

Key Text 4.2 Arend Lijphart and Consociationalism

We have noted that comparative political theory can be developed through a careful examination of a single country. This is certainly the case with Arend Lijphart's study of the Netherlands. Lijphart was interested in how a country that was deeply divided by religious cleavages could survive politically without overt conflict, and indeed with a good deal of cooperation and government effectiveness. His examination of Dutch politics lead him to develop the idea of 'consociationalism'.

Lijphart argued that the three religious groups in the Netherlands were organised into three 'pillars' (Roman Catholic, Calvinist, and secular) that effectively minimised the interaction of ordinary members of the groups; almost all aspects of socio-economic life of the Netherlands were organised within the pillars. This separation minimised conflict between the rank and file members of the groups. The separation could minimise conflict but it could not allow for effective management of the political system; that requires cooperation among the groups. That cooperation, Lijphart found, did occur at the élite level of Dutch politics so that the leadership were capable of running the political and economic systems.

This consociational system of governance functioned because of the existence of horizontal and vertical trust. Within each of the pillars there was vertical trust between the mass membership and the élite. That vertical trust enabled the élites to negotiate with one another with a good deal of latitude. At the élite level there is sufficient trust among the élites that enables them to reach binding deals among themselves. While this produced apparently secret and closed negotiations among the élite that was accepted as necessary to maintain the other aspects of democracy within the Netherlands.

The consociational system was effective in the Netherlands for a number of years, although it appears that the system has now become more secularised and 'depillarised' (Mierlo, 1986). The concept of consociationalism has, however, been extended to explain politics in a number of other culturally divided systems such as Canada, Malaya, and India (Lijphart, 1997). The concept has not been as successful in describing politics within those other societies, but it still has provided substantial conceptual leverage in understanding more generally how to cope politically with strong cultural divisions in a society. This concept has been able to travel better than have many others in the social sciences, but still appears to have some content that is purely Dutch.

democratic systems, which could then be used to explain and predict behaviour within the systems. Similarly, Karl (1990) uses a typology based on relative actor strength and strategies to discuss alternative models of the process of democratisation in Latin America (Figure 4.1).

A typology is more than a simple measurement question; it is the initial stage of a theory of politics. In the case of the Lijphart typology, this proto-theory is arguing that the *interaction* of these two levels of culture shapes the nature of politics in these systems, rather than either of the two variables alone. In this case, the logic of the typology is that although politics in Sweden, for example, are distinctive and have their national peculiarities (Heclo and Madsen, 1987), Sweden can also be understood as a case of centripetal politics. As such, its politics is sufficiently similar to that of other countries such as Norway and Denmark found in the same cell of the typology for it to be treated as a homogeneous group (Elder *et al.*, 1988). Therefore, this is a step in moving comparative politics away from the study of proper names to the development of theories based upon variables and classes of countries. While typologies may move comparative politics in the direction of statistical analysis (see Crepaz, 1996), rather than more classic forms of comparative analysis, it certainly is a major contribution to comparative theory development; for another example of moving from variable names in the place of countries in the development of theory by typology, see Thomassen's (1994) work on the linkage of voters and representatives.

Another good example of the relationship of typologies to measurement and to theory is Jeffrey Paige's (1975) classification of agrarian revolutions in a range of less developed countries (see Figure 4.2). This was a typology based upon the sources of income of cultivators and non-cultivators in agrarian society, with the dependent variable being the type of agrarian unrest that should be expected. When this

FIGURE 4.2
Typology of agrarian revolutions

		Income of non-cultivators	
		Land	**Capital**
Income of cultivators	**Land**	Agrarian revolt	Market reform
	Wages	Revolution	Labour reform

Source: Paige (1975).

model is tested empirically (Anderson and Seligson, 1994) in one Central American country, however, it proves to be under-specified, and several other variables need to be added in order to generate stable predictions of the outcomes. Also, it is not clear if the same dynamics would have been expected for agrarian change in pre-modern Europe. Still, this typology and the associated theory did provoke a much better understanding of these processes.

Although typologies can certainly contribute to the development of empirical political theory, there are also some potential pitfalls to this form of measurement. The first is the common reliance upon the dichotomisation or trichotomisation of continuua that appears inherent in this approach. This concern about typologies actually is just another example of the 'degreeism' mentioned above as a problem for measurement (p. 103). That is, in each dimension of a typology there is usually an underlying continuum that then is divided arbitrarily into two or three segments. For example, in the Lijphart typology there is an underlying dimension of mass political integration. This dimension may be anchored by the extreme fragmentation of Switzerland, divided into four linguistic and two religious communities, in addition to the usual socio-economic cleavages; Lane and Ersson (1994a) provide a quantitative evaluation of cleavages among European countries, based upon the number and intensity of socio-economic differences, that demonstrates the extreme position of Switzerland. At the other end of the dimension might be Sweden, with few significant cleavages other than the fundamental socio-economic division. Where along this continuum should the researcher divide the democratic countries? That is no simple decision, given that the choice of the dividing line will to some extent determine the research outcomes.

Aaron Wildavsky (1987) makes the point about the artificial nature of some of the divisions in typologies very well in his examination of Mary Douglas's (1982) typology of culture. Wildavsky examined the impact of culture on the way in which knowledge was used in industrial regulation in six industrialised democracies. He found that several of the countries fit very neatly into the cells of the typology, but that the United States and European social democracies tended to bridge the cells. As well as pointing to the arbitrary nature of the way in which the dividing lines between categories are drawn, this finding also points to the reliance on individual scholars to define words like 'few' and 'weak' that are used to define the ends of the continuua. One person's weak may be another person's strong, especially when those persons themselves are drawn from different political cultures.

Another potential problem arising with typologies is the reverse of the dichotomisation problem. The temptation for scholars is often to elaborate typologies with a large number of different categories for each of the variables. Some of the work of Sartori (Sartori *et al.*, 1975) and others in the COCTA (Committee on Conceptual and Terminological Analysis) group within political science demonstrate this tendency very clearly. While this strategy can certainly point to all logical possibilities, it can also produce confusion and unnecessary complexity. In that case, 'reduction of the property space' (see Marradi, 1990) may be needed to produce a usable classification scheme.

The final potential problem concerning typologies as a means of measurement is that they tend to push towards whole system comparisons. Within the Lijphart typology, for example, the United Kingdom is seen, rather clearly, as an Anglo–American, centrifugal democracy. There may, however, be some policy areas or some issues on which the British government behaves more like a centripetal regime – for example, agriculture. Further, some parts of the United Kingdom may display significantly different political values – Scotland can be described as being more like Continental countries politically. This variation within countries is to some extent a problem inherent to comparative analysis; Freeman (1983; see also Muller, 1985) argues that there are greater differences across policy areas within countries than in the same policy area across countries. The classification of entire systems on the two (or more) variables, however, tends to make that rather homogeneous classification more apparent, and also appear more suspect.

Triangulation

Given the numerous problems of measurement that arise in comparative politics, we should also think about using multiple measures to address the same phenomenon. This basic strategy – triangulation – has been proposed for social science in general (Webb *et al.*, 1967; Denzin, 1978). The argument being made is that many of the research methods on which we rely in the social sciences are intrusive and obtrusive. People know that they are being observed and measured, and therefore react differently from how they might in a more natural setting. Reliance on obtrusive measures, even those such as surveys that generally are administered in a respondent's own home, then obviously becomes a major threat to the external validity of social research.

The strategy proposed was to supplement the obtrusive measures with a series of unobtrusive ones that would allow respondents to behave more naturally. For example, suppose a researcher is interested in the manner in which citizens are treated by public servants in a variety of settings – post offices, welfare offices, passport offices, and so on Some available evidence (Katz *et al.*, 1975; Bodiguel and Rouban, 1991; Goodsell, 1995) is that citizens are treated about as well in these situations as they are in the offices of private organisations, or even better, although the public sector rarely receives credit for its good treatment of clients. The researchers could ask clients how they are dealt with, and they could also ask public servants how they think they are treating their clients. This will provide some evidence, but it may be coloured by factors such as the possibility that social service clients may not report inadequate service for fear of losing benefits, and that public employees will always give the socially desirable answers for fear of poor performance ratings. On the other hand, however, the generalised denigration of the public sector in many societies may mean that reports are excessively negative; triangulation might allow using some more objective standards of quality to test the reliability of respondents (see Pollitt and Bouckaert, 1995).

The survey data are useful, but they could be supplemented with unobtrusive measures. A researcher could sit or stand (unobtrusively, of course) in an office, and watch the interactions between client and government officials as decisions are made (see Goodsell, 1976; Almond and Lasswell, 1934). He or she might also role-play, and pretend to be a prospective client in order to see how they are treated, a 'ethnomethodological' style of research that may produce some questions on ethics as well as problems of its reliability. The researcher might examine case files or complaints to determine how different types of clients (defined by race or gender perhaps) fare with government officials. All these methods can supplement and enrich the evidence gained by simply asking people what is happening for them when they visit government offices.

Triangulation need not just be the use of unobtrusive measures to supplement more intrusive ones. It may also involve the use of various types of obtrusive measures, each designed to check on the validity of the others, or to elicit different forms of information from the research subjects. For example, the information gained from a survey may be supplemented by an even more intrusive method such as a social experiment. This latter method might be used to control the stimuli presented to the respondents, especially when the issue at hand has relatively little salience to a mass political audience. Similarly, scales may be constructed from several unobtrusive indicators – voting behaviour, membership in certain groups, political violence, and so on – to characterise the nations or the various subnational units within a country for comparative examination.

Triangulation may be especially important for coping with variables that carry social stigma or even legal penalties (see Brewer and Hunter, 1989). For example, if we are interested in tax evasion as an indicator of popular disaffection with government (Listhaug and Miller, 1985), it is difficult to go up to someone's doorstep and ask them in a survey instrument if they have been evading taxes. There are, however, several seemingly effective ways of getting at this issue (see Peters, 1993). One is to ask them if they believe that their neighbours evade taxes – people who commit an anti-social act often justify it by assuming that others do the same thing. There are also less obtrusive ways to measure the level of tax evasion, for example, the amount of cash used in the economy and the error terms of national accounts such as gross national product. (GNP is measured by income and expenditure; expenditure figures are almost always higher than income figures, because people hide income to evade its being taxed.) A combination of all these varieties of measures should give a good picture of the comparative levels of evasion in relatively similar economies.

The strategy of triangulation can also be seen as a means of validating measurements to be used in comparative analysis. Any comparative researcher will be aware that his or her measures may not travel, and there is a need to see if indeed they do 'work' in a particular context. This discussion is phrased in terms of surveys and attitudinal scales, but is more generally applicable. For example, to attempt to validate the meaning of voting for a particular political party, the researcher might want to test the correlation with membership in groups such as trade unions, or look at the socio-economic correlates of areas with a large voting strength for that party. Campbell and Fiske (1959) some time ago pointed to using the triangulation method for validation of a new measure, or for validating a familiar measure in a new setting. What this requires is the application of a series of measures, some similar to and some dissimilar from the scale or other measurement technique in question. A sample is then given all these scales. If the measure is valid then it should correlate positively with the already validated measures to which it is assumed to be similar, and negatively with those measures from which it is thought to be different.

Also, the use of unobtrusive measures should not be seen as a panacea for social research. While it has the advantage of not intruding into social settings, it has the disadvantage of not always being readily interpretable. Abraham Kaplan (1965) makes this point, when he distinguishes between act and action meanings in social research. 'Act meaning' is the meaning attached to behaviour by the observer, while 'action meaning' is the meaning attached to that same behaviour by the participants. Let us return to our example of assessing the behaviour of government bureaucrats. The observer may see an apparently unhappy client at the wicket and assume that he or she is being mistreated. In reality, however, that apparent anger may be a conscious strategy on the part of the client to get even better treatment. Indeed, it may be only in those situations where the client expects good treatment that he or she will engage in these ploys.

The difference between act meaning and action meaning is especially important for comparative analysis. When researchers begin to transfer their measurements across cultures, the difficulties of interpretation increase, and if unobtrusive measures are particularly subject to these differences then they quickly become suspect. One rather obvious example has been voting for communist parties in many countries of Western Europe during most of the post-war period. Without placing that behaviour in context, the 34 per cent vote for the communists in Italy (1976) or the 22 per cent in France (1967) might appear to be strong support for Marxism. When these votes are understood in context, however, they more often reflected protest against the political system as a whole, rather than adherence to any particular political ideology (Pierce and Converse, 1986; Blackmer and Tarrow, 1975). The problem with replying upon unobtrusive measures, then, is that there is no one to tell the researcher when he or she has interpreted the measure incorrectly, as there might be when subjects are involved more directly in the measurement.

As well as thinking about triangulating measurements of political phenomena, we should think about triangulating theory and measurement. Most measures are, or at least should be, related to a theory. Therefore, a researcher can triangulate all he or she wants, but if the theory is inadequate then the measures probably will be also. If we think about the matrix in Figure 4.3, we can see that it is possible to have studies that fall into at least three of the four cells (it is unlikely to have multiple theories but no differences among the measures). Most researchers enter the field with a clear idea of what they are after, and how they expect to find it. Perhaps too often they find what they set out to find. Some greater attention to the possibilities of multiple measurement and testing multiple theories, even if qualitatively, may help advance the discipline.

The classic example of triangulating theory is Graham Allison's study (1971) of the Cuban Missile Crisis. The possibilities are demonstrated even more clearly in Bobrow *et al.*'s study (1996) of development in South-East Asia, using five different developmental scenarios and multiple measures of change. Also, Ruth Collier (1993) addressed directly the need to triangulate in qualitative studies as well as in quantitative studies. She attempts to understand several aspects of regime change in Latin America during the 1940s, using external factors in the political economy and internal patterns of change as alternative explanations.

Despite its potential pitfalls, triangulation is an important measurement device for comparative research. It can help the researcher go into geographical and cultural settings with which he or she is relatively unfamiliar without committing egregious errors of interpretation. Although no technique can save a researcher from poorly

FIGURE 4.3
Triangulation matrix

x_1	—					
x_2	i	—				
x_3	i	h	—			
x_4	h	i	i	—		
x_5	h	i	i	h	—	
x_6	i	h	h	i	i	—
T	h	i	i	h	h	i

Test variable T is highly correlated with variables x_1, x_4 and x_5, but uncorrelated with the other variables. Therefore, T can be said to share some of the attributes of those other variables and to be a potentially valid measure of a characteristic similar to the variables with which it is correlated.

Key Text 4.3 Richard Rose and Party Government

One of the fundamental questions of democratic politics is whether political institutions are capable of translating the preferences of voters into effective public policies. Richard Rose (1974b) developed a set of questions about the capacity of governing systems to perform this function, including whether the parties presented clear statements of goals and means from which voters could choose, whether the ministers selected for office had the time and the skills necessary to put policies into effect, and whether the rest of government would follow the directives developed by elected executive.

Rose developed his intellectual model within the context of British government, finding that there were a number of serious impediments to making 'party government' function in that country. Although the original work was based on the single country, it clearly provided a basis for more comparative analysis. That comparison could be across countries (Castles and Wildenmann, 1986), across institutions (Peters, 1973) and across time. For example, while British cabinet ministers are encumbered with parliamentary and constituency duties their counterparts in France, by virtue of having to relinquish their parliamentary seats, have more time to manage the ministry and pursue policy objectives. Similarly, Austria tends to recruit a number of ministers from outside parliament while the convention in British (and other Westminster) government is that ministers must come from one house or the other of parliament. This feature appears to make Austrian government more effective in implementing party programmes than are many other similar political systems. Finally, changes in British government creating a number of autonomous and quasi-autonomous agencies for implementing policy may actually make party government less likely.

This book points out first how a study of a single country can foster comparative analysis, if the research is directed at basic theoretical and analytic questions. Britain should be a case in which party government functions well, so that if it fails there it may be in trouble in many other settings. It also points out how important normative questions, for example the nature of democracy, can be dealt with in a more empirical manner. Rose's research does not redefine the nature of democracy itself, but it does show how democracy does or does not function in practice.

developed theory or inadequate measurement, the various 'tricks' discussed in this chapter should alert the researcher to the pitfalls of measurement that is extended across cultural boundaries and to some ways of at least checking on the problems which are arising.

Nominal Categories

More than any other branch of political science, comparative politics depends upon nominal categories for its analytic power. Using nominal categories is a long-standing tradition in comparative politics, going back to some of the very early attempts to use descriptive and analytic categories (Wilson, 1898; Woolsey, 1893). Despite the development of more complex models and measures, the use of nominal categories has continued. For example, Carl Friedrich and Z. Brzezinski wrote a classic book (1956) in the field entitled *Totalitarian Dictatorship and Autocracy*. Not only do the words in that title provoke political and even emotional reactions, but they also require a good deal of specification if they are to be measured cross-nationally.

Even terms that are used commonly in the discipline and in everyday political discussions require careful definition – the recent spate of research on 'democratisation' raises the need to specify concepts very clearly. There are a variety of conceptual and empirical meanings for democracy, so that any statement about democratisation requires classification.

The use of nominal categories need not be confined to single terms, but rather taxonomies can be developed that classify different political systems. These differ from the typologies already discussed in being simple lists of names, rather than the product of the interaction of two or more variables. Take, for example, the taxonomy of African political systems contained in Table 1.1. There is some underlying dimension in these categories (democratisation, perhaps), but the categories are not even really ordered, much less have any knowable distance between them. Further, each of the terms used will require some more precise definition in order to be useful for comparative analysis – just how do we differentiate a party-mobilising from a party-centralist regime?

In some instances, a clear definition of a conceptual term will make measurement relatively easy, even for a nominal term. For example, Phillipe Schmitter (1974) provided a litany of terms to characterise corporatism. For him, corporatism is:

> a system of interest representation in which the constituent units are organized into a limited number of singular, compulsory, noncompetitive, hierarchically ordered and functionally differentiated categories, recognized or licensed (if not created) by the state

> and granted a deliberate representation monopoly within their respective categories in exchange for observing certain controls on the selection of leaders and articulation of demands and supports. (p. 93)

Given that clear definition, a researcher can measure the extent to which pressure group structures in a country are corporatist. For example, Schmitter (1981) himself provided one set of measurements of corporatism for European countries, as did Klaus von Beyme (1981). In the case of this important concept, there also have been attempts to make it travel effectively across national boundaries. Some of Schmitter's initial analysis was based on Latin American cases (see also Wiarda, 1997) as well as European ones, but subsequent analyses have extended the concept to African countries, and even China (Zhang, 1994), as well as prompting questions about why the United States has no corporatism. Also, Japan has been described (Pempel and Tsunekawa, 1979) as having 'corporatism without labor'. Even for the United States, however, it can be argued that corporatism does exist at the state level (Hansen, 1989).

Despite this, however, the problems here may not be solved entirely. What, for example, does the term 'singular' mean, and how singular is singular enough to fit within the definition? Can there be one principal organisation with some minor ones involved, or is only one permissible? The categories contained within the measurement scheme all appear to be affected by what Sartori (1991) called 'degreeism' (see above, pp. 96–7). If we choose one point along the dimension to split the concept of singular, we may get one result, but if we choose another we may get another result. The problem is endemic in the social sciences. We have few natural measures of the concepts that have become crucial for our thinking about the social and economic world. Even a commonly used concept, such as gross national product in economics, something that countries use as a central component of their economic policy-making, is a dimension that often is made into a dichotomy – high and low, rich and poor.

One major danger with the use of nominal categories is that, given that they reflect no underlying metric, they can rapidly become stretched beyond all recognition. For example, the Brzezinski and Friedrich category of 'totalitarian' mentioned above was designed to fit the particular case of the former Soviet Union, and even then at a particular point in its history. Applying the concept to other cases deemed to be 'totalitarian' risks losing all meaning from the term. On the other hand, totalitarian might be used as a standard against which to compare the characteristics of other countries, in which case comparative political analysis could be well-served. In fairness the fault, to extent that there is any, lies as much with the formulators of these concepts as with the later adopters. When the characteristic of a particular country is converted from a country into a category, this invites the later, inappropriate application of the concept.

We thus encounter another of the many dilemmas involved in comparative research in political science. On the one hand, one of the goals of this research is to eliminate proper names of countries, so that we can deal with conceptual categories and theoretical explanations. On the other, however, if those conceptual categories remain too closely linked to the countries for which they were developed, then there is a danger that the measures are artificial and disguise more than they reveal. To phrase this another way, we must be very careful to avoid the problems of conceptual stretching described so well by Sartori (1970). On the other hand, however, if we do not stretch some then concepts may remain too parochial, and the possibility of any genuine comparison is reduced or even eliminated.

Ideal-Type Analysis and Measurement

One important measurement technique for comparative analysis is the use of ideal-type analysis, as advocated by Max Weber (1949) and others. Most of our comparative analysis is based upon empirical evidence and concepts that emerge from analysis of real world countries. There may however, be instances in which rather than comparing a country with other countries we would want to compare it with some intellectual standard. The logic of this methodology is not that the standard is 'ideal' in the sense of being perfect, but rather that it is 'ideal' in the sense of being an intellectual construct that may never exist in the real world.

Weber's idea of bureaucracy is probably the most famous case of ideal-type analysis. Weber develops a model of bureaucracy containing a number of elements, including:

(1) a hierarchy of offices,
(2) segmentation of the official role,
(3) defined competencies,
(4) appointment on the basis of technical competence,

(5) formalised compensation schemes; and,
(6) a formalised career structure.

Although this model is to some extent based on the characteristics of Wilhelmine public administration of the time at which Weber was writing, it still was an abstraction from that reality. Bureaucracy was intended to reflect the ultimate and ideal achievement of rational–legal development in society, rather than the system of Weber's time or perhaps any other.

Subsequent scholars have attempted to use Weber's characterisations as a means of assessing real-world organisations. Diamant (1962) explicated the model with respect to public organisations, and that treatment was expanded by Page (1985), who used Weber's categories as a framework for comparing European public bureaucracies. Page examined administration in France, Germany and the United Kingdom, and found that even in nominally 'bureaucratic' administrative systems Weber's ideal was never matched. In addition to the studies of bureaucracy in the public sector, there are a number of examinations of private sector organisations using Weber's model. Constas (1958) and Udy (1958), for example, identified a number of measurable factors that would characterise a bureaucracy. They found that no formal organisation conformed to this model of a bureaucracy, despite their being described as such.

There have been some uses of ideal-type analysis that are closer to the usual concerns of comparative politics. For example, in the study of socio-economic development, the Parsonian pattern variables (see list below) have been utilised to create ideal types of the developed society and the underdeveloped society. Once again, no society would be so perfectly developed or underdeveloped that it would manifest these variables completely. Still, these variables could be used as a means of examining individual cases against the intellectual and presumably objective standard, with the comparison coming from the relationship to those variables rather than with other countries.

Harold Lasswell (1950) advocated another version of the ideal type, which he referred to as the 'developmental construct'. The idea, very much like an ideal type, is that of a state or condition that may never be achieved in reality, but may be something against which to assess the actual characteristics of a political system. The clearest example of a construct of this type is the 'garrison state', as a political system threatened by external forces and willing to suspend civil liberties in response to that threat. That fear was raised with respect to the United States during the cold war, and has since been applied to other systems (Gibney, 1992).

A somewhat more complex version of ideal-type analysis relies on several dichotomies to characterise political systems and behaviours. For example, the 'pattern variables' developed by Talcott Parsons (1939; see also Levy, 1966) to characterise the development of societies also could be utilised to analyse political development. The six patterned variables were a series of dichotomies, or in practice actually continua, that can be used to describe societies:

Universalism .... Particularism
Specificity .... Diffuseness
Achievement .... Ascription
Affective neutrality .... Affection
Self .... Collectivity
Rational .... Traditional

To some extent, any intellectual construct possesses some features of ideal-type analysis or a developmental concept. For example, Lijphart's conception (1975a) of consociational democracy was developed on the basis of Dutch politics, but it was also an abstraction from that reality. As it has been applied to other multi-cultural settings such as Colombia (Dix, 1980), Lebanon (Hudson, 1969), Canada (MacRae, 1974), India (Lijphart, 1996), Malaysia (Nagata, 1975) and Kenya (Berg-Schlosser, 1985), the concept has been stretched, but it also has come to be treated as something of an ideal-type concept. The conditions that Lijphart specified in his discussion of the Netherlands could be used to judge the extent to which the other societies conformed to that model. Further, the basic pattern of consociational conflict management among social groups could function even if all the conditions of the model were not met, so that researchers could understand which elements of the full model might be essential in which contexts.

Summary

Measurement is a crucial first stage in any comparative research project. If we cannot clearly define and then measure a concept then it is difficult to include it in a comparative study. Measurement is a difficult enterprise in a homogeneous, monocultural setting, but it is an even more difficult enterprise in a comparative concept. Even seemingly simple factors such as differences in language can introduce error into studies that require questioning respondents, and inadequate translations make respondents in one setting respond to stimuli different from those in other settings. The potential problems with measurement go well beyond simply translating questionnaires adequately. The problems are based on the differences in conceptual meaning that concepts can have in different cultures, and the perhaps untranslatable elements of social understanding that define cultures, including political cultures. Even when there is no need to use intrusive methods such as questionnaires to measure concepts, there are important conceptual problems associated with measurement. Concepts do not travel as easily as do comparative political scientists, and caution must be exercised in developing measures so that they remain valid in the full range of settings in which they are used.

The travelling problem is yet another reason to think about using intermediate-range comparisons rather than attempting to compare the full range of nations. There may yet be some problems even within nominally homogeneous areas, for example, Western Europe, but they may be much more controllable and much more knowable than in studies of the range of world systems. The social scientist is also not entirely defenceless against these measurement difficulties. There are ways of addressing differences in cultural contexts, whether through validations of measurements or through the triangulation of measurement. As with so many issues in comparative analysis, there is no complete remedy for the problem but with an understanding of what is involved the researcher can take some ameliorative actions.

5

The Role of Theory

We already have argued at several places for the importance of empirical political theory as a potential saviour for the methodological problems facing a good deal of comparative political analysis. If there are too many variables and an insufficient number of cases, then good comparative theory is expected to ride to the rescue and to enable the researcher to identify more parsimonious explanations. In addition, theory is expected to assist researchers in selecting the cases that should be included in their samples of political units for effective comparative analysis. Finally, political theory is expected to provide a basis for better-informed and more effective measurement of the concepts used in analysis. Can existing comparative theories sustain the weight of the responsibility that is being placed upon them?

There is not adequate space in this volume to assess fully the range of theories that are usually applied in comparative politics (see, for example, Dogan and Pelassey, 1990; Wiarda, 1985; Mayer, 1989). These theories range from very general ones attempting to explain the behaviour of entire systems to micro-level approaches that focus on individuals and their behaviour. We will, however, attempt to demonstrate how each version of the various theories available assists comparative researchers in their task of developing adequate explanations. Each of these various theories functions with a variety of assumptions about the sources of political behaviour and the most appropriate locale at which to begin (and to end) the quest for explanations. Despite the claims of generality of several of these theoretical approaches, we will argue that none of the theories provides a sufficient explanation for all political outcomes and political behaviour. Researchers therefore should look at a variety of explanations in order to gain that more complete explanation.

As we point to the utility of theory as a source of research questions and as a source of explanation, we should also be cognizant of the potential dangers of reliance on theory. As Thomas Kuhn (1970) and others have pointed out, theories constrain vision as well as opening visions. Political science may not have had the firmly established 'paradigms' characteristic of the natural sciences, but still there are theoretical approaches that dominate thinking and shape understanding. These approaches illuminate our thinking, but they can also prevent scholars from considering new problems, accepting innovation, or evaluating fairly new forms of explanation. The struggle in the discipline to accept behavioural theory (Eulau, 1963; Dahl, 1961), and then more recently rational choice analysis (Green and Shapiro, 1994; Friedman, 1996), is indicative of the difficulties of displacing prevailing patterns of thought.

Examining political theories and their influence on comparative politics requires thinking about how these paradigmatic perspectives can change in response to new information and new problems. It often appears that fad and fashion dominate the search for explanation through political theory; a more positive formulation would argue that comparative research is (and should be) driven by real-world problems (Kholi, 1995). For example, comparative politics during the 1960s and 1970s was dominated by concerns with political development and bringing the experience of Third World countries into the ambit of comparative research. Those geographical concerns, therefore, tended to focus attention on developmental issues, even when that orientation may have been inappropriate. The 1970s, and into the 1980s, especially for the more industrialised democracies, was definitely still the 'century of corporatism' while for the less developed world it appears to have been primarily the decade of clientelism.

All of the above theories offer valuable perspectives on political behaviour, but while popular they have tended to be abused as much as used. More recently, rational choice theories have been the most popular approaches to political phenomena, although these have made perhaps less impact on comparative analysis than on other parts of the discipline. Some scholars (Bates, 1988; but see Budge, 1993) have pointed to the utility of approach in a variety of comparative settings, but the focus of so much comparative work on the systemic level of analysis tends to make rational choice less useful. To the extent that rational choice perspectives have been adopted, those relying on game theory (Tsebelis, 1990; 1994) appear to have been more successful in capturing the reality of the issues than have others.

Levels of Explanation

As noted, the theories used to explain politics comparatively range from the systemic level to the individual level. Each level of explanation can help to understand politics, but each also has a number of potential weaknesses. As mentioned above, system level theories run the risk of excessive personification, or assigning the characteristics of human actors to non-human constructs. Systems analyses can ignore individuals and the necessity that those individuals should make decisions that are manifested at the system level. On the other hand, theories that concentrate on individuals run the risk of ignoring institutional and system level variables that can shape and constrain the autonomous behaviour of those individuals. This distinction between 'structure' and 'agency' (Dessler, 1989; see also Lane and Ersson, 1994b; Hay, 1995) remains one of the fundamental questions in social and political theory, asking whether structures or the individuals within them are the most important source of explanation.

Macro-Level Theories

Comparative politics generally operates at the macro-level, comparing whole political systems. The descriptive tradition of comparative politics had done that in its own manner for most of the history of the discipline. What was being sought then, however, was a version of comparative analysis that could cope with entire systems, yet could say something more about them analytically. The two principal versions of macro-theory were systems theory and structural-functionalism. Although it is now fashionable to denigrate these approaches, and indeed they have their weaknesses, they also continue to have some utility. If nothing else, much of the language used in comparative politics – the political system, feedback, interest aggregation – came from these approaches.

Systems Theory

Some of the earliest versions of theories at the macro-level of analysis were so-called 'systems theories'. The development of systems level theories was characteristic of the early stages of the 'behavioural revolution' in politics during the 1950s and 1960s. This theoretical development was in large part a reaction to the descriptive character of almost all studies in 'comparative politics' before then. Further, these theories were designed to be sufficiently general to be applicable to almost all political systems. This generality was designed to be in clear contrast to most comparative politics up till then, which had concentrated on the countries of Europe and North America. The generalisability of systems theory was especially important during an era in which a number of former colonial countries were gaining independence and had political practices and traditions very different from those of Western governments. Therefore, these theories tended to function at an extremely high level of generality, and could be applied to every system from tribal governments to the most advanced democratic political system.

Among these general theories of politics, the most general of all were the 'systems theories', usually associated with David Easton (1965; 1979; see also Finkle and Gable, 1971). Systems approaches to politics were derived from open-systems theories in biology. The fundamental argument of systems theories was that politics and government could be conceptualised as a system of input, throughput and output functioning in an environment that provided the 'energy' required by the system. In the case of politics, that energy was 'demands and supports'. Those factors comprised demands from groups and individuals for policy changes, the political support from the population in general, and other necessary resources such as tax money. The outputs of the system were policies, with a feedback loop reflecting responses to the policies that then initiated another round of political demands from the public to which the system would respond.

In this theory, or set of theories, the government became the 'black box' linking inputs to outputs. There was almost no specification of the institutions and processes that would be used to link inputs to outputs. This lack of specificity is perhaps understandable, given the goals of the scholars involved to eliminate any dependence upon specific and possibly ethnocentric ideas about how government should be conducted. Still, it made 'government' as we conventionally think about it appear an almost automatic process. The assumption was that the internal functioning of the system would make some direct linkage between 'wants and demands' expressed (in some manner) by the public and policies of government. This was a rather optimistic, democratic perspective, but it also ignored all the politics that we know takes place within that 'black box', and the marked differences between what goes into the box and what eventually comes out. There was some attempt to develop an idea of 'withinputs' to describe the machinations of governing, but that seemed to do little to clarify the process.

Despite its several weaknesses, systems theory did make some real contributions to comparative politics. In the first place, the theory did accomplish what it intended, that is to provide a very general perspective on political life, which could be applied almost anywhere. Further, systems theory pointed out that government, like all systems, was dependent upon its environment, so that the importance of the social and economic underpinnings of government was reinforced. Despite that dependence on the environment, systems were conceptualised as having the capacity to make decisions that would reflect internal political realities; this was to some extent the beginning of discussions about the 'autonomy of the state' (Nordlinger, 1981; Migdal, 1988). Third, systems theory did point out than even in apparently totalitarian systems there had to be some connection between the demands of the public and the policies enacted. Relatedly, this approach also pointed out the degree of interconnections between all aspects of economy, society and the political system, as well as the complex (if unspecified) interactions that may occur within the political system itself (see Lipset and Rokkan, 1967).

Finally, systems theory pointed to the importance of feedback, and the need of governments to take into account their own previous actions when making policies. As a number of scholars (Wildavsky, 1980; Hogwood and Peters, 1985) have pointed out, policy is very often its own cause, and one round of policy-making almost inevitably produces political reactions, new policy problems, and a subsequent round of policy-making. This feedback–dominant perspective on governing was elaborated by Karl Deutsch in his conception of government as a cybernetic system – *The Nerves of Government* (1963). Deutsch developed an elaborate conceptualisation of government as a system responding to changes in its environment, with the information-processing capacity of the public sector being its primary attribute for making that linkage and in governing successfully, work that easily can be related to Deutsch's other work (1966) stressing the importance of political communications. Although again highly abstracted from the descriptive reality of any one political system, Deutsch's approach did provide a general model for understanding better how governments relate to their environments, and the centrality of information in political life. Further, governments can be compared on their capacity to respond effectively and efficiently to the environment.

Structural-Functionalism

Structural-functionalism was the intellectual companion of systems theory in examining politics at a very high level of abstraction and at the systemic level. Structural-functionalism, derived originally from anthropological theory (Radcliffe-Brown, 1957; Stocking, 1984) assumed that all political systems would have certain functions that they would have to perform. Almond and Coleman (1960), for example, argued that governments had the requisite functions of: interest articulation, interest aggregation, rule-making, rule-application, rule-adjudication, political communication and socialisation and recruitment. This list was later expanded (Almond and Powell, 1966; see Key Text 1.1) to include requisite capabilities of systems such as extraction, distribution, regulation and responsiveness. The functionalist perspective was that no matter how primitive or developed the political system, it would have to perform these functions, and the researcher could then compare how the different systems performed whose tasks. Thus, like systems theory, one purpose of the structural-functional approach was to permit political science to break out of the Western parochialism that had been argued to characterise much of the traditional literature (see Eckstein, 1963; Macridis, 1955), and to be able to make meaningful statements about almost any political system.

This comparison of the means of performing a function led to the structural element of the approach. Rather than necessarily identifying rule-making in government with legislatures, this question was left more open. So, for example, we know that in almost all contemporary political systems the public bureaucracy makes more rules than does the legislature (Kerwin, 1994), and that in many countries the courts are also active rule-makers (Alter and Meunier-Aitsahalia, 1994). The argument of the structural-functionalists was that all structures were multi-functional and all functions were multi-structural. As developed within political science structural-functionalism also had a developmental aspect, with additional variables – secularisation, role differentiation, and subsystem autonomy – argued to gauge just how far the political development process had proceeded, especially in its structural and cultural elements. This line of argument was related to the pattern variables developed by the sociologist Talcott Parsons (1939). Political systems, it was contended, became more divorced from religious and ascriptive criteria, and to become more differentiated from other parts of the social system as they developed.

Being significantly less abstract, structural-functionalism did not have the extreme disconnection from empirical description that afflicted systems analysis. It was much easier to relate concepts such as 'rule formation' to traditional activities and institutions of the public sector, and to employ the functionalist framework for more detailed analysis of actual governments, than it is to apply systems to specific institutional structures. This analysis could be performed while maintaining much of the generality that enabled systems analysis to apply to virtually any type of system. Finally, in the later versions of this approach, there was a strong policy emphasis that prepared the way for the policy movement in political science. Despite all those virtues, however, the critics still found functionalist theory excessively divorced from the empirical reality of politics. As Barrington Moore (see LaPalombara, 1970) once said, 'they were forever packing their bags for a voyage they never intend to take'.

By shunning some of the extreme generality characteristic of the systems approach, the structural-functional approach to politics left itself vulnerable to claims of reintroducing some of the ethnocentrism that critics argued had afflicted the traditional study of comparative politics. For example, the three pattern variables that were used to assess development were closely related to political patterns observed in Western countries; in some instances, however, very traditional patterns persisted in the industrialised democracies and were functional for their survival (Rose, 1965). Thus, to be considered developed, a less developed country had to follow the same path that the Western democracies had followed before. Even a particular version of Western democracy tended to be favoured in these functionalist models of development. All these assumptions were considered highly suspect by the numerous critics of this strand of theorising.

On the other hand, it was argued that structural-functional approaches should be conceptualised as extremely conservative and static. As usually presented, structural-functionalism lacked even an identifiable element such as the feedback loop that gave systems theory some dynamism, and enabled it to incorporate popular reaction to government policy. The structural-functional assumption appeared to be that the institutions that had evolved and survived within a system were indeed 'functional' for it, and that there was little need to reform or change them significantly. Thus, on the one hand, the critics argued that there was only a single permissible direction for change implied in the model, while on the other hand they argued that the theory did not admit change readily. The problem is that both of these criticisms could be accurate, and largely were.

If nothing else, however, structural-functionalism did help to fuel the growing concern with development and change. A great deal of theory in comparative politics has been, and continues to be, static. The concerns with development associated with structural-functionalism were expanded and elaborated through a number of additional approaches to political change. Politics and government are always in flux, but the theories of political science are often very static. The concern with political change has been reasserted during the late 1980s and into the 1990s through studies of democratisation and political transformations in a variety of political systems.

In the contemporary theories of democratisation, there is some echo of the structural-functionalists and their basic argument that all governments must perform the same functions, the question being *how* they are performed. Indeed, there has been some effort to resuscitate structural-functional analysis (Lane, 1994). The argument being advanced is that structural-functionalism can be cast in a more testable, 'scientific' manner than was characteristic of most work in the 1960s and 1970s. This would involve blending the macro-level perspective of functionalism with the individual motivational and action assumptions of rational choice theory. While this is an interesting attempt to bridge the two levels of analysis, the end result may be more a product of rational choice theory than of functionalism.

Both systems analysis and structural-functionalism worked at the level of the political system, and had difficulty in relating that level of analysis to the level of individuals or even groups of people. While it was not the intention of these approaches to explain individual behaviour, this still constituted a serious weakness in both approaches. The problem is that these theories were almost forced to reify the systems as the actors. Especially in systems analysis, there was no place for individuals, and political élites which converted inputs into outputs and exercised some independent judgment in doing, so seemed to have no place in the theory. Given that all government decision-making ultimately comes down to decisions made by individuals or groups of individuals, the failure to build in more realistic assumptions about how humans influence system behaviour is an almost fatal flaw for these theories.

Meso-Level Theories

If we move down a ladder of generality, comparative politics can also be conducted at the meso-level, concerned with the functioning of specific institutions, processes, and perhaps groups of countries. As noted above, Joseph LaPalombara (1968) argued that the best strategy for comparative analysis would be to develop middle-range theories that could subsequently function as the building blocks for more general theories. As Roy Macridis (1986: 22) later argued:

> clustering, as opposed to the search for grand theory, has given to the field a new vitality, and may ultimately pave the way to the development of some unifying models and priorities.

Working at this level of analysis would avoid the problems of excessive generality and inadequate specification already argued to characterise much macro-level analysis. It would also therefore avoid at least some of the 'conceptual stretching' problem advanced by Sartori. Further, middle-range theorising could draw on the talents of scholars who are well versed in a single region of the world, or a single institution, without having to develop a whole new set of generalists to do comparative work. Organising research around regions does not avoid this problem entirely. If we take Europe as a region (see below), there are marked differences between Norway and, for example, Greece or Portugal.

Whether consciously or not, comparative politics appears to have been following LaPalombara's advice. A very large number of theories and analytic schemes have been developed covering virtually all parts of the world, and all structures within the political system, and all political processes. There are so many such schemes, in fact, that it would be virtually impossible to identify and discuss all of them in this one chapter. Therefore, I will do some highly selective sampling of approaches in order to illustrate the strengths and weaknesses of this level of analysis, and to provide some guidance for approaches that touch on other areas and other institutions.

Theories by Region: Europe and Others

There are by now theories intended to describe and explain politics in almost all world areas. For example, Hydén and Bratton (1992; see above, pp. 18–19) have developed a theory to describe and explain governance in Africa. This is in addition to other theories of African politics, such as that of that of Fortes and Evans-Pritchard (1940) for pre-independence Africa, and those of Welch (1990) and Young (1982) for more contemporary systems on that continent. In Latin America, Collier and Collier (1991), Cardozo and Faletto (1979) and O'Donnell (1978) all have developed broad approaches for explaining politics in the region. The former communist countries of Eastern and Central Europe have had any number of theoretical perspectives applied to their transformation, including those of political development (Nagel and Rukavishnikov, 1994), consolidation and democratisation (Bova, 1991).

The above list could be extended to cover other regions, and could also be extended take into account theories that bridged a number of regions, such as theories of political development (Higgott, 1983), and a few covering the industrialised democracies (Dahl, 1971; Lijphart, 1984). However, to get a better idea of how theories developed for one geographical region might work, we will focus on theories covering Western Europe. As these have developed, they have evolved from being ways to locate the variety of European national systems along some continuum or in some typology (Katz, 1987; Kitschelt, 1994) to being ways of understanding the evolution of politics within, or at least in reference to, the European Union (George, 1992; Lesquesne, 1994). As European politics has been developing, it is difficult to conceptualise politics, even for countries not members of the European Union, for example, Norway (Olsen, 1995), without taking the EU into account (see Meny *et al.*, 1996).

One explicit attempt to build a theory of European politics was Martin Heisler's (1974) 'European polity model'. This was derived largely from the experience of the smaller European democracies, although the implicit argument was that it could be used to explain policy-making in at least some of the larger European countries, especially (then West) Germany, with a strong corporatist tradition. Heisler's approach appeared, however, to be of little applicability to Britain, which lacked that crucial trait of a legitimate role for interest groups, although Jordan and Richardson (1987) characterised British politics as more open to the influence of interest groups than the conventional wisdom would have us believe. Heisler argued that the openness of the smaller European governments to legitimate interactions from societal groups, and the desire of the groups within society to participate in those interactions, explained the capacity of otherwise deeply divided societies to make and implement policies. The roots of the openness could be cultural, as in Scandinavia (Meijer,

1969), or lie in a more explicit political desire to maintain the polity (Lorwin, 1971), but in any case it worked. Further, this characterisation of individual countries also appears to work in many ways as a description of politics within the contemporary European Union (Peters, 1997), with the segmented Commission being extremely open to the demands, and ideas, of groups in the society.

Jeremy Richardson (1982, 1984; see Key Text 5.1 and also Mazey and Richardson, 1993) has provided another approach to understanding politics in Western Europe, using the concept of 'policy styles'. Unlike the Heisler approach, which concentrates more on the motivations and strategies of participants – public and private – in the political process, Richardson focuses his analysis on the policy-making system as a whole. His characterisations of four types of policy-making encountered among the European democracies are intended to predict the manner in which the systems will make policy and react to changes in the external environment. This approach to policy-making also can be utilised to understand the emerging politics of the European Union, and the relationships of the member countries to the Union.

Also for Western Europe, there are approaches that address the relationship of individual nation-states to the European Union and the manner in which these systems correspond or not to the demands of supranational integration. A series of studies of the individual member countries *and* the Union point to the different ways in which political traditions play a role in shaping the interactions between Union and nation (George, 1992). The differential relationships between nations and the EU can also be seen in the apparent decline in nationalism in most Western European countries at the national level (Dogan, 1994a), despite its apparent force at the subnational level.

Finally, the emergence of autonomous countries in Eastern and Central Europe has led to the development of a variety of theories and classifications of these systems. In the first instance, these approaches have focused on transitions and the democratisation of these systems (Campbell and Pedersen, 1996; Derlien and Szablowski, 1993). These studies included a number of attempts to compare democratisation in these systems with similar processes in other parts of the world (Higley and Gunther, 1992). As these systems have continued to develop, there is some evidence that they will revert to type, and re-establish some of the political patterns that they had established prior to domination by the communist regimes.

Key Text 5.1 Jeremy Richardson and Policy Styles

One strategy for comparative political analysis is to develop typologies or taxonomies that capture some underlying dimensions of political systems. The idea of typology is that two (or possibly more) variables interact to create and describe groups of political systems. Those classes will, in turn, be used to predict some aspects of behaviour of the political systems to which the typology applies.

Jeremy Richardson has developed such a typology for the countries of Western Europe. Richardson's typology was developed to predict the policy choices, or 'policy styles' of those European countries. Richardson argued that these policy styles were based upon the degree of imposition that a government was willing to use to achieve its policy goals, as well as on whether the government tended to be active or reactive. Using these two variables policy-making in countries such as Sweden is classified as being interventionist and active, with the expectation that they would act to anticipate problems and then intervene forcefully to ameliorate the problems. In contrast, Britain's policy style is argued to be consensual and reactive.

This mode of analysis is useful for providing predictions about policy that can then be 'tested' with more empirical analysis, as they were in the country chapters in Richardson's book. Further, this is an excellent example of creating a 'mid-level' theory, both because it is concerned with policy rather than the full range of political institutions and behaviours, and because it is concerned only with one segment of the world. Despite the modest geographical claims, the approach may be applicable to more countries, and perhaps to the full range of political systems of the world.

Characterising entire political systems with these few variables is always laden with danger, and indeed it could be argued that some policy areas would behave very differently than would the general characterisation of the system – the Celtic Fringe of Britain may see the system as being more concerned with imposition than might the English. Further, it could be argued that the argument about policy style is actually a tautology. We can see that some countries tend to respond crises slower than do others, and this characteristic (the presumed dependent variable) is then used to define the nature of the policy style – the independent variable. Even with those problems, however, the discussion of policy styles has helped to advanced the comparative study of public policy.

Theories by Institution

Just as there have been meso-theories dividing the world geographically, there have been others that divide it along institutional lines. Systems theorists might have a very difficult time accepting this division, given that it tends to place at the centre of the theory rather traditional ideas about how politics and policy-making are done. Still, in almost all countries now it is possible to identify institutions such as political parties, legislatures, executives, and so on These institutions may be shaped very differently, and many nominally democratic institutions such as legislatures or parties clearly would not conform to the standards of Western scholars for a functioning institution of that type. Still, these do provide the grist for a theoretical and comparative mill; if they are different, then how and why?

The New Institutionalism

At the most general level are a group of theories that use institutional analysis as a general approach to politics, rather than as a focus on any particular institution. As noted, the tradition in comparative politics was institutional, although institutional in that context meant almost entirely descriptive, a characterisation that may be very unfair (Wilson, 1898). The contemporary version of institutionalism takes into account all the theoretical and methodological developments of the 1950s onwards, but still attributes most important variations in policy and politics to the institutional actors involved rather than to individuals (Abbott, 1992). For example, James March and Johan Olsen (1989; 1994) argue that institutions are governed by 'logics of appropriateness' that define what the institution and its members should and should not do. Other institutional theorists accept the logic of rational choice analysis, but focus on the importance of structural explanations rather than on the methodological individualism that characterises most of that approach (Tsebelis, 1990; Laver and Shepsle, 1996). Still other versions of the new institutionalism attempt to test the empirical effects of macro-institutional structures, for example, presidential versus parliamentary government or divided government, on political performance (Weaver and Rockman, 1993 – see Key Text 5.3; Stepan and Skach, 1993; Fiorina, 1991; Pierce, 1991).

It is almost certainly true that institutions do matter; these theories have the burden of saying when and how. Despite their common

Key Text 5.2 James March and John Olsen, and the New Institutionalism

For much of the second half of the twentieth century political science has been dominated by either behavioural theories or rational choice theories. Both of these approaches to explaining political phenomena assume that the individual is the appropriate unit of analysis and that all political action is a function of either individual values or individual rational calculations of utility. In these versions of comparative politics institutions often became the 'black box' within which transformations of preferences into policy occurred, but that was not considered a worthy object of enquiry.

March and Olsen set out to challenge those dominant assumptions about political life, arguing that organisations and institutions should be seen as the source of a great deal of political behaviour, and that indeed one could understand behaviour better by beginning with institutions. In their view institutions have a 'logic of appropriateness' that is transmitted to their members and which those members in turn use to structure their own behaviour. Given that they were reacting more against the rational choice assumptions of part of the discipline than against behavioural assumptions they contrasted the logic of appropriateness with a 'logic of consequentiality' in which organisations (and individual members) made choices based on the expected utility outcomes.

This work by March and Olsen, as well as their earlier (1984) article, and their later (1994) book were central in the restoration of institutional theory to a central place in comparative political science. Theirs is one of many versions of institutionalism that have become used in the field, but their challenge to the dominance of more individualistic theories was sufficiently compelling to open the field to a broader array of approaches. While it might be argued that this was merely restating the past of comparative politics and that this was a retrograde rather than progressive move in the discipline, this version of institutionalism is more consciously theoretical than the older versions. In addition, the March and Olsen version of institutionalism paved the way for other institutionalisms (see Key Text 5.3) that were much more empirical than the older versions. In short, by restating the position that instituting do matter, but doing so in a way that was familiar to people working in the contemporary social sciences, March and Olsen redirected the course of this subdiscipline.

focus on institutions as the major factor in explanation, this body of theory uses very different means to create those explanations and hence require very different research methods. The original March and Olsen (1989) version of the new institutionalism would require understanding organisational cultures and the values held by participants in the governing process (see Key Text 5.2). Both the rational choice and the more empirical explanations would focus attention on structural features of government. The historical institutionalists (Thelen *et al.*, 1992) focus on the initial formation of institutions and policies and argue for persistence and 'path dependency' thereafter. For example, Liebried and Pierson (1995) examine the development of the welfare state over decades and argue that the initial policy ideas still dominate and tend to shape existing systems, even after attempts to downsize them dramatically.

Thus, although parading under the same banner, this body of theory is actually a variety of approaches to looking at governing and policy. Further, it is not always clear how these approaches help us to compare (but see Peters, 1996b) across countries. The major exception to that generalisation are the empirical institutionalists, whose approach is fundamentally directed towards comparison. Weaver and Rockman (1993) (see Key Text 5.3) and their collaborators analysed a number of different policy areas using a variety of different countries as examples. Although coming up with somewhat unsatisfying answers – basically the answer is that 'It depends' – this research did address directly the question of the impact of institutions on policies across countries.

Bureaucracy

At a more specific level, there have been comparative theories developed for almost all political institutions. Many of these theories have focused on the developed countries, for reasons of greater familiarity, of access, or of presumed comparability. For example, there are several studies of political executives in the developed democracies (Blondel and Mueller-Rommel, 1988; 1993), but only a limited amount of work (Blondel, 1985 – see Key Text 6.2) extending the analysis of political executives to the less developed countries. Similarly, there are a number of theories of political parties, going back at least to Duverger (1954), but these also tend to concentrate on the more developed countries (Sartori, 1966; Panebianco, 1988). One major exception was the study (now dated) of the role of political parties in political development (LaPalombara and Weiner, 1966). There have been some comparative studies of

Key Text 5.3 Kent Weaver and Bert Rockman, and Institutions

The title of Weaver and Rockman's book – *Do Institutions Matter?* – clearly states one of the principal questions of contemporary comparative politics. With a return to institutional analysis in political science comparative politics becomes a natural laboratory for testing whether institutions have the influence on policy and behaviour that they are assumed to have. It is not possible for political scientists to manipulate government structures, except perhaps in formal models or simulations, so that the use of comparative analysis may be the only means of assessing the validity of the predictions coming from institutional analysis.

The Weaver and Rockman book addressed one of the central questions emerging in comparative institutional analysis – the difference between presidential and parliamentary systems. The basic assumption of this differentiation of systems types is that the integration and party discipline found in parliamentary systems would produce greater capacity of governments to change policy and to impose losses on citizens even in entitlement programmemes that might be considered to be inviolable politically (see Pierson and Weaver, 1993). In contrast the divisions found in presidential governments might be associated with less policy-making capacity. The majority of papers in the Weaver and Rockman book contrast American presidentialism with various parliamentary systems, using the experiences in a number of policy areas as the tests of the hypotheses.

This volume represents a major test of the impact of the basic institutional differences between presidential and parliamentary systems. One major problem in the analysis is that given that the United States is the principal (and sole) example of a purely presidential system among the advanced democracies it may be difficult to separate the impact of presidentialism from the peculiarities of American politics. The authors can identify several important differences among types of parliamentary regimes but are unable to do the same for presidential government. In addition, although they expend a great deal of effort at addressing the issue, the dependent variable in the analysis – government capability – remains somewhat underspecified. The capacity to identify government capacity becomes all the more important as arguments about the 'hollowing' of the state become endemic in comparative politics. Despite those problems, the topics addressed, and the careful manner in which they are addressed, make this book one of the most important statements about comparative institutional analysis.

legislatures (Olson, 1994; Kornberg and Muslof, 1970), and a smaller number concerned with the courts (Tate, 1987; Cappelletti, 1989), but in general these have been some of the less developed areas of enquiry, perhaps because of their association with particular types of political system.

Although public administration is often considered unfashionable in political science, one type of institution has been subjected to a great amount of comparative analysis, namely the public bureaucracy. This is in part because it is perhaps the most directly comparable of all governmental institutions, both across countries and across time. Governments have relied on bureaucratic structures for almost as long as they have been in the business of governing (Eisenstadt, 1963). Further, bureaucracies and administrative structures exist in rather similar formats (despite some important differences) in countries at almost all levels of socio-economic and political development (Heady, 1996). Within the public sector there are some clear problems in the measurement of administrative variables (Peters, 1988; 1996b) but these structures are in principle the most comparable in that sector.

The process of comparing bureaucracies has been undertaken in a variety of manners. One has been to examine the nature of the individuals recruited into the bureaucracy, whether it is through the lens of representative bureaucracy (Meier, 1975; Kim, 1992), or through the lens of the attitudes about their role in the political system that they bring with them (Aberbach *et al.*, 1981; Mayntz and Derlien, 1989). Another approach is to look at the roles that the bureaucracy plays in the policy process (Suleiman, 1974; Dogan, 1975; Schneider, 1991). The structures of bureaucratic systems also can be compared (Silberman, 1993), although structures tend to be more similar than do other parts. Finally, bureaucracy can be compared in developmental terms, ranging from very traditional systems (Farazmand, 1989) through transitional regimes of several sorts (Riggs, 1964; Derlien and Szablowski, 1993), to fully modern political systems (Pierre, 1994). That development analysis was, in reality, what Weber was doing with his development of the ideal-type model of a fully modern bureaucracy.

Although the comparative approaches to public bureaucracy may have somewhat different purposes, they have the advantage of having more readily comparable units than do most other comparative research foci. In most systems, bureaucracies have primary responsibility for implementing public policies, and have also acquired a significant role in policy advice. Most bureaucratic systems are structured hierarchically, although contemporary management theory tends to produce flatter, more participative organisations. Also, most public bureaucracies have some nominal form of merit recruitment, with the real question being the extent to which this is honoured in practice as well as in theory. This is an institution for which comparative analysis appears extremely appropriate, and one in which partial theories and well-documented cases can provide guidance for the researcher.

Micro-Level Approaches

Finally, we can look at theories of comparative politics that focus on the individual as the unit of analysis. These approaches present problems that are the antithesis of the problems encountered with the macro-level approaches discussed above. The macro-approaches had difficulty in identifying the human actors who would account for the decisions taken within their stylised models, and therefore had difficulty in explaining the decisions that were made. Micro-level analysis, on the other hand, has all the individual actors anyone could need, but what it finds difficulty in doing is incorporating the systemic element. Although these studies must be done somewhere, the important element appears to be the individuals, not the nature of the system.

There are any number of individual approaches to political behaviour that have been used comparatively, most of them derived from a general behavioural conception of politics. One of the most common approaches of this type is the examination of voting behaviour. To some extent derived from the voting behaviour literature in the United States, studies have taken place of voting behaviour in almost every country that votes. Many have been within a single country (Butler and Kavanagh, 1992; Conradt, 1995; Gilbert, 1995; Miles, 1988; Von Mettenheim, 1995), but some also have attempted to apply the same models of behaviour across a number of political systems (Booth and Seligson, 1989; Rose, 1974). To explain voting behaviour, most of these models depend upon individual level characteristics such as social class, partisan identification and group membership.

A huge volume of public opinion research also enriches the comparative understanding of politics. These studies have in many ways supported the voting behaviour literature by examining the attitudinal roots of voting behaviour (Dalton, 1996; Dominiguez and McCann, 1996). Public opinion research can also address questions of political participation more broadly than just voting (Dalton, 1996), as well as the attitudinal bases of support for old and new political systems (Kornberg and Clarke, 1992; Janssen, 1991). Thus, while many approaches to comparative politics examine the formation of states from the top down, as an almost entirely élite process, micro-level theorists look at the social and attitudinal foundations for the formation of successful regimes, and the maintenance of existing regimes.

Finally, beginning at least with the *Civic Culture* (Almond and Verba, 1967) micro-level theories have sought to assess the nature of political culture and the influence of those complexes of values on the way in which politics functions in different countries (Calvert and Calvert, 1989; Kedourie, 1992; Gaffney and Kolinsky, 1991). One of the most important strands of this literature has been Inglehart's work (1977) on changes in cultural values in the industrialised democracies. The basic argument is that political concerns have shifted from materialism to post-materialism, or from a concern with economic issues to concern with issues such as participation, the environment and equality. This shift, in turn, is argued to influence the strength of traditional political parties.

Despite the contributions to our understanding, the micro-level behavioural studies have not always appeared as comparative as might be desirable (but see Dalton, 1996). Often the independent variables used to explain behaviour also are found at the micro-level, rather than at the level of the systems being compared. The result is actually a series of micro-level analyses that just happen to occur in different geographical settings. That being the case, if there are differences in the findings then the researcher is often forced to go outside the theory to find explanations at the systemic level that account for the differences. There has been a strong tradition in European political sociology linking the macro-structural characteristics of states with political behaviour (Lipset and Rokkan, 1967; Lane and Ersson, 1994a), especially around the structure of political cleavages, but that tradition appears to have been largely ignored recently in favour of more individualistic approaches to political behaviour. The reverse can also be true. Pateman (1980) and others have argued that the Almond and Verba *Civic Culture* study (see Key Text 2.1) attributed too many of the differences in their findings to features of the country and too few to socio-economic differences within the countries. In this particular case, an individual level explanation may have been more appropriate.

There has, of course, been some work at incorporating these spatial and contextual factors into micro-level theories (Sprague, 1982; Agnew, 1996; Goertz, 1994), but even here the basic thrust has been to characterise that context in terms of other micro-level variables rather than in terms of its more structural and institutional features. For example, a number of studies of voting behaviour in Britain (Butler and Stokes, 1970; Johnston *et al.*, 1992; Rose and McAllister, 1986) have argued that working class voters are more likely to choose Labour in disproportionately working-class neighbourhoods than in other neighbourhoods – there is a definite reinforcing effect from the social composition of the surroundings and the types of individual contacts that voters are likely to have in that surrounding. Eulau (1994) describes a 'contextual revolution' in voting studies, but most of the work cited remained largely at an individual level of analysis.

The above critique of micro-level approaches to comparative politics can be illustrated with several studies of political attitudes and voting behaviour that have been conducted in a number of different settings. Silverman (1991), for example, points to the relative dearth of 'structural' factors in voting studies. Scarborough (1987) points to the failure to integrate those structural factors into the study of voting behaviour in Britain, and indicates that individual level and ecological level analyses tend to move along parallel but unconnected paths. The major comparative study of voting behaviour and the economy by Michael Lewis-Beck (1988) makes an attempt to include economic contextual factors in the analysis, but these tend to be more continuous economic variables, rather than the structural features of political or social systems.

One interesting exception to this characterisation of the inadequacy of contextual theories of is Jackman and Miller's (1995) study of the institutional factors affecting political participation, and especially voter turnout, in industrialised democracies. This research built on Jackman's earlier (1987) work, and studied the impact of formal institutional factors such as the nature of electoral laws, as well as the nature of the party system. It tested the impact of contextual factors against those of cultural and individual level factor, and found a significant impact, even when the usual factors explaining turnout are included.

Although the theoretical basis for linking macro- and micro-level concerns is still not particularly well developed, the methodological and statistical methods are. There has been a return to an interest in cross-level inference in social statistics (Achen and Shively, 1995; Flanigan and Zingale, 1985) that had largely been lost when survey data replaced aggregate data in the study of voting behaviour and similar political phenomena. The individualistic and ecological fallacies had largely been forgotten, but yet still presented major inferential and theoretical problems (Hannan, 1991). We must hope that a return to a concern with the methods will produce some greater concerns about the theory as well.

As well as the behavioural studies of attitudes and voting, the contemporary domination of rational choice analysis in political science has added another micro-level mode of analysis. Even more than the behavioural approaches, the rational choice perspective on political behaviour tends to assume no significant differences in behaviour across political units. Assuming that individuals act in their own self-interest provides a perspective that can travel across geographical and political boundaries very easily, even if the circumstances within which the individuals are expected to maximise do vary quite dramatically. Therefore, peasants considering some form of political mobilisation in a Third World village (Scott, 1976; Popkin, 1979; but see Foley, 1993) may be understandable through the same theoretical lens as rational voters in Paris or Stockholm.

This said, however, the rational choice versions of institutionalism discussed briefly above do link the individual with larger structures. It may be that over the long run rational choice analysis will provide a better avenue for linking individual and collective level phenomena than will the behavioural approaches. One of the problems motivating much of this body of literature (Weingast, 1996; Ostrom, 1990) is the need to construct institutions that can restrain individual free choice, and thus provide some means of solving problems such as the 'tragedy of the commons' (Hardin and Baden, 1977) that continue to plague governments.

What the micro-level approaches to comparative politics can do is test general theories about individual political behaviour. By looking at behaviour in a variety of settings, these approaches can assess whether the relationships hold true regardless of setting, or whether they are conditioned by the setting in which they occur. For example, the Beliefs in Government project (Kaase and Newton, 1996) in Western Europe attempted to examine the ways in which changes in government over the past several decades have influenced public attitudes and been influenced by them. Putting these two levels of analysis is together is very important for comparative politics. As Mayer (1989: 46) argued, the importance of comparative analysis arises from putting structural factors together with micro-level analysis to extend the capacity for explanation.

State and Society

As well as dividing comparative theories by the level of analysis at which they work, we can also divide the field by whether the theories focus on the state as the source of explanation or whether they focus on social actors. This will, to some extent, replicate the above discussion, given that almost all macro-theories tend to be state-centric, but there are some interesting and important distinctions. Further, asking whether the state is in and of itself a significant actor tends to illuminate some questions about the comparative functioning of political institutions. It is easier to argue that states and their institutions are autonomous actors in some societies than it is in others, and that is itself an important dimension for comparative analysis.

This discussion can be phrased in terms of the four explanatory '*is*' now popular in the study of political economy: institutions, ideas, interests and individuals. Each of these four factors can be said to have some influence over policy, the theoretical problem being to decide which one to focus on and whether to focus on one of the exclusion of others. Much of the theoretical discussion in political science tends to be exclusive, with claims that one factor or another is the important independent variable. This may be correct, but our measures and our analysis are rarely well enough developed to support arguments of that sort. As we will show below, more inclusive strategies may provide fuller explanations, yet leave theory in the same muddle that it has been in for years.

State Theory

The question of the role of the state is rather different in Anglo–American political science from what it is in political science in most other countries. The United States has been described as a 'stateless society', and although the state is clearly a more important actor in Britain (but see Rhodes, 1997) thinking about governing tends to be more Lockean and contractual than state-centred. Thus, when major scholars in the USA argued for 'bringing the state back in', scholars in Continental Europe and much of Asia wondered where the state had been – as far as they knew it was always a central part of the explanation for political phenomena.

State-centric explanatory theory argues that political activity in a society can best be understood by beginning with the state and then working outwards toward society. Most international relations theory assumes the state as the central actor, and much of the international political economy literature that has come into comparative political science from international relations makes many of the same assumptions. Take, for example, the views of Peter Evans (1995) concerning the role of states in economic development in the 'little tigers' of Asia. Evans argues that the best way to understand the success of these systems is not through the strength of markets but rather through the role of the state in promoting industry, and especially export industries (see also Haggard and Moon, 1995).

Society-Centred Theory

Society-centred explanations have been a major part of comparative analysis in the behavioural discussion of political science. For example, the *Civic Culture* (Almond and Verba, 1967 – see Key Text 2.1; see also Almond, 1980) was one of the dominant icons of comparative research in the behavioural tradition. The basic argument was that the success or failure of political democracy was a function of the social and cultural underpinnings existing in society. More recently, Robert Putnam *et al.* (1993 – see Key Text 5.4) and Victor Perez-Diaz (1994) have documented the importance of social factors for the continued vitality of democracy in some parts of Italy in contrast to others, and for the democratisation of Spain after the death of Franco (but see Tarrow, 1996). These studies used a much broader conceptualisation of the social supports for democracy existing in these systems, and tended to triangulate (see pp. 97–103; Laitin, 1995) the role of society in democracy. However, like the *Civic Culture*, these studies tended to assume that democracy was the dependent variable, social patterns the independent ones.

If we return to the 'four Is' that often are advanced as explanations for political outcomes, and especially for public policy choices, we can see clearly that three are more society-centred than state-centred. Interests, individuals, and ideas all tend to arise from a social basis,

Key Text 5.4 Robert Putnam *et al.*, and Social Capital

The spate of democratisation in the late 1980s and early 1990s raised questions (theoretical and practical) about what conditions were necessary and sufficient for an effective democratic system (see Key Text 6.3). There were some remarkable instances of viable democracies being created in what appeared to be hostile circumstances, while at the same time attempts to build democracy in seemingly more favourable circumstances produced instability or a return to authoritarianism.

One important answer to the puzzles arising out of attempts at democratisation was provided by Robert Putnam and his colleagues. Putnam's answer was based on studying Italian politics for over two decades, and argued for the importance of a strong *civil society* for explaining successful democracy. Putnam had been following developments in a number of local communities in Italy and found that those communities that had a strong associational life were more likely to produce effective democratic government than were those localities without such associations. It did not appear to matter if those associations were political or were as far removed from politics as choral societies; what mattered was that citizens were involved in organisations outside the immediate family.

The argument that Putnam develops from these observations is that civic life is essential to democracy. Through their membership in organisations citizens are able both to gain experience in working within organisations outside the family and to develop more positive attitudes towards democracy and other citizens. The *social capital* created through these extra-political experiences provides the bedrock for political democracy.

The Putnam thesis has been very influential in the democracy debate, but has not been without very strong criticisms. For example, some critics have argued that he has placed excessive emphasis on the role of individuals in political life, as opposed to the role of the numerous states that have influenced politics in Italy, especially southern Italy where the most obvious problems of democracy arose. Further, the assumed causal linkage between associative behaviour on the part of citizens and the effectiveness of democracy remains at the level of an association; it is argued that there is not a good theoretical 'story' to make that linkage. Despite these claims, as significant as they may be, this volume has raised many of the right questions about democratisation and the link between state and society, and will continue to influence both theory and practice.

although both individuals and ideas must function through formal institutions to have their impact. Thus, there is a huge range of theory available for the comparative researcher who wishes to develop society-based explanations, especially when society here includes the economy and the role of national and international economic actors. Indeed, to some extent, economic and social explanations often have dominated political science, explaining the relative success of democracy and policy (Linz, 1988), with some scholars seeming to argue that political variables are irrelevant. This is yet another instance in which drawing the line clearly between these types of explanation is difficult. The economy may be argued to be an institution – the market – or it may be argued to be a set of interests and even ideas.

Even with the extensive availability of theory, the researcher may be misguided into believing that any one of these society-based explanations is sufficient to cope with the complexity of the political situations that must be explained. The surrounding society and economy may have a substantial influence over politics, but there must still be a political mechanism to translate all that pressure into political action, and then into policy decisions. Thus, countries with similar socio-economic cleavages or similar levels of development may still behave differently. The socio-economic conditions may establish parameters for possible actions, but political institutions, political actors, and political values must still determine how to function within those parameters.

Coda

It is important to note that state-centric theory and society-centric theory can concentrate on the same actors, but still have different assumptions about the dynamics involved in the political process. Take, for example, explaining public policy through the role of interest groups. On the one hand there is corporatist political theory of all sorts (Schmitter, 1974; Cawson, 1986; Pross, 1992). Even for the variety of corporatism that Schmitter (1974: 88) labels as 'societal', the dominant actor appears to be the state. In this view, it is the state that accepts one interest group or another as the legitimate representative of the economic or social sector, and it is also the state that structures the interest intermediation and ultimately makes the decision about policy. The interest groups may have formed autonomously and may have autonomous views about policy, but the public sector tends to define how the system of interest intermediation will operate and who gets to play the game, even in more decentralised versions such as corporate pluralism.

The above view of the relationship between government and interest groups can be contrasted with familiar pluralist conceptions (Gunnell, 1996; Dahl, 1980; Kariel, 1961). In such conceptions, which are usually associated with American political science, government was merely the arena within which the interest groups worked out their own competitive games over policy and influence. This conception of interest intermediation is much more society-centred. Interest groups are assumed to arise autonomously in society, and governments rarely accord them any special status. Governments will make policies in part as a function of the political pressure exerted by interest groups, but they do not provide the virtual guarantees of such influence that exist within the corporatist framework. Somewhat ironically, the characterisation of the state that emerges from the pluralist model is of a more autonomous actor than that which emerges from the more state-centric corporatist arguments (see Dunleavy and O'Leary, 1987).

It is not only in interest intermediation that both state- and society-centred views of the policy process can be sustained at the same time. While political economy was advanced as a subfield of the discipline in which state-centric views were dominant, more society-centred views of the field also abound. Take, for example, Joel Migdal's (1988) arguments concerning 'weak states and strong societies' existing in many underdeveloped countries. The argument here is that states in these countries are not yet sufficiently powerful to overcome the entrenched interests in society, with the consequence that policies can best be understood as reflecting societal rather than state preferences. This, in turn, may perpetuate patterns that contribute to the poor levels of economic growth and development.

Another example of the contestation between state- and society-centred explanations of public policy arises in Jonas Pontussen's (1995) review of several books arguing for explanations both state-centred and institutional-centred. Pontussen admitted the importance of the institutionalist arguments, but also pointed to the central role of societal interests, especially the economic structures of 'global capitalism', in shaping public policy. Pontussen's arguments may reflect yet another instance in which the complexity of government and public policy overwhelms any simple explanatory structure, and is yet another implicit plea for the triangulation of measurement and theory in the development of political theory.

The conflicting theories existing in these fields do not provide any clear answers; they are much better at framing interesting questions. Further, the theories provide questions that are, in principle, testable and that may be further contextualised. If we consider the state-centric versus society-centric views of political economy, for example, then we should inquire whether both theories are not correct. In some situations, the state may be the dominant actor, while in others social factors may be more important for explanation. Are these empirical differences systematic, and can they say anything more about the nature of the different political systems? In particular, are there certain challenges that some states face at points in their development that require one form of governance as opposed to the other? For example, the United States is usually thought of as the quintessential case of society domination, but during parts of its history government was a major development actor (Hughes, 1993; Sbragia, 1996).

Summary

There is no shortage of available theory in political science that might be used to inform comparative political analysis; if anything, there is too much theory and not enough measurement and application of those existing theories. Hubert Blalock (1984), among others, has argued that one of the fundamental problems of the social sciences is the failure to dismiss theories that do not perform adequately. Whether because of the complexity of causation of most social phenomena, or the difficulty inherent in developing adequate measures for the principal concepts, or simple soft-heartedness, the social sciences tend to keep a number of moribund theories on life support.

The above having been said, however, there may be a shortage of theory that provides the comparative thrust needed for advancing this particular segment of the discipline of political science. A good deal of the explicitly comparative theory now existing functions at a level of extreme generality. That generality prevents the development of sufficiently specific hypotheses for effective comparison. Further, many available theories of political behaviour assume that political behaviour is the same in almost any setting, and that comparison, therefore, is not particularly valuable. What may be needed most is some means of assembling these various approaches and using them together. For example, approaches such as rational choice tend to assume that behaviour is the same in all places. This universalistic assumption should then be assessed in light of the more directly comparative hypotheses of other types of theory.

6

The Case Study

We have already discussed the possibility of conducting comparative research with small samples of countries, including the seeming impossibility of doing meaningful comparison with a sample of only one. These small-N comparisons all depend upon the capacity of the researcher to perform effective case-research. The case-study remains by far the most common method of research in political science in general, and more particularly in comparative politics. Despite its frequent use, case-research is often denigrated by more 'modern' and 'scientific' researchers, who rely on statistical analysis and other more quantitative methods to collect their data. Also, it must be said that case studies are often conducted poorly, and without sufficient understanding of the theoretical and methodological issues involved in doing proper case-research. Sir Geoffrey Vickers (1965: 173) provides a trenchant critique of case studies (whether done well or poorly) when he argues that:

> Case histories are a laborious approach to understanding. For situations are so varied that even a large number of cases may be a misleading sample, while each is so complex that even a detailed description may be too summary; and none is comprehensible outside the historical sequence in which it grew.

We all understand that cases may at times merely present themselves to the researcher, but even when investigating such a research windfall, some attention should still be given as to how best to fit that single case into more general analytic and theoretical concerns. Even a single case can be used to identify some way to compare – whether through comparison with theories or directly with other cases. A single case, if properly constructed and researched, can be used to expand the analytic knowledge of political science and to illuminate, and even test directly, theories commonly used in the discipline. For example, an exceptional occurrence such as the political mobilisation in Belgium over the murder of young children can be used to understand both that country and political movements (Van Ouvride, 1998).

In addition to doing the best job possible with the single cases, there are also a number of ways of taking a number of cases and aggregating their results to make a coherent theoretical argument. If these techniques for assembling case materials are understood and propagated, then there will be a much better chance for extending the theoretical grasp of comparative politics. These aggregative methods permit the accumulation of the large body of existing case material into a more interesting theoretical structure, and may guide in the subsequent development of more carefully designed matched case studies. As with all techniques, there are questions and potential pitfalls in these. These cumulation methods do appear, however, to provide an option for extending the capacity of comparative politics to make more general statements without massive (and unlikely) injections of money for large-scale field research in a number of countries.

This chapter will begin with a discussion of the case method, and the methodological issues that have been raised about this format for research. A descriptive case-study often can make a contribution to understanding, but there are means of making the results of the case-research more useful and more valid in its their right. Further, cases have a number of possible uses for the development of theory in political science. There are several ways to look at those possible contributions, and this chapter will also evaluate how individual cases can be, at least in some cases, crucial for theory development.

After this discussion of the role of individual cases, we will proceed in the following chapter to examine two methods for taking the results from case studies and aggregating them. The first method is termed 'meta-analysis', and has been developed as a means of facilitating more general theoretical development on the basis of quantitative results garnered from more limited studies. The second method, using Boolean algebra, goes even further, and attempts to do more direct tests of theoretical propositions using the results of cases.

Improving Case-Research

The prevailing model of social science research is variable-oriented research, with the possibility of multiple causation and complex interactions among variables. These complexities can be sorted out through a variety of statistical manipulations if there is a sufficiently large sample of observations. That social-scientific model is often a difficult standard to meet in comparative research, especially when there is an opportunity only for a limited examination of one or a few cases. In the first place, the availability of only a single case means that almost every variable has an equal chance of being a cause; without some comparison (across time or across cases) there is no means to sort out the causes of the differences. The plausibility of putative causes, as a kind of face validity, can be used to sort out explanations, but often there are any number of 'stories' about causation that are equally plausible, and hence no possibility of rejecting causes.

Further, even if there were some means to include more variables and to evaluate them, any individual researcher can only examine a few, and probably those will be the ones that led the researcher to look at the case in the first instance. Most researchers do not undertake to do case-research at random; he or she will be attracted to the case because the issues it represents are interesting, and it will be difficult to overcome that initial interest. That initial interest, and the subjective probabilities that go with it (Tversky and Kahneman, 1974), will tend to shape research outcomes despite real efforts by the researcher at preserving objectivity.

If we begin to move beyond the single case-study and to develop a capacity to utilise collections of case methods for more theoretical purposes, we begin to face several important questions. The first of these is how to make the individual case studies more comparable. One of the standard responses to attempts to compare cases, other than those that already enjoy a very strong 'family resemblance' (Collier and Mahon, 1993; see also Castles and Mitchell, 1993), is tosay that the cases are not comparable, and that therefore the results of the proposed exercise are inherently flawed or even meaningless. How does a researcher know if cases are comparable, and indeed, what makes cases comparable or not? The tendency to assume that cases must be relatively similar in order to be included in comparison institutionalises the 'most similar' design discussed by Przeworski and Teune (1970), perhaps to the detriment of the development of

Key Text 6.1 Ronald Inglehart and the Study of Political Values

The behavioural approach to political science, and to comparative politics, assumes that individuals and their attitudes are the root of political behaviour. In this view, rather than looking at institutions or even at structures such as political parties or interest groups political analysis must begin with individuals. Ronald Inglehart (1977, 1990, 1997) was concerned initially with the shift in values between what he termed 'materialist' and 'post-materialist' values. 'Materialist values' in politics focus on economic issues as the basic motivation in politics, assuming that politics is a means for people and groups to improve their economic positions. 'Post-materialist values', on the other hand, focus on other societal goals, such as freedom, participation, and improving the environment. These values tend not to benefit individuals directly but rather improve the quality of life within the entire society.

Inglehart argued that there appeared to have been a shift from materialist to post-materialist values beginning at least in the 1960s. That shift was most evident for younger people and for the better educated. These findings, along with the general shift away from traditional class-based politics towards a politics of ideas and of values. Inglehart's work was to some extent the sequel to Rokkan's (see Key Text 3.1). Rokkan had demonstrated the importance of cleavages arising before the industrial revolution, and Inglehart demonstrated that new cleavages were emerging.

Inglehart's work has played a major role in the development of political science but also has raised some major questions. The most obvious question is whether this view of politics is not also locked in time, just as was the class-based, economic conception. Talking about the rise of post-materialist values seemed natural in the 1960s but the oil crises of the 1970s reintroduced scarcity into the minds of many people, even in the most affluent countries of Europe and North America, so that there was some waning of post-materialism. Further, it was not always apparent how these changes in values actually translated themselves into real political action, at least not to the extent that post-materialist concerns could supplant the existing political parties and patterns of voting. It appeared easy for people to respond positively to post-material values but then the act politically in a more self-serving manner. Once again, however, Inglehart's work has shaped the continuing discussions in comparative politics.

comparative theory. Also, if their degree of comparability is inherently low, are there ways still to make cases more comparable, and still to utilise them within an effective comparative analysis? These questions are central to the pursuit of comparison through the case method, and hence become crucial for the development of the study of comparative politics.

Despite the potential weaknesses of case-research, it is important not to be excessively apologetic for doing this type of research. Indeed, this method has some advantages over the conventional statistical research more usually identified as 'good social science'. In the first place, good case researchers accept complexity and multiple causation as a crucial characteristic of their research, rather than as a bother to be eliminated, as it appears to be in some variable-oriented research. It is difficult to believe that complex political events are always the consequence of a few variables that are capable of being measured at the interval level.

In addition, the case-study attempts to locate its findings in its particular historical and cultural milieu, rather than assuming some degree of isolation of political events from their surroundings. As a result of that 'embededness', the case-study can look directly at the sequence of events that produced an outcome, rather than just at the outcome. We have argued above (pp. 19–22) that, despite the importance of process and procedure in the political system, research using process variables is relatively rare, and rather weak, in political science. The focus of cases on process is therefore a real advantages for one type of understanding of politics, albeit not always the best basis for making generalisations.

We should also note that some scholars may utilise the case method as their fundamental basis for methodology but then themselves accumulate a number of cases that create a theoretical whole from the seemingly disparate parts. We have already mentioned the major historical and comparative analyses of scholars such as Moore (1966), Bendix (1964) and Skocpol (1979). These scholars had a common theoretical framework, which they then applied to a series of cases, each case selected to demonstrate a relatively wide range of variation so that their basic hypotheses about social change could be tested. This purposive selection would not meet the canons of experimental or statistical methodology, but it still permitted these scholars to make reasonable theoretical statements with a strong comparative basis. Also, this style of research imposed (before it was formulated) the 'most different systems' design.

Case Studies

Any time a researcher investigates a single instance of a phenomenon within a single setting, we call that exercise a case-study. The boundaries of the term 'case-study' are themselves rather fuzzy. For example, if the researcher collects data about several decisions made in the same issue area over a short period of time by the same political institution, is that still a single case-study or several? And if he or she examines different types of decisions made within that same setting, has that research moved beyond being a simple case-study? Also, if this mythical researcher looks at the same issue being resolved in different but very similar settings, cities in the same country, or in the same state in Germany or Australia, is that still a case-study, or has it already become a comparative study in its own right? Eckstein (1975: 85) would give a precise definition of the case, but perhaps an excessively narrow one. He would limit the definition of case to a single observation, making it more a data point than a case. These are important definitional questions that need to be considered when embarking on case-research, given that they will shape to some extent the methods and interpretation of the findings. The purpose here is not to dwell on definitions for the sake of definitions, but rather to be sure that we examine the full range of possibilities for case-research, and thus not dismiss its utility too quickly.

Conducting Case-Research

No matter what form a case-study is to take (see below), there are several fundamental methodological issues that must be addressed. These can be summarised in terms of the questions about variance that we have been using throughout the discussion of comparative analysis. The generation of experimental variance is fundamentally a problem for the selection of cases, and for assuring that there is indeed variance along some important theoretical dimension or dimensions. Of course, if a scholar chooses to work with a single case then that experimental variance must be assumed rather than observed directly. This remains the dominant approach to case-study research, given limitations of time, money, language skills, and so on This in turn means that 'comparison' comes later, either with a theoretical standard or with other known cases. It must be assumed that a case selected for a particular reason will actually reside somewhere along a

Key Text 6.2 Jean Blondel and the Study of Government Institutions

The renewed interest in institutionalism in political science has pointed to the importance of formal structures in determining the outcomes of the policy process. Even before it became fashionable to do so Jean Blondel was documenting the nature of government institutions and showing their influence on the policy process. In a number of books and articles Blondel (1980, 1982, 1985) and colleagues (Blondel and Mueller-Rommel, 1988, 1993) have described the nature of cabinet government and other aspects of the structure of governments. This published research was done primarily on the industrialised democracies, but some of the work has generalised the concepts to the universe of political systems. This is particularly true of Blondel's textbooks in comparative politics (1969, 1996) that use much of the same approach to politics to analyse a range of countries and issues.

Blondel's approach to the comparison of political institutions has been very straightforward. This strategy has been to collect a great deal of basic quantitative and qualitative information about institutions, and to then provide several analytic lenses through which to understand the differences that emerged from the data. For example, his book *The Organization of Government* (1982) asked some deceptively simple question about the organisation of the public sector around the world. Answering these questions with evidence from dozens of political systems enables Blondel to provide the reader with a wealth of information about how governments are organised, with some implications about how they would function.

Although heavily empirical, these studies also have substantial theoretical relevance. In particular, given the return of concern with institutions and institutionalism in political science this research provides a source of hypotheses, as well as numerous empirical examples for institutional analysis. Also, the conceptions of institutions in Blondel's work goes beyond the dichotomy between presidential and parliamentary systems that has dominated much empirical institutional analysis (see Weaver and Rockman – see Key Text 5.4). It presents a more nuanced vision of differences among executive institutions, especially within parliamentary regimes.

It is easy to criticise some aspects of Blondel's work on institutions. It tends to be data-rich and relatively theory-poor. It tends to count all cases as equal, whereas major cases (the United States, France, Japan) that have served as exemplars for other systems should perhaps be weighted. Despite that, he has made a very great contribution in extending our understanding of the nature of political institutions and the choices that governments make about their own organisation.

continuum of some independent variable, and that if a different case had been selected then there would have been different results. That remains, in most cases, however, only an assumption, albeit one that can be tested by the methods of cumulating studies discussed in the next chapter.

If we remember Przeworski and Teune's (1970) admonitions concerning 'most different case' research designs, and the search for the general rather than the particular, then there are rather different uses for the single case design. In this mode of reasoning, the only real utility of a single case would come in selecting a case that was as deviant as possible from other cases in which a certain pattern had been discovered. If the pattern of relationship among variables holds up in that 'most different' case, then we have even greater assurance that the relationship is indeed very robust, and there is reason to accept that there is some stable and reliable pattern of political behaviour.

The control of extraneous variation and the reduction of error variance are more important questions for the conduct of the research itself. In case-study research, the researcher himself or herself is the major source of error variance, as well as a major source of extraneous variance. The problem is that, unlike in most other forms of social science research, there are few, if any, checks on the observations made by the researcher. The observer can be a major source of extraneous variance. He or she will learn a number of things in the course of conducting a case-study, and therefore observations made towards the end of the study will be different from those made early. Similarly, the researcher brings a number of biases – theoretical or otherwise – so that the research will tend to be a personal expression as well as a direct reflection of the facts of the case.

Error variance is the result of an unsystematic mistake in research. Again, case studies are very open to this type of error, simply because they are usually not subject to replication. Most case studies are unique opportunities to observe a political process, and without several scholars working on the same case it is unlikely that there will be any cross-checking. Even if there are multiple reports of the same case, different theoretical perspectives may mean that the researchers will not be interested in the same data. Theory offers something of a test of findings; if the findings differ significantly from theoretical expectations then there may well be error involved. The theory available is often not sufficiently powerful to provide clear expectations that can provide such a check.

Defining Cases

In addition to the above boundary questions, case studies also can be differentiated and classified by their origins, their purposes and the manner in which they use the information available. Ragin (1992: 8–9) differentiates between cases that are 'found' and those that are 'made' by the researcher. The question raised here is the position of theory, and with theory the role of the individual scholar, in the development of the case and its selection. Some cases appear naturally to the researcher; the *Challenger* disaster was very obvious, and demonstrated a number of very important points about public administration in the United States and in the rest of the world (Vaughan, 1990; Casamayou, 1993). Other cases must be constructed or 'discovered', and the nature of that construction depends upon an analytic or theoretical framework being imposed on the facts of the case. Bovens and t'Hart (1996; see also Hall, 1973), for example, are concerned generally with policy fiascos and disasters, so they identify, construct and catalogue a number of failures that might have escaped more casual observers but that enable them to develop a framework for analysis.

Ragin also differentiates cases on the basis of their generality. By 'generality', he means the extent to which the researcher can know *a priori* what the case is a case *of*. Sometimes a case that appears intriguing is not clearly defined before the researcher enters the scene. That researcher will have to spend some time simply deciding how to classify the case, and then how to fit it into the descriptive and theoretical frameworks of the discipline. For example, is the famous Suez case in Britain (Lucas, 1996; Bowie, 1974) a case about foreign policy decision making, or a case about ministerial responsibility, or what? On the other hand, some cases are clearly questions of budgeting, or of interest group influence, or whatever – their categorisation is never in doubt from their inception, even though the researcher may still want to apply a particular analytic framework to the case.

There is always a danger of premature closure in the classification of a case, and of assuming that one of many possible facets of a case is *the* important factor. One means of addressing the indeterminacy and multiple facets of the cases that we frequently encounter in comparative politics is to attempt to triangulate the information, just as we advocated in general (pp. 97–103) for measurement above. The classic example of this strategy is Graham Allison's study (1971; for a recent critique see Bendor and Hammond, 1992) of the Cuban missile crisis. Allison examined the missile crisis through three independent theoretical lenses, attempting to determine what the case really exemplified, and how it could best be understood.

Relatively few cases may have the richness of the one addressed by Allison, but the theoretical triangulation strategy is still a useful option when there is some real dispute over just what the nature, and even the facts, of the case are. The multiple lenses employed could lead to several alternative sets of questions concerning the case, which should, in turn, lead to a more complete understanding of the case. The danger, of course, is that the multiple lens strategy will disguise a real preference of the researcher for one or another of the explanations, with the use of the multiple lens providing the reader with a false sense of security in accepting the *a priori* interpretation of the researcher.

Another purpose to which case-analysis can be put is in defining deviant examples and using those cases as a means of exploring causation (see Smelser, 1973). Ali Kazancigil (1994), for example, explores the nature of both modern Turkish government and Islamic patterns of governance by using Turkey explicitly as a deviant case. How does a state with a governing system copied primarily from Western models function within an Islamic environment, one lacking a great deal of the economic wealth that appears to undergird the stability of governments in Western Europe? This deviant case-analysis raises interesting questions, not only as a means of describing politics within the single country but also as an entry point for understanding a more general set of questions about governance and the role of religion in politics. Likewise, American (Lipset, 1990), Japanese (Pempel, 1990) and Singaporean (Quah, 1990) exceptionalism can serve as useful ways to explore more general theoretical questions about politics and governance.

Ultimately, all cases must be constructed. That is, even if it is evident from the beginning what it may be a case *of*, the case itself must still be socially constructed by the researcher. That scholar must decide what the boundaries are for the case, what the relevant questions are, and what the relevant evidence is. In particular, if the research is to be of any real utility for the discipline generally then the researcher must develop or adapt a conceptual framework into which the case can be fitted, and with which to make it more comparable to other, similar cases. What cases it will be similar to will be defined by the conceptual framework is chosen and how the researcher constructs the case, and that construction does not occur naturally. Even when the strategy of deviant case-analysis is being used, there must be some regularity of other cases assumed, or demonstrated, in order to argue that the one case actually is a deviant.

Social scientists inevitably approach a case with a set of ideas and concepts that define it. Too often, those concepts are implicit rather than stated, and it is incumbent on them to explicate those assumptions so that readers can better assess their findings. Not all constructions of a case are equally valid, so a researcher may define the case in a way that ultimately will be demonstrated to be unsuitable. For example, Edward Banfield (1958) did a major case-study of a village in southern Italy. With it he explicated a conception of 'amoral familialism' that was used to describe the seemingly asocial nature of life in this part of Europe. Subsequent research has tended to bring that conception into doubt, and to demonstrate a much livelier civic life in much of Italy than Banfield described (Putnam *et al.*, 1993 – see Key Text 5.4). In all case-method research there is the danger that the researcher brings along too much intellectual baggage when constructing his or her image of the case, something that subsequent critiques through the operation of a discipline will have to correct. This characteristic of research presents the interesting problem, noted by Thomas Kuhn (1970), of how this correction is to come about if the discipline is shaped by influential scholars and influential studies.

Purposes

Case-research can also be conducted for a variety of purposes. Although they often are done just because the individual scholar is interested, cases can be thought of as fulfilling several purposes. Eckstein (1975), for example, lists five purposes for case-study research in comparative politics. The first of these purposes, the 'configurative–idiographic' study, can be thought of as a case-study conducted simply for Dragnet purposes – 'just the facts'. One entirely valid reason for doing a case-study is to collect information on the topic in question, especially while the case is still in progress. Once the issue is settled, the memories of the respondents often become selective, and, knowing the outcome, they often tell a rather simplified story about how the decision was reached. The real lines of political division and the indeterminacy of most public decisions will be more apparent while the case is in progress. Examining the political process while it is in progress may be especially valuable in comparative politics, given that the researcher may be less familiar with the national setting of the case than he or she would be for their own country, and hence examining the process is even more important.

As well as simply collecting information on a particularly interesting event or decision, case-research can be used to typify a process or the politics of a country, or even type of country. This is similar to what Eckstein referred to as a 'heuristic' case-study. While in the first, descriptive use of cases above we may be looking for the exceptional, in this instance we are looking for the typical. Any number of collections of case studies (Macridis, 1968; Linz and Stepan, 1978a; 1978b; O'Donnell *et al.*, 1986) have been developed to demonstrate how politics in a country or set of countries actually work (see Key Text 6.3). These collections can have a great deal of pedagogical value, because they take the abstractions about the way in which politics works somewhere and translate them into more tangible examinations of the political dynamics. As such, they are useful 'heuristics' about how these systems function.

Case studies can also be used to teach in other ways. Many business schools teach through the use of cases, giving students the facts of a case and then allowing them to make their own decisions about what the best course of action would be. In comparative politics *per se*, this style of instruction is not often appropriate, but it may be so in the comparative study of public administration or public policy. Comparative cases can be used as a means of exposing to students the assumptions and biases of their own policy systems, and what the options for improving existing public policies could be, were the net for ideas cast more broadly (Bennett, 1991; Dolowitz and Marsh, 1996). Further, these cases may explore just what the limits are of 'pinching ideas' (Ingram and Schneider, 1988) to make policy in one country better than in the past.

Finally, cases can, and should, be used in a more consciously theoretical manner in testing and elaborating theory. If we are interested in theoretical development in the discipline of political science then this goal is the most important application of the case-study method. Eckstein develops three ways in which cases can be applied directly to the construction and testing of theory. The first is through what he calls the 'disciplined–configurative' study. This is a case-study in which there is an attempt to utilise the case-study to illustrate a general hypothesis or theory. As Howard Scarrow (1969: 7) pointed out some years ago, a case-study has the capacity to be

Key Text 6.3 Alfred Stepan and the Study of Democratisation and the Consolidation of Democracy

Political events beginning in the 1970s and continuing through the 1980s and 1990s have presented a new empirical and theoretical challenge to comparative politics. In Southern Europe, Latin America, Asia and particularly in Central and Eastern Europe there have been breakdowns of authoritarian regimes and movements towards some form of political democracy. These political changes have been far from uniform, and hence there has been a need to develop theories that can account for both the similarities and the differences in these cases.

From the wealth of empirical evidence now becoming available a number of intellectual approaches to democratisation have been developed. Some of these approaches focus on the role of political élites, and the development of 'pacts' that can manage in what might otherwise be conflictual circumstances. Other approaches have focused their attention on the nature of civil society (see Key Text 5.4) and the importance of 'social capital' for democracy. Still other studies of democratisation have been concerned with the selection of the appropriate institutions and writing the types of constitutions that can make democracy effective.

Alfred Stepan and several of his colleagues (especially Juan Linz) have been central to the debates over democratisation and in the development of theory about the processes of breakdown, democratisation and consolidation. Their recent work has been concerned with the consolidation of democracy, or the process through which new democracies can ensure the continuance of an open and participatory form of governing. Unlike many other scholars they concentrate on the development of appropriate institutions for democracy, especially a *Rechtstaat* and an effective bureaucracy. The argument being made is that civil society may help create or sustain democracy, but is more likely to be a barrier, especially in societies with little experience with democracy. Therefore, if the right institutions can be created and can be operated then there is a chance that the system will be effective and can create legitimacy. Especially important in this process is developing the rule of law in societies in which government has a tradition of being arbitrary and capricious. Finally, Stepan and Linz have been concerned with the problem of dual transitions, as many countries are forced to change from centrally planned economies to market economies at the same time that they democratise. This places a tremendous strain on any political system, but also emphasises the importance of robust institutions for policy-making and implementation.

comparative and theoretical, if 'the analysis is made within a comparative perspective [which] mandates that description of the particular be cast in terms of broadly analytic constructs'. The theory has been developed outside the case, the case being an attempt to illustrate that the theory does indeed work. A good example of this use of cases is the set of cases edited by Linz and Stepan (1978a; 1978b) to compare the breakdown of democracy in Europe and Latin America. These cases had a clear theoretical focus that was applied in most instances and ranged across a number of countries.

The second possible theoretical use of cases discussed by Eckstein is the 'plausibility probe', in which there is not yet a general theory to be tested and confirmed or disconfirmed. Rather, there is a proto-theory that the researcher wants to try out by using the particular case. If the case provides some support for the theory, or it at least is useful in exposing some features of the landscape covered in the theory, then the researcher may feel more confident in moving on to more extensive field research. Eckstein cites his own early research (1966) on Norway as an example of a case-study that explored the plausibility of a concept. He was not very certain about the utility of the cultural theory he was developing, but he did have the opportunity to apply it to the interesting case of Norway, in the main successfully.

Finally, Eckstein discusses the use of the 'crucial case' as a means of testing theory. While no amount of case-study research can confirm a theory definitively, it may be that if a theory works in a situation where it might be thought to have been a difficult test, then the researcher can have greater confidence about that theory. On the other hand, if a very likely case is studied and the theory does not hold in that case then there may be good grounds for rejecting the theory. In either of these instances, we can argue that there has been a crucial case-analysis. What this discussion may also imply is that it is easier to get the crucial confirming type of study published than it is the disconfirming evidence. Journal reviewers and book editors would seem to prefer to publish positive results, so that a manuscript demonstrating that a theory appears to work is more likely to find its way into print than one that rejects the theory. This tendency may help explain why there are perhaps too many theories available for the researcher. The social statistician Hubert Blalock has argued (1984) that the social sciences in general tend not to disconfirm enough theories. This 'weakness in our culture' (his phrase) means that the scientific aspect of the disciplines has been slower to take hold than in the natural sciences.

One interesting variation on the crucial case-study would be a country that makes a major change in some political variable. That change can be seen as a quasi-experiment and a crucial test of the presumed relationship between variables. For example, in the 1990s New Zealand has changed from a single-member district electoral system similar to that found in the United Kingdom and the United States to a limited proportional-representation system (Vowles, 1995). This change appears to have led to a multi-party system, even in a country without many cross-cutting cleavages, but will that change persist? The two months required to seat a government after the first elections under the new rules may lead to some rethinking (Hall, 1996). Japan, on the other hand, moved in 1996 from proportional representation (PR) to electing its Diet by a mixture of PR and single-member districts; will this reduce the number of small parties represented in the Diet? Similarly, in 1996 Israel chose to move to an independently elected prime minister, rather than having the prime minister drawn from the Knesset (parliament) as before. What effect will this movement towards a presidential system have on government and policy? Are any effects purely a function of Israeli politics, or are the implications more generalisable?

This is a rather complete list of the purposes to which case-research can be put. It is important to remember, however, that these purposes are not a once-and-for-all thing, and one case may fulfil several of these purposes. A case that is conducted simply as a configurative exercise may later be used as a crucial test for some hypothesis or another (Stinchcombe, 1968). This often reflects the passing of time and the development of new theories into which to slot old cases. This style of theory testing may, however, encounter a number of dangers along the way. A researcher who went into the case with one set of assumptions, and who was operating in one research tradition, may produce results that are subject to severe misinterpretation by someone operating with different assumptions. As Ragin points out, cases are sometimes made rather than occurring naturally, and the craft of the case makers may ultimately show through even when the cases are put to different uses.

The Case as Process

We have to this point been discussing the case largely as an event, almost in the highly restricted manner that Eckstein advocated (1975: 85 ff.). That is, a case for Eckstein is a single event – a decision for example – at a single point in time. That restriction may have some utility as a means of delimiting cases for further analysis, but may also be excessively restrictive. The alternative is to structure the analysis of the case as a *process*, and examine the way in which the issues at hand develop during the course of the case. This strategy may mean that instead of a single observation there are a number of linked (and therefore not independent) observations, with changes on perhaps both the nominal independent and dependent variables. This strategy still generates a case in a very real sense, but it is also a comparative study across time.

The *developmental case-study* is one way to think of this process of multiple measurement in the analysis of a political process. Bartolini (1993: 141 ff.) advocates this method as a means of studying political processes that are extended across time, and then using these case studies as a foundation for better understanding some fundamental political processes, for example, decision-making or implementation. For example, case studies have been crucial for the development of implementation theory, beginning with the original extended one by Pressman and Wildavsky (1976). The implementation literature has also been developed comparatively through case studies, including some in places such as the United Kingdom (Barrett and Fudge, 1981), Germany (Mayntz and Scharpf, 1975), the Netherlands (Hanf and Toonen, 1985) and the Third World (Grindle, 1980).

In addition to just implementation as one stage of the process, the study of public policy may be particularly amenable to process-tracing forms of comparative analysis. There is a well-known model of the policy process (Jones, 1984), which, although developed in the context of American government and not without its critics (Nakamura, 1987), appears sufficiently general to be applied to a variety of research settings. Does the process of agenda-setting, for example, differ between the European Union (Peters, 1994b) and the United States? If so, how and why? Does policy formulation in Mexico (Mendez, 1996) differ markedly from that in the more industrialised countries to its north? These and similar questions provide a means of approaching the *process* of policy-making comparatively.

Alexander George (1979) has been an important advocate of case-study methodology, especially with respect to case studies that focus on processes rather than individual decisions. George's own research has focused on foreign policy decisions and the development of foreign policy through those particular choices. The methodological points he raises, however, apply easily to case-study research in comparative politics. In particular, he discusses the interaction between statistical and case modes of explanation, and the role that history plays in explanation in the social sciences. The history in which George is interested is not, however, a series of idiosyncratic explanations for events, but rather the development of generalisations on the basis of multiple cases occurring through time.

Rather than developing a classificatory scheme for case studies as Eckstein and Lijphart have, George instead discusses a series of essential tasks for case-study research. Those tasks are divided into three basic phases. The first phase is the initial design of the research. In that phase, the basic tasks are to specify the problem to be investigated and the nature of the independent, dependent and control variables to be central to that research. Once those issues are resolved the next task is to select the particular cases that will comprise the research, as well as the particular forms of data that will be needed, and to specify how the expected findings would relate to the theory that has guided the selection of the cases.

The second phase of the research process involves the actual execution of the case studies required by the designs developed in the first phase. George is careful to point out that anyone conducting case-research must be extremely careful to consider all possible explanations for the outcomes of the case, and not just find evidence that supports the preselected theory. Unlike statistical analysis, case studies do not have clear means for determining how the evidence supports a theory, nor what level of support is sufficient to justify the (at least temporary) acceptance of one explanation. Because the case researcher is the judge for evidence, he or she must be careful to be as open as possible to alternative evidence and ideas.

The final stage of George's plan for case-study analysis is to move from the case materials to the theoretical implications of the comparisons. George posited that the development of theories was through the route of selected, controlled comparisons and the development of typologies. In this controlled comparison, the researcher should, it is argued, consider each case both as a deviant case and as an indication of the basic theoretical line of research for which the case was originally developed. It is then up to the researcher to separate the elements that come bundled in each case, or to classify the cases as predominantly one type or the other. That is a difficult task at best, but even having to address the issues may force the researcher to think about what he or she has actually found in any one case, and to relate that case to broader theoretical issues.

Issues in Case-Study Research

The above discussion has focused on the relationship of case-study methods to theory. These are certainly crucial issues, but we should also look at a few more practical issues. We have noted that the standard issues of maximising experimental variance, minimising error variance and controlling extraneous variance arise very clearly in case-study research. Although case-research by definition raises these problems in a more extreme form than other forms of social research, it is not impossible to do valid case-research. As with most other methods, the most important factor is being cognizant of the potential problems and being able to understand the problems that may arise in his or her own analysis.

The Role of the Case Researcher

More than any other form of research in political science, case-analysis places a burden on the individual researcher to address these problems. Further, in comparative analysis, the role of the researcher becomes even more of an issue, given that he or she is a product of a particular political and intellectual culture, and almost inevitably brings that set of values to bear on the research. In some instances, those values are brought to bear very explicitly in the research, as when the research focuses on issues such as democratisation. Similarly, a good deal of comparative policy research also has a normative element, assuming that policies that provide certain types of benefits to the public are preferable to others (Heidenheimer, Heclo and Adams, 1990).

In addition to the explicit use of normative standards in case-analysis, researchers bring other, less explicit values to a case. For example, scholars accustomed to a unitary and centralised government such as that of the United Kingdom may find the complexity and indeterminacy of federal systems – especially highly decentralised ones such as Canada (Simeon, 1985) or Switzerland – difficult to understand, and also somewhat suspect normatively. Similarly, Americans may find the absence of checks and balances in a Westminster parliamentary political system such as that of Britain to be tantamount to an authoritarian government.

The question for comparative analysis is whether an observer from one culture can effectively understand and interpret the politics of another culture. For countries such as Canada and the United Kingdom, which share many cultural and political values, that comprehension may not be particularly difficult, although even then there may be sufficient difference to lead to misunderstandings, especially of features such as a written charter of basic freedoms that appear in one country but not the other. When the country studied and the country of the researcher are more diverse, the possibilities of error and inadequate understanding are exacerbated.

Just as cultures may imprint a researcher with certain preconceptions about what the case may mean, so too can a theoretical commitment on the part of a researcher. The problem with case-research is that there is little or no check on the findings of the researcher, except in the rare instances in which several scholars are working on the same case. Although not in comparative politics *per se*, the *Challenger* disaster in the United States has had a number of independent and to some extent varying case studies performed on it. The case of the Suez decision and entry into the European Community have had similar multiple treatments in Britain. As we have noted above, theories provide social scientists with a set of questions, and to some extent also a set of answers, for any issues that they may encounter. In some cases, asking a scholar to eliminate these biases may be more difficult than getting him or her to recognise the cultural biases that are being brought to the research. Part of being a social scientist is that commitment to a theory, while a cultural bias is definitely not a component of the prescribed toolkit.

7

Building on Case Analysis

The preceding chapter has pointed to the utility, and some of the potential pitfalls, of case studies in comparative analysis. One of the major issues is that each case is only a case, and it is difficult to build any theoretical generalisations from the individual cases. Any one case may be conducted extremely well, and be very valid as a representation of the reality that it investigates. The problem may be that it is also very atypical of the population of similar cases, whether that population is within a single country or across a number of countries. The probability that a case is atypical is higher in comparative research, given that there is almost certainly more variance within the more diverse population of instances that are likely to be encountered, so the need to move beyond single cases is more important in this area of the discipline.

This chapter will discuss several ways that have been developed for cumulating individual case studies. Cumulation of case-research that has been performed for the particular purposes of individual scholars will present inherent difficulties of its own. Even if those researchers were interested in the same issues, and were working within the same intellectual framework, differences in the ways in which the research is conducted may easily introduce extraneous sources of variance. It is sometimes argued that in case-research the researcher is the major independent variable; even if that is an overstatement, it does point to the possible sources of difference in research outcomes that can make cumulation more difficult.

An extension of the above argument can point to one of many peculiarities in the way in which academic research is conducted, and the values expressed in that research. Scholars tend to make their reputations by identifying the unique and the unusual, rather than by working with cases that correspond easily to other cases. Scholarly reputations are made by claiming a case is unique or at least unusual, and that makes cumulation of cases more difficult. Claims of uniqueness, however, are sometimes overstated, and if cases are examined together then there is the capacity to create some generalisations out of apparently disparate cases. For example, the European Union is often claimed to be a unique political system, but its operational reality is not significantly different from that of many federal states (Sbragia, 1992). The description of the cases by their proud 'discoverers' may emphasise the unique, but the underlying reality may be more mundane.

The basic argument of this chapter is that even with all the potential problems, cumulation of case materials is preferable to no cumulation. First, as interesting as individual cases may be, and conceding that they can say a good deal about individual countries or decisions, they can only be single cases. The major purpose of comparative politics is to create generalisations. The development of those generalisations may require focusing on the central elements of the many cases that may be included in an analysis. That is in contrast to the usual pattern of focusing on the details that make each case interesting (and important) for students of a particular country or policy issue. At the level of the basic 'story' – the relationship between independent and dependent variables – the biases and idiosyncratic concerns of individual scholars may not be such a barrier to the cumulation of findings.

In addition to building generalisations, assembling a number of individual cases can help identify those that are the outliers. The findings in those cases may still be quite valid, but they do merit somewhat greater consideration and scrutiny than the more conventional findings. For example, post-apartheid South Africa has been characterised by a capacity for accommodation and internal peacemaking that is atypical of societies with such a history of violence and oppression. Why has that country been able to move towards some form of political forgiveness, while others have had reprisals and bloodshed? This case would probably stand out even without a formal attempt at cumulating cases, but an attempt at cumulation would permit identifying factors present and absent in a range of cases to see what causal assumptions might be viable.

The focus on outliers reminds us that although comparative politics is primarily concerned with developing generalisations, it is also about identifying the exceptional cases. Careful understanding of the

Key Text 7.1 Arnold Heidenheimer *et al.*, and Comparative Policy Studies

It is somewhat unusual to list a book that began its life as a textbook as one of the most influential works in the sub- discipline, but this book appears to deserve that classification. We have already pointed to several other books that focus on public policy in comparative perspective, but those books all owe some debt to the Heidenheimer, Heclo and Adams' work.

Unlike the typical textbook this volume defined the field, and to some extent created it. These three authors defined 'public policy' in terms of social choices, and the effects that those choices have on individuals. They then marshalled a great deal of evidence about the differences among policy areas in these countries and were able to demonstrate some consistent patterns in the choices made.

Despite its importance, there are some obvious problems with the Heidenheimer, Heclo and Adams version of comparative policy Studies. Perhaps the most obvious question about the volume is why does it focus on such a limited range of policy issues? Certainly the range of social polices covered account for a good deal of public expenditure and public employment, but there are also a number of important policy areas – defence, economic regulation (in any depth) and agriculture, as examples – that are excluded. Do the analytics developed to account for differences in these policies also hold true for other policy areas? Further, some of the more important differences appear to be among the policy areas rather than among the countries and that dimension of comparison is largely unexplored. Also, the work covers only a limited range of countries, being concerned only with the developed democracies and then primarily with only a few of those. This is understandable given that there are often different policy problems in less developed or in centrally planned economies, but there is also a need to think about the possible extensions of the basic models developed here. This is all the more true as the 'little tigers' in Asia begin to challenge common assumptions about paths of development and the ways in which state-society relationships should be organised.

As with all of the works we have highlighted in this book there are obvious and important problems, but there is still an significant and lasting contribution to comparative politics. If nothing else, the book made the point very clearly that politics is, as Lasswell argued, about who gets what.

exceptional cases can themselves bear substantial theoretical fruit. Indeed, the 'most-different systems' approach to comparison discussed above, as well as a concern for critical cases, would argue that we should consciously search out those outliers as a means of enriching our theories. Some of the exceptional cases may be very familiar – there are arguments that both American and Japanese politics are exceptional (Lewis, 1975) – but when seen in the light of the modal political system or the modal political decision, they are indeed exceptional cases.

The question, then, is not whether to attempt to cumulate cases but rather how to accomplish that task as effectively and as efficiently as possible. If conducting individual case studies raises questions of measurement, then attempting to do a number of cases and put them together raises those questions to an even higher level of concern. In case studies, the researchers are themselves the principal instruments, and thus can be a source of extraordinary levels of extraneous variance. Take, for example, a book such as Moran and Prosser (1994) on the experience of privatisation in a number of countries in Europe – east and west of the former Iron Curtain. It contains a number of interesting case studies written by scholars from the respective countries, all of whom bring with them to the process their own traditions and concepts, so that the findings are to some extent conditioned by those conceptual differences. This is true despite the best efforts of the editors to bring the cases into a common framework.

Similarly, the selection of the cases themselves is another potential source of extraneous and error variance over which a scholar seeking to cumulate studies can exercise little or no control. We have already pointed out that there is a pronounced tendency for scholars to pick some cases more readily than others. It is much more convenient to select English-speaking countries – for their presumed cultural similarities, as well as the ease of using the language. Thus, even where there are attempts to cumulate cases, the 'sample' will be far from random, and hence there are pronounced threats to the external validity (the ability to generalise) of the results.

Again, case-research is done at different times for different purposes, so that many of the threats to validity discussed by Campbell and Stanley (see pp. 46–53) arise with limited possibility to understand and control the sources of error. Sincere, dedicated, scholarly work may still be flawed when there are factors in the environment of that research that introduce error, and which permit the excessive influence of factors that are beyond the control of the researcher. A researcher inevitably goes into a project with an underlying thesis about cause and effect, even if this is not stated in such positivist language, and thus will look at only some parts of the total evidence. The researcher therefore runs the risk of excluding crucial causal factors. For example, studies of domestic politics and public policy in the 1990s are increasingly suspect if they do not take into account the influence of the international political economy and 'globalisation' (Strange, 1996).

The methodologies we will discuss in this chapter deal with the question of cumulation from individual studies in different ways. The principal method discussed will be Boolean algebra. This approach is especially well suited for use with case studies, given that it depends upon relatively gross levels of measurement (dichotomies are used for both independent and dependent variables); a researcher can code information from already published analyses in order to assess the relative frequency of occurrence of patterns of causation. Boolean algebra need not be used only for the cumulation of other studies, but could be the basis of a research design that will classify all the variables as dichotomies.

Meta-analysis, on the other hand, is a method for amassing information from studies that are themselves statistical. It therefore requires greater *a priori* agreement on measurement and method, something that is often lacking in comparative politics. Still, there are a number of variables that have been used frequently enough – party identification, social class and levels of education as independent variables explaining voting behaviour, for example – to provide some opportunities for pulling together statistical studies to produce generalisations about the statistical relationships of variables. Even with these familiar concepts and variables, however, care should be exercised, given that a seemingly simple concept may be interpreted differently in different settings. For example, it appears that British respondents in voting studies tend to regard 'partisan identification' as the party for which they intend to vote, while American respondents, as evidenced in the classic study *The American Voter* (Campbell *et al.*, 1960), tend to think of this as a more enduring commitment to a party.

Meta-Analysis

The discussion in the previous chapter centres on the potential benefits of individual case studies. While if done properly a case can add a good deal to political theory, the accumulation of cases is likely to be more valuable still. Even if cases are conducted initially with a configurative or descriptive intention, they may later be cumulated and applied to the purpose of theory construction and testing. This can be done in relatively informal manners, and it can also be done more formally and statistically. The development of the tool of meta-analysis (Cook *et al.*, 1992; Hunter and Schmidt, 1990) enables cumulation of cases with some greater confidence of the capacity to use the cases appropriately. Thus, meta-analysis goes beyond the usual literature review, to attempt a more systematic compilation of available research findings.

Meta-analysis can be carried on at a number of levels of statistical sophistication. Although almost all of the method has been developed for assembling studies that have quantitative methods, and for making some inferential sense out the seeming jungle of findings, there are ways to use the method that do not depend upon existing statistics. The most common is the simple voting technique of tabulating the number of votes for one explanation of a finding or another. Once there are statistics – even simple means or measures of difference – then the possibilities of combining the research findings increases dramatically (Glass *et al.*, 1981). These methods make a number of sometimes dubious assumptions about the underlying nature of the statistical evidence, but still greater confidence in cumulation than would otherwise be possible.

This method may be especially useful for comparative studies of micro-level political phenomena that already have a sufficient *N* of cases to compute statistical measures, but which may produce disparate findings in different settings. We have argued already that, paradoxically, the comparison of quantitative results from different settings is one of the weakest areas in comparative politics. The availability of the statistical evidence within single settings tends to focus attention on the particular rather than on comparison across cases. This method will not address the differences directly, but will force researchers to think about the sources of observed differences, especially when there are some clearer generalities. There are such a large number of studies now using relatively similar measures and techniques that this cumulation should be very fruitful.

In addition to the development of generalities, meta-analysis may direct micro-level analysis towards looking more at the deviant cases and what they add to comparative analysis (see above). Kazancigil (1994) points to the utility of deviant cases in the study of comparative politics, using the case of Turkey as a Muslim country behaving more as a European state, although the success of an Islamic Party, Welfare Party, in 1996 may make Turkey less a deviant case. Also, in the Newton and Kaase (1995) compilation of research – some data original and some secondary – on political values in Europe there are some obviously deviant cases. For example, why should the residents of Norway be so much less concerned with some aspects of social policy than are other Europeans (Pettersen, 1995)?

It should already be clear that this set of techniques is not the answer to all the problems of case-analysis in political science. It depends in large part upon the existence of clear research findings that subsequently can be coded by another analyst, even if there is no formal statistical analysis. This means that some of the equivocation and nuance that are important in case-research may appear to be lost. Further, if a researcher is attempting to cumulate what is known about a hypothesis, or what is contained in a research tradition, then he or she is at the mercy of what has been published. This dependence tends, in particular, to drive the findings in favour of positive effects, because there is still that bias in publishing in the discipline. Further, there tends to be a bias in favour of certain areas of the world, so that some, such as Scandinavia, may be over-represented in any cumulation of findings and may thus affect the results. Like any technique, the results of meta-analysis should be viewed with some healthy scepticism, but that should not preclude its presence in the armoury of comparative analysts.

Boolean Algebra and Cumulation

If quantitative research faces difficulties in cumulating research findings, then qualitative researchers must be facing seemingly insurmountable obstacles. The very language that dominates in qualitative research tends to soften and temporise research findings. Not wanting to place all their analytic eggs in one basket, researchers will describe their research findings as 'suggestive' and 'heuristic', and say that their presumed independent variable 'appears' to be related to their dependent variable. All this hedging may save some future embarrassment, and it reflects appropriate uncertainty given the less precise nature of qualitative research.

The modesty expressed by qualitative researchers also makes all the more difficult the job of scholars attempting to extract any more comprehensive sense out of this work. Making temporising statements adds to the vagueness of any outcomes of the research. In addition, I have already argued that social scientists tend to advance their careers by including causal factors in the armoury of the discipline, rather than eliminating presumed causes that really do not work. In almost any case-study, we find (no surprise) that the presumed independent variable does indeed have some relationship with the presumed dependent variable. That inclusiveness may help academic careers, but it may actually slow scientific progress!

The sociologist Charles Ragin (1987) has borrowed the mathematical techniques of Boolean algebra to develop a technique for aggregating case findings and testing theory on the basis of the available case materials. As we will point out below, this method is far from foolproof, but it does offer a procedure for utilising the rich array of case materials in comparative political science for building more theoretical generalisations. This method is a technique that can take the wealth of case-oriented materials and case-derived 'data' in political science and convert them into a form suitable for variable-based research and the systematic testing of hypotheses. This method allows use of some of the very real advantages of cases (see above, pp. 139–42; see also Ragin, 1994: 304–8), while still being able to examine systematically cause-and-effect relationships existing in the outputs of many cases.

Basis of Analysis

The basic tool of the Boolean approach is the 'truth table', in which findings from all available cases are presented and codified (see Table 7.1). In such a table, the available cases are classified according to the presence or absence of certain presumed causal variables, the presence or absence of some condition that functions as the dependent variable, and the number of instances in which the particular configuration of cases occurred in the 'sample' of cases available to the researcher. That visual presentation of the data in itself often makes it clearer what sort of relationship exists between the presumed independent variables and the dependent variable than any conventional descriptive summary of findings.

For example, in Table 7.1 there is a study of whether managerialist (Pollitt, 1990; Hood, 1991) reforms occurred in various OECD countries. In this case, rather than relying totally on published cases, much of the coding was done by the present author using annual surveys of public management coming from the Organisation for

TABLE 7.1

Adoption of pay for performance

Independent variables				*Cases*	
Right	*Deficit*	*Scandal*	*Culture*	Y	N
N	N	N	N	0	0
Y	N	N	N	0	2
N	Y	N	N	2	0
N	N	Y	N	0	1
N	N	N	Y	0	0
Y	Y	N	N	1	0
Y	N	Y	N	2	1
Y	N	N	Y	0	2
N	Y	Y	N	3	1
N	Y	N	Y	0	0
N	N	Y	Y	0	0
Y	Y	Y	N	0	0
Y	N	Y	Y	0	1
Y	Y	N	Y	0	0
N	Y	Y	Y	0	0
Y	Y	Y	Y	1	1

Economic Cooperation and Development. Other sources for these data include Aucoin, (1995) and Olsen, (1991). The argument is often made that there is a world-wide diffusion of policy ideas (Dolowitz and Marsh, 1996), including ideas about public management. In this case, we are examining 13 forms of reform occurring over 6 years, so that there are 78 possible adoptions of reform in each country. Given that there are 24 countries for which we have data, that makes a total of several thousand possible adoptions. In this case, the independent variables include control of government by a party of the political right, a perceived economic crisis, and the occurrence of major scandals or reports of major administrative malfunctions. The question is what best explains why these reforms have been adopted in some countries, but not in others.

For the purposes of simplicity in presentation, we have not presented all the available data. Instead we are focusing on one particular reform – pay for performance – and amalgamating all six years, so that if the reform was adopted in any one year is counted as an adoption in the data. This table, then, is suggestive of general patterns, but by no means a complete explication. In some ways, however, it is more valuable to look at individual reforms, rather than the total, given that there can be marked differences in the nature of the reforms, and hence in the politics that would lead to their adoption by the public sector (Peters, 1997).

Notice that the truth table presents all possible combinations of the various values of the 'independent variables'. Rather than looking necessarily for a single cause, the Boolean approach enables the researcher to look for more complex relationships among the identified causes. In this way, the method provides some of the strength of the techniques, such as multiple regression, that are usually associated with variable-oriented research. It may be, for example, that conservative political leaders are successful in changing the nature of the public service only in the presence of financial problems, or only when there has been a major administrative scandal. Thus, this method enables the researcher to establish necessary and sufficient conditions for the occurrence of events.

In this case, it appears that presence of a party of the political right, by itself, is not a necessary cause of administrative reforms, despite the widespread identification of these changes with political leaders such as Margaret Thatcher and Ronald Reagan (Savoie, 1994). Some of the most notable instances of administrative reform (New Zealand in particular) occurred under Labour or social-democratic governments. The argument that economic problems generate the desire to reform appears better supported in these data, although again far from perfectly – Norway is a clear exception to that hypothesis. Finally, there does not appear to be a strong relationship at all between the presence of a major administrative fiasco and attempts to impose reform. Thus, no variable by itself can be seen as a major cause of attempts at reform.

We can now proceed to examine the combinations of variables, again seeing that in case-research it is the ability to look at a multiplicity of causes, rather than a single cause, that is a virtue. The presence of these three dichotomous causal factors yields a set of an additional five combinations of variables (plus the three instances in which a single posited cause is present – there are *x* combinations of causal factors in these studies using dichotomous variables). In this particular case, it appears that the presence of a party of the political right, combined with the presence of an economic crisis of some sort, is an important pairing for producing reforms, a combination more important than either of the variables by itself. As important as that combination is, however, the independent impact of administrative culture on the acceptability of reforms appears even more significant.

Boolean Operators

There are two fundamental logical operators in Boolean algebra – a method that is indeed more like formal logic than like mathematics. The two operators are called 'addition' and 'multiplication', but are not really analogous to those operators in ordinary arithmetic. If Y is the dependent variable and A, B and C are the independent variables, then the addition operator – $A + B + C = Y$ – is actually saying that A or B or C produces Y. That is, if any one of those conditions is present then Y will be present, or have a positive value. In that form of the Boolean approach to analysis, any of the three independent variables could be determined to be sufficient to produce the existence of the dependent variable, although none is a necessary condition. The truth table will, of course, provide the data to determine whether this additive assumption is correct.

The 'multiplication' operator in Boolean algebra is actually the means of looking at the 'and' condition for the occurrence of the dependent variable. If that condition holds then each of the independent variables determined to be important can be said to be *necessary*, but probably not sufficient, to produce the existence of the dependent variable. Rather than focusing single causes, even if multiple causes are found to be sufficient in the additive look at the data, this version of Boolean analysis looks at the interaction of variables and the occurrence of the dependent variable only when there is a particular combination of independent variables. This is then analogous to the use of interaction terms in regression analysis.

In addition to the two logical operators, there is another important operation in Boolean analysis that moves beyond the simple explications of the truth table. This is called 'reduction', and is an attempt to simplify what might otherwise be rather formidable presentations of the data. This operation is an attempt to move from simply identifying sufficient conditions and crucial combinations of variables to looking at the Boolean process in almost experimental terms (Ragin, 1994: 302–4). That is, if we can hold all other factors constant (the presence or absence of a condition), then we should be able to tell if the one remaining variable that does vary has any influence.

The fundamental logic for employing reduction in Boolean analysis is:

If a Boolean expression differs in only one causal condition yet produces the same outcome, then the causal condition that distinguishes the two expressions can be considered irrelevant and discarded.

Again, this is the aspect of the analysis that is experimental. If the presence or absence of a condition – agrarian disruption, in combination with rebellious cultures and agrarian structure in Wickham-Crowley's analysis of revolutions – makes no difference to the outcomes observed then that variable obviously cannot be a causal factor, and should be excluded to simplify the theory. As Wickham-Crowley (1991: 307) argues, this is Occam's razor in practice. Such an approach has the further virtue of eliminating possible causes, something that, we have argued above (pp. 30–3) appears to be difficult for the social sciences to do.

For the analysis of reform discussed above, we can resolve the basic findings into simpler explanations of the patterns of reform. We can begin by expressing the relationships among variables, in which a capital letter represents the presence of a trait and a lower-case letter represents its absence. Thus, the Boolean expression:

$$X = aBc$$

indicates that the dependent variable X occurs when B is present and when A and C are not. If we also find that the expression:

$$X = aBC$$

is also true in a number of cases then we can eliminate C as a relevant variable in the analysis. The presence or absence of that one variable appears to make no difference to the outcome of the process in question, and hence can be eliminated safely from additional consideration.

Using the above process of simplification, we can proceed to eliminate variables and perhaps reduce the causal pattern found to relatively few potential combinations. For example, using this method, Wickham-Crowley was able to reduce the number of causal patterns of interest in his study of peasant support for revolutions from 13 'variants' to 4 combinations of factors (1991: 308–9). These included the presence of conducive agrarian structures combined with agrarian disruption in the area, and with substantial pre-existing linkages of guerillas to the peasantry. Support could also come when the agrarian structure was combined with a historically rebellious peasantry, and when that rebellious peasantry was associated with pre-existing linkages of guerillas with the peasantry. Finally, the pre-existing linkages of peasants and guerillas may have some effect even when other conditions are absent.

Potential Problems in Boolean Analysis

Although an extremely useful method for the comparative scholar, these Boolean techniques are not without their problems and pitfalls. There is some tendency to think that the real problems of comparative analysis, and political analysis more generally, are problems of technique, but neither Boolean analysis nor any other technique is a magic bullet for our research problems. In the first place, the method depends heavily upon theoretical and conceptual developments to define what factors should be included in the analysis (Markoff, 1990). As with any other methodology, if the proper variables are not included from the outset then the results will not, and cannot, be valid.

As well as having the right variables theoretically, those variables must be included, or in some way includable, in the full range of cases if the method is being applied to studies already conducted. In the examples used above, there is relatively little need for extensive case-analysis prior to inclusion in the Boolean analysis – this is largely primary research using the technique. In other cases, however, for example, Wickham-Crowley's (1991) analysis of revolutions, there is such a need. The cases in that latter study were conducted much less within a common framework of research, and therefore had to be placed into such a framework, with some additional coding from other case materials necessary to fit the data to the requirements of the model. While secondary coding may be necessary to maximise the 'sample' size, it may also involve the risk of importing a systematic bias by a researcher who already has a theory that is expected to explain the outcomes. This coding can also generate unsystematic error from inferences by coders who did not have primary knowledge of the case.

Another other potential problem with the Boolean approach is the question of the dichotomisation of variables. All the variables included in these analyses – independent and dependent – have been made into dichotomies. This requirement presents two potential problems for the analysis. The first is a practical, measurement problem, namely, When do we say that an event has occurred? This can be illustrated with the study of administrative reform used as the example above. Given the pervasiveness of ideas for reforming the public sector during the 1980s and 1990s, almost any government in the world will have considered this option and will doubtless have tinkered somewhat with their machinery; the government of Germany is usually cited as having made perhaps the least change of any public sector, but even there changes have been implemented (Reichard, 1997). How much change is enough to push them into the 'reformed' camp?

The related problem is the problem of degree and 'degreeism' (Sartori, 1991), again a measurement problem. For some variables, we may have the problem of identifying an occurrence, or non-occurrence, of an event. For others, however, there may be reasonably good measurement of the variable, but to be usable that information must be transformed into a simple dichotomy. The dichotomisation appears to require the loss of a great deal of valuable information. The selection of a particular point along a continuum to dichotomise also may bias the findings. If the division point is moved along the continuum then the outcomes of the analysis may be changed. Relatedly, this dichotomisation tends to lump together cases that may be in many significant ways extremely dissimilar. Again, in the case of administrative reform above, New Zealand has undergone a massive shift in the manner in which government business has been conducted (Boston *et al.*, 1996) while Canada has undergone very meagre changes (Peters, 1995a). Still, the two may still be classified as equal if a simple dichotomy is employed. For the independent variables, it may be that the variable has an effect only at very high values, even though it may be coded as occurring at lower levels, again producing potential bias in the results. This dependence upon dichotomisation also puts the research outcome very much at the mercy of the individual researcher.

Thus, while the use of dichotomous variables has a number of advantages, it also may have some serious disadvantages. Coding outcomes as simply occur/non-occur may appear uncomplicated, but in fact that choice may disguise substantial impositions of judgement, and also some potential for bias by the researcher. In some ways, a more extensive coding scheme would be more accurate, as well as more reliable and precise, despite the seeming difficulties in classifying data into a larger number of categories. There are well-developed means of verifying coding, and these may be particularly useful for a method such as this, which can be so dependent upon the judgements of coders.

The utilisation of Boolean analysis can also present problems of sampling and the existence of cases. For example, in studies of successful revolutions using this method, the sample is biased by the relative number of attempts at revolution occurring in different countries. If country *X* (Cuba) has one successful and well-institutionalised revolution, then its attributes are understated in the sample, while another country that has a succession of revolutions, even if successful, may have its attributes overstated in the sample. Unless there is some mechanism for using each year as a 'trial', and judging whether an event occurred or not for all countries in that year, there can well be significant sampling problems.

Finally, and perhaps most importantly, Boolean algebra as a method of case-analysis depends upon the existence of relatively clear conditions of necessity and sufficiency among the variables. If these conditions can be satisfied then this method does do something well that most social science analyses find difficult to do: eliminate some possible causes for a political phenomenon. That is, if few if any cases having a certain value on the dependent variable display a certain factor presumed to be an important cause of the dependent variable, then researchers can comfortably eliminate that cause as either a necessary condition or a sufficient one. Unfortunately, however, few things in the social sciences are so sharply defined. Rather, the causal patterns tend to be more mixed, especially as the numerous variables available from the literature are added and considered as possible causes, or at least conditioning factors, for the outcomes in which the researcher is interested.

In summary, the Boolean approach offers a number of real advantages for dealing with case-level materials. It enables the researcher to cumulate case materials and to begin to make some theoretical statements about information that otherwise would remain rather under-utilised in theory development. The method also has some serious drawbacks that must be understood before it is used. As with any research method, this approach depends upon measurement, and the classification of the variables that are then fed into the research. In this case, the need is to identify clearly the presence or absence of a variable and to dichotomise variables that may be continua.

Another Possibility

Another way of culmulating cases involves some features of both meta-analysis, with its reliance on conventional statistical analysis, and the Boolean approach, with its reliance on case-research. Statistical methods for coping with dichotomous dependent variables have been improving steadily, so that it is possible to develop statistical models using the outcomes of case-research as a dependent variable related to a number of interval-level independent variables. This would enable using case materials, again assuming that the dependent variable could be classified into 'yes/no', 'success/fail' categories, and from that produce results that might correspond well to the usual canons of social science research.

In particular, log–linear or logit analysis provides a general method of analysis of data that produces results analogous to those of conventional regression models with dichotomous dependent variables (DeMaris, 1992). More precisely, the method provides a measure of the odds of a correct prediction of cases into the two classes. This model can also use categorical independent variables and still produce estimates of the differential odds of an outcome. For example, it could take Wickham-Crowley's data on revolutions and provide an estimate of the differential odds of a successful one occurring, given the particular values of the independent variable or variables chosen.

We could apply the log–linear model to the same data for which we have been using Boolean analysis. There is a clear dependent variable expressed as a dichotomy. There are also a number of independent variables that can be expressed as categorical variables. The cultural variable could be presented either as the dummy variables used in the Boolean analysis or as the four types that we argue exist among administrative systems. The political variable can be presented as partisan control by the Left or not, again as we did in the Boolean analysis. The deficit and union strength variables are somewhat more of a problem. These can be dichotomised around the mean or median values, but this appears to lose a good deal of usable information, given that these are expressible as interval-level measures, though it enables them to be included in the logit analysis more readily.

TABLE 7.2

Logit estimates of impacts on probability of adoption of administrative reform

Pseudo-R^2 = 0.278	
Political right	0.22
Culture[a]	–0.46
Deficit	–0.04
Scandal	0.17

[a] Coded Germanic/non-Germanic.

Table 7.2 provides the outcome of the logit analysis for the data on the diffusion of administrative innovation in the OECD countries. These data very much confirm the findings from the Boolean analysis, but do so in a somewhat more precise manner. That is, we now have some idea that there is more of a real impact of parties from the political Right than appeared in the earlier analysis. When this political variable is simply dichotmised, the effect is almost non-existent. On the other hand, when the magnitude of domination by the Right is taken into account, there does appear to be a slight influence. It would be interesting in light of recent political changes in Britain in particular to then determine if large majorities from the political Left were to be associated with other types of changes in government, for example, freedom in information.

We could also apply discriminant analysis (Klecka, 1980) to these data, utilising the interval values of the independent variables to attempt to predict the placement of cases into the two categories ('adopt' or 'non-adopt'). In this instance, we would want to include the Left control variable as an interval-level variable, such as the percentage of seats in parliament held by parties of the Left, or the percentage of cabinet seats held by those parties. Including the administrative culture variable would, however, prove more difficult except as a series of dichotomous 'dummy' variables.

How can we choose among all of these various ways in which to aggregate the evidence coming from a series of case studies? One obvious factor would be the level of measurement available, and the confidence that we had in the measurement. If there is not a great deal of confidence in the measures then the Boolean analysis may be the best choice. It does not require (or permit) anything more than simple dichotomies for all the variables. While that in itself may introduce some sources of error, because of the choice of how to split a variable into the classes, there are far fewer problems than when we assume that there is adequate information to use a continuous measure.

The log–linear technique might be appropriate when there is a higher level of confidence in the measurements. For example, despite various disputes over the best ways to measure public sector deficits, these measures tend to co-vary, so that as long as the same definition is used for all countries there can be some confidence about the adequacy of the data for a more elaborate form of analysis. Even higher levels of confidence might be required for discriminant analysis, given that the variables are all measured at an interval level.

Summary

Case-research remains the most common and most fundamental way to conduct research in comparative politics. Despite the frequency of its use, there are very real problems in the method. It can provide detailed and interesting information on the cases and provide insights into the real world of politics as it is practised in the countries studied. Case studies also permit inclusion of a much wider array of information into the explanation of an outcome than would be possible with the statistical techniques associated with 'modern' political science. The case method therefore is suitable for interpretative analysis, but seems to be ill-suited for developing scientific generalisations. In the case method, each case remains a special undertaking, with the researcher focusing attention on the particulars of that case alone, and being content to provide a good explanation of that one case.

There is, however, some hope for developing generalisations based on primary case materials. First, the cases themselves can be researched and developed so that they are related more directly to political science theory. As George (1979) argued, case-research should be done by designing the cases with theory clearly in mind, or with the direct comparison with other cases in mind. Further, the usual characterisation of a case as comprising only a single observation at a single point in time is perhaps an excessively restrictive criterion, so that processes and more extensive longitudinal analyses can still be concluded as components of cases analysis. A case can be examined over time as a means of observing the play of variables under different conditions in order to gain a better understanding of cause and effect. Similarly, a number of cases can be collected in order to test the theory in question in a variety of socio-cultural settings.

Also, if those case materials include any sort of statistical information then they can be compiled through a meta-analysis, which can provide some reliable assessment of the available quantitative evidence concerning a hypothesis. If the evidence available from the cases is less quantitative then the Boolean approach can, with some manipulations of it, pull it together to produce an assessment of cause and effect, if any appears to be present. Even if there is no discernible pattern of causation, the Boolean mode of analysis still will have done its job, simply by allowing researchers to reject some of the large number of possible causes for political phenomena that litter the field. Even then, however, the limited number of cases available for most studies may make firm rejection of the hypotheses difficult.

We should emphasise again that all of these methods of cumulating case studies depend entirely upon the quality of the raw material fed into them. The first research task, therefore, is to ensure that the individual case studies themselves are done with regard for all the potential threats of validity, and further that they are conducted with some attention to developing theory. Cases should not be just something to do when other forms of analysis appear inappropriate, but themselves can be a worthwhile means of addressing social science problems. Case-analysis cannot answer all our research questions, but neither can any other method. Case-analysis can, however, address some questions that more 'sophisticated' research techniques cannot, so it should retain a proud place in the arsenal of comparative political analysis.

8

Events Data and Change Over Time

The tendency of many scholars is to think of comparative politics as contemporary politics, with the data that researchers should use being measures of contemporary attitudes, votes, decisions, and policies. Indeed, although political scientists sometimes sneer at journalists for their instant analyses of complex events, we ourselves engage in the same behaviour now and again, providing immediate theoretical explanations for complex political phenomena. These events range from the most recent election in our own country through the collapse of the former Soviet Union to democratisation in Latin America. Political science, in contrast to history, generally thinks of itself as the study of contemporary political life and events, and seeks to be as current as the morning newspaper, although much more analytic.

Despite the appeal of contemporary events, the student of comparative politics can augment understanding substantially by somewhat greater attention to the development of political systems over time, and the occurrence of certain types of events. The historical institutionalists (Krasner, 1984; Thelen *et al.*, 1992; King, 1995; Pierson, 1996), for example, emphasise the 'path dependency' of political life and the impact of formative events on contemporary politics, especially contemporary political structures. If students of comparative politics are searching for law-like statements about political behaviour then those laws should be as applicable in the past as they are at present. Further, some events may not occur sufficiently frequently to provide a reliable database if we depend entirely upon the contemporary period. For example, political parties do not come and go all that frequently, so if we are interested in the formation and durability of parties then we may need to look at changes over a reasonably long time period (see Mair, 1997). Taking a longer time perspective can open up the discipline to a variety of interesting data sources, as well as to a variety of interesting research questions that might otherwise be ignored.

This chapter and Chapter 9 will each discuss several approaches to studying political events and political change across time. We have discussed questions about research across time in passing in several of the earlier chapters, but in these two chapters we will address these questions more directly. Studying politics across time presents a number of interesting theoretical and methodological questions, but also can provide some answers to questions that could not be addressed adequately with a more static conceptualisation of the political world. Therefore, if researchers attempt to be at all perceptive about the current state of politics, it is often necessary to understand how those events were manifested, and were shaped, across time. Given that most socio-economic and political variables come packaged in large bundles called 'nation-states' examining change may be the only effective means of sorting out causal relationships among the variables.

Political science also must be able to provide explanations for change and development, as well as for the final static distributions on the dependent variable in which nations and individuals find themselves. Some of the most important questions in comparative politics are those of change – political development, democratisation, institutionalisation. As we will point out in these two chapters, any explanation that is effective for that distribution at the single point in time may not work in explaining the developmental pattern that generated that final distribution. The researcher therefore may have to make difficult choices about which explanations he or she is really interested in. Explaining both the final distribution and patterns of change are important and useful exercises, but also often are different exercises.

Events Data

A particular form of data that can be collected across time is called 'events data' (Allison, 1984). The idea of events data is deceptively simple. We can visualise the political world as manifesting itself in a series of discrete events that occur – wars break out and end, organisations are created and later dissolved, policies and programmes are initiated or terminated – or do not. When these events are cumulated, they can say a good deal about the nature of the political world within which they did or did not occur. Many of the variables that we use in political science are perceived as being more or less continuous – budgetary expenditures ranging (theoretically at least) from 0 to 100 per cent of gross domestic product – or are already aggregated – voting percentages are aggregations of individual occurrences in the polling booth. Events data tend to identify actions and events more discretely and to then create identifiable patterns directly out of those multiple occurrences.

The roots of events history analysis comes from the study of demographic variables like births, deaths and survival rates (Lawless, 1982). In the social sciences events data analysis has been used extensively in the study of private sector organisations such as restaurants, gas stations and newspapers (Hannan and Carroll, 1992; Carroll, 1987). The questions being addressed in these studies have to do primarily with the ability of organisations to survive in a particular environment, as well as the nature of the environments within which organisations function. The events that are utilised in these analyses are the creation and the eventual demise of those organisations, indicating at least indirectly the carrying capacity of their environment. In the cases of these private sector organisations, the analogy is often made to a population of biological organisms attempting to survive in a particular ecological setting. A biological environment can 'carry' only so many organisms of each type, because of the limitations of food, water, shelter, and so on When more than the limit of organisms attempt to live within the setting, inevitably some must die, or perhaps migrate.

Economic and social environments have limited carrying capacities, just as do natural environments. There are only so many customers for restaurants or gas stations, and there is only so much capital available for investment in businesses, so that some attempts to start new businesses will fail – in many cities today it appears that there must be a limitless supply of customers for Italian coffee-shops and fast-food outlets. The theory would predict, however, that some of these must fail if too many enter the market. Some businesses may be able to survive by adapting themselves to very specialised niches, just as some animals (the polar bear for example) have adapted to survive in seemingly hostile surroundings. Of course, some failures of businesses may be a function of their own poor management or simple misfortune. The fundamental argument, however, is that the environment and its capacity to absorb and to nurture organisations of certain types will also play a major role in determining the number of each type that do eventually survive. No matter how good the management, so the argument goes, only so many organisations will be able to survive, with management perhaps determining which ones do.

This world of gas stations and restaurants may appear to be a very long way from the world of comparative politics, but that is not necessarily the case. Many of the same questions that have been raised about those private sector organisations can also be asked about organisations in the public sector, or about social organisations that attempt to influence government. Lowery and Gray (1995), for example, have examined the rate of formation and dissolution of interest groups in the American states, doing so comparatively across the fifty states. They found that these organisations had a relatively close linkages with their environments, and high rates of formation. Other scholars (King *et al.*, 1990) have examined the formation and dissolution of cabinets in parliamentary governments using variants of events history analysis. This mode of analysis has provided an understanding of the dynamics of making and dissolving governments different from those provided by others, and is useful to supplement if not replace the analytical techniques more commonly used across time.

The rate of formation of political parties could be an interesting example of a phenomenon of this type, especially given that national electoral laws create very different 'ecologies' for parties in different countries (Lawson, 1994; Taagepera and Shugart, 1989). What is the carrying capacity for political parties of an environment with proportional representation, for example, as compared with that in a country with more restrictive policies for rewarding political parties with representation for winning votes in elections, as in the United Kingdom and the United States? What happens to those parties when changes in electoral laws significantly alter that environment, as has happened when New Zealand moved from single-member districts to proportional representation in 1996, with the early indications being for an increase in the number of parties on the political Left, and with that a marked decline in voting for the Labour Party? Also, how do threshold values at which parties gain representation affect the carrying capacity of the political environment? Electoral laws may specify that parties which gain below certain levels of the vote, typically 4 or 5 per cent, can get no seats in parliament. This is a way to prevent small, and possibly extreme, parties from gaining an official status in government, and hence this environment has a smaller carrying capacity than it would with other electoral laws.

Events history analysis also is able to provide a fresh look at classical political science questions such as regime change. Several of the earliest applications of events history to political phenomena – conducted by sociologists rather than political scientists – investigated the impact of a number of variables to changes in political regimes over time. Hannan and Carroll (1981) looked at regime change over twenty-five years, using a variety of economic development and world systems variables to explain regime stability. In this research, events were transitions among five different regime types. Also earlier, Hannan (1979) had examined the impact of ethnicity on the formation of nation-state boundaries and conceptualised this process as one of defining the availability of niches for various ethnic groups within the individual countries.

One example of using population ecology models for political science purposes is Peters and Hogwood's (1991) study of the survival of organisations in the US federal government, while others include some of Hogwood's later work (1996) utilising similar models for studying organisations in the British government. One of the most enduring of conventional wisdoms about politics is that government organisations tend to persist in the face of virtually any sort of challenge. The adage 'Nothing is so permanent as a temporary government organisation' captures that common perception rather well. This conventional wisdom was substantiated by the scholarly work of Herbert Kaufman (1976) on the US federal government, who found that federal government organisations were indeed virtually immortal.

The Peters and Hogwood study challenged the findings of Kaufman and other scholars (Casstevens, 1984) concerning the immortality of public organisations. Taking a longer time period, using a somewhat different definition of survival as well as a substantially larger sample of organisations, they found that government organisations 'died' and went through identifiable metamorphoses at almost the same rate as did most reported populations of private sector organisations. In particular, Kaufman's sample was based on all the organisations in existence in 1935, offer which he then determined what percentage still existed in 1972. This strategy ignored, for example, all the organisations that were created during the New Deal and World War II but then went out of existence, a problem referred to as 'middle censorship' in events history analysis (For a later discussion of the persistence of organisations see Kaufman, 1991). The Hogwood and Peters study used events history data analysis very explicitly. The data used in their study were a compilation of the formation, termination and transformation ('succession') events through which federal organisations went from 1933 to 1989. Organisations did change very frequently, but they tended to persist in a recognisable form for long periods.

These events history studies address some very important political questions. This importance is not just in debunking the popular misperception of the ability of government organisations to remain in business after their utility is exhausted; the research also addressed questions about what factors might affect the rate at which public sector organisations are created and dissolved. For example, one hypothesis that could be studied with these data is that political leaders (Bunce, 1984) have a 'honeymoon period' at the beginning of their term of office in which they have the capacity to make change that erodes thereafter. Also, this study could examine the effects of the political control of government on the tendency to create or dissolve organisations. The use of events data is therefore potentially an extremely valuable, and under-exploited, manner of looking at political change in comparative perspective. In this case it revealed something of the dynamics of change that could not have been understood with the more static methodology used by Kaufman and others.

The Method

The above discussion should provide some sense of how the logic of events data may be used to address political questions. What is needed now is to develop a better understanding of the particular techniques that are used to generate these findings. As we have been pointing out in reference to every method that we have looked at in comparative context, there are any number of potential problems with events data (see Tuma and Hannan, 1984). Still, there is also the potential to reveal a great deal about political processes and about political organisations that could not easily be identified through other means.

The first stage of the process is to identify what sorts of events will be included in the analysis, and what the operational definitions of those events will be. This task is fundamentally no different from the definition of any other variable, but, somewhat like the variables that are used in the Boolean approach, these variables are always dichotomies – the events in question either occurred or they did not. The number of occurrences of the events in which the researcher is interested then becomes the data from which subsequent analysis is developed. As with the Boolean analysis, the seemingly simple coding of occurrence or non-occurrence of an event is not always as simple as it appears. For example, if the dependent variable is to be changes in government, when is change sufficient to say that a genuine change has occurred (see Strom, 1988)? Governments change constantly, but when is the transformation great enough to count?

The coding problems are especially evident in political science, when incremental change tends to be more apparent than the discrete 'state changes' that are employed in some sociological work using this method – it is usually clear when a birth occurs or does not; issues such as 'common law' marriage can further confound these statistics. Take, for example, political party research and the history of the Conservative Party in the United Kingdom. This is clearly a political party now, but at what date did it become one – was it under Robert Peel in the 1830s, or at a later date when the party structure became more institutionalised? And has the Liberal Party in Britain really gone out of existence, or only been changed by its various mergers with other political groups? The researcher must develop very clear rules to code these potentially ambiguous events.

In events data analysis, there are really two types of coding decisions that must be made. The first is whether a unit is in or out of a sample. For comparative political research, these units frequently are organisations. So, for example, a researcher must decide what constitutes a political party for the purposes of his or her research. What criteria will distinguish a party from an interest group or a social movement? What level of formal structure is required before the party exists as an organisation, and in how many elections must it participate before being considered a real political entity, and not just a temporary manifestation of discontent (see Mackie and Rose, 1990)? For other types of research, for example, the outbreak and termination of wars, similar types of coding decisions must be made (Small and Singer, 1982: 31–61).

For comparative analysis it is especially important to remember that different political systems may pose different measurement problems and thus can bias the research. For example, in the United

States the creation or termination of a public organisation tends to require some form of official action, such as an act of Congress. This can be contrasted to changes under the United Kingdom or other parliamentary regimes, in which internal changes in an executive department are accomplished easily at the will of the minister and may not be formally recorded (Peters, 1988). The incautious researcher may assume, therefore, from official records that one of these political systems was much more stable (organisationally) than the other. That may be true, but the evidence from which the conclusion might be drawn would be inadequate for the conclusion, and change may be as common in one as in the other.

One of the more technical questions that arises in the definition of events is whether or not they are repeatable. Individuals are born and die only once. On the other hand, a single country may experience a number of regime changes. This is perhaps less a problem of defining the variable than of the analysis that can be applied to them. Repeated events raise questions about the independence of the observations that may undermine the assumptions of statistical methods. Further, when we think about political events, we need to be careful that the events are indeed meaningful watersheds in political life that are sufficiently important to be counted.

It is also clear that time is a crucial element in this method. The data are collected across time, and the researcher must be very certain that the 'sample' of time selected for analysis is representative, just as another style of comparative researcher would have to ascertain that the sample of countries selected was representative. The simplest statistical models are based on continuous time, with the events being distributed throughout time as they occur. The problem is that events may be rather sparsely distributed, so that any time period sampled is not likely to have any positive observations.

The tendency has been to favour using relatively long stretches of time for analysis, for a variety of reasons. One is to be sure that selecting a shorter period does not bias the results of the research. Also, even if the time period in question occurs relatively infrequently then a longer time-span is needed to have a reasonable N for analysis. Further, having the longer-time span enables subsequent manipulation, so that the researcher can determine if the survival rate of organisations changed after some crucial event.

As well as the total quantity of time, researchers must be very concerned with how events are counted within the time period. This is called 'censorship' within the method. It has nothing to do with the freedom of the press, but rather has to do with how we calculate the population of organisations or events in the sample. Left censorship, for example, would exclude organisations existing before the beginning of the designated research period, and would look only at those formed within the period. If the question were the durability of cabinets from 1973 (the first oil crisis) onward then left censorship would not look at cabinets already in existence prior to that time, probably an inappropriate research decision. Right censorship, on the other hand, does not take into account the termination of organisations formed after the end of the period – usually a more acceptable decision. This is in part if the researcher is bringing the analysis up as close to the present as possible – it is impossible to know the future, so that a certain amount of right censorship is inevitable.

If we return to the example of Kaufman's (1976) research on government organisations in the United States mentioned above, the practice there was 'middle censorship'. That is, Kaufman looked only at organisations that existed prior to the beginning of his time frame (1935) and then determined which ones survived until the end of the period (1972). As noted above, this research strategy had the effect of excluding a number of organisations newly formed during the intervening several decades. Given that new organisations tend to be the most vulnerable to termination, and that the period excluded was one of intense organisational activity, this form of censorship biased the research heavily in the direction of finding permanence.

Once we have made the decisions about the organisations and the actions to be counted, and about the time period in which they are to be counted, the remainder of the analysis can begin. As discussed throughout, the major questions that arise with these data have to do with the persistence of events and organisations. Just as business researchers or organisational sociologists want to know how long a restaurant may last on average, the comparative political scientist wants to know how long a political party or a cabinet is likely to persist. This persistence question becomes especially interesting if the researcher can also assess survival rates under differing conditions. For example, do political parties survive longer in proportional representation systems or not? One might hypothesise yes, but the persistence of the Democratic and Republican parties in the United States and the Progressive Conservatives and Liberals in Canada might bring that view into question.

At the simplest level of analysis, the researcher can justify tabulate the survival and persistence results for different types of organisations.

For example, Usui (1994) did an events history analysis of the adoption of social insurance programmes in some sixty countries from 1880 to 1960. In this case, the researcher initially was less interested in the persistence of the programmes than in the time and circumstances of their first adoption in each country. Thus the first portion of the analysis was determining the dates of initiation of the programmes in every country and then tabulating them across time. This, of course, depended upon a prior definition of the nature of programmes to be included and the sample of the countries to be studied. Further, the analysis was restricted in part by looking at only the first adoption of any programme. It might have been extended by looking at a group of five or six types of social insurance (for example, old-age pensions, sickness insurance, industrial accidents insurance, unemployment insurance and health insurance) and then having a 'sample' of up to 360 events. It can be argued that this would not fit with the theoretical purpose of Usui's research, but it could be an interesting extension of the analysis.

A similar form of enumeration of results was developed form the Peters and Hogwood study of changes in the US federal bureaucracy. They show that three major types of events were measured for each decade from the 1930s to the 1980s. These were 'births, deaths and marriages' (Peters and Hogwood, 1991), or the formation, termination and change in organisations over the time period. The first two events were relatively easy to identify, but the third took somewhat more effort and coding. When did an organisation change so much that it ceased to be the same organisation, and was in effect terminated? Almost all government organisations now have a very diverse genetic composition, reflecting various episodes of organisation and reorganisation (Grafton, 1984). Again, although the determination of the events that go into these analyses may appear simple, it actually involves a good deal of judgement and a thorough knowledge of the research site.

To move beyond the simple enumerations of events and transition matrices, events data also can deal with sequencing of events. For example, in the transition from non-democratic forms of government to more democratic forms, is there a particular sequence through which this occurs, or can moves into functioning democracy be made in any pattern? Hannan and Carroll (1981, 24) for example, found 30 different sequences of change in the 90 countries included in their study. Likewise, Peters and Hogwood (1991) identified a pattern of organisational change that appeared to be associated with the later termination of organisations. In understanding these transformation processes, what is important is not only that events occur, but the order they occur in; understanding the sequencing is crucial, but it is also difficult with the statistical methodologies usually used in political science (Abbott, 1983).

This simple enumeration of events data can say a good deal about the research question, but it is usually necessary to go further and investigate the rate of survival and the rate of failure of organisations. This form of analysis can be used to tell the researcher a number of things. For example, in Usui's study, the 'rate of success' was, in effect, the rate at which countries adopted the social insurance programmes. Hence, this is in practice another means of studying the diffusion of policy innovations (Collier and Messick, 1975). The theoretical basis for the analysis, and some of the assumptions, different from those in most diffusion studies, but the basic questions are the same. Both styles of research look at the rate at which the proportion of systems remaining in the 'non-adopter' category changes, as more and more countries go into the 'adopter' category, with both finding an S-shaped curve of adoption over time (Ramirez and Boli, 1987). The events history analysis, however, can add social structural variables to the analysis of diffusion (Strang, 1990) while most diffusion studies look only at something.

There are a variety of models of the survival of the members of a population of organisms, whether they are organisations or states that have not adopted a particular policy. The most common of these models are based on logarithmic survival, or 'hazard rates'. That is, survival rates tend to vary as the logarithm of the time that the entity had come into existence. The rate of 'death' of those entities tends to decline across time, given that new organisations tend not to be capable of sustaining themselves as well as do those with an opportunity to have established their place in one of the environmental niches. The cumulative probability of the entity in question being terminated tends, however, to increase over time. The rate at which death occurs can also be affected by a number of other factors in addition to just time, and if they are known then those factors can be included in the calculations for the rates of survival. Gasiorowski (1985), for example, found that the rate of survival of regimes (or, in his research, the probability of transition) was a function of something.

There has been some debate over the suitability of simple hazard rates for the study of political phenomena (Alt and King, 1994).

Hazard rates are useful descriptions of phenomena such as the death of organisms, but they are perhaps less useful when we attempt to explain political phenomena – the ultimate purpose of comparative politics. The alternative proposed is to calculate hazard rates, taking into account the effects of possible independent variables, so that in addition to dependence simply upon time there are also other influences, such as the number of parties included in the cabinet, the majority or minority status of the cabinet, and so forth. A number of studies (Warwick and Easton, 1992; King *et al.*, 1990) are now beginning to develop these more sophisticated analyses of cabinet stability, with the methods also being applicable to a variety of other political events.

Relationships with Other Methods

Although events history analysis has a clear standing as a research method in its own right, it also has some clear relationships with other methodologies. In particular, it appears closely related with the Boolean approach (Chapter 6) and with time-series regression (Chapter 9). In almost any research situation, the comparative scholar attempting to quantify his or her results has available a range of alternative research methods. Researchers often attempt to utilise their data within the most 'high-powered' method possible, often violating the assumptions of the method and making the research less valuable than it might have been using somewhat more modest methods. The task that the researcher faces is choosing the method that can best answer the research questions and for which the data available are suitable.

The relationships between the events history method and Boolean algebra are relatively clear. Both methods use dichotomous dependent variables, and both methods therefore depend upon the ability to identify those dichotomies adequately. Furthermore, the events identified in the events method could become dependent variables in the Boolean approach if each event could have the dichotomous independent variables associated with it. For example, in the Usui study discussed above, each of the cases of adoption of social insurance could be matched with a number of possible independent variables: control of government by left parties, the presence of labour unrest, economic crises, and so on We could then move on from relatively mechanistic explanations of diffusion, based largely on the density of the populations of adopters and non-adopters, to more politically motivated assessment of the same process of change.

Relating events history to times series regression analysis may require somewhat greater effort. Whereas time in events analysis can be somewhat free in form, with researchers able to count events when and if they occur, the coding requirements for regression analysis tend to be somewhat more restrictive. In time series regression, there should be an observation for each month or year, if nothing more than the presence or absence of an event. In a study that to some extent updates the Hannan and Carroll (1981) analysis of political change, Gasiorowski (1995) examined regime transitions in Third World countries from the 1950s through to the 1980s. This analysis took the events data and then fitted them into a logit regression model to examine the effects of various possible independent variables, especially economic variables. Logit regression, unlike conventional regression models, assumes a dichotomous dependent variable. It is an estimate of the odds of an event occurring, given the presence or absence of the independent variables (DeMaris, 1992). Using this combination of methods, Gasiorowski could detect a shift in the impact of economic factors across time, with rapid inflation shifting from inhibiting democratisation to facilitating it during the 1980s.

Potential Problems

As with all approaches and methods in political science, the use of events history is not without its almost inherent problems. Some of these shortcomings have been alluded to in the course of the discussion, but they should be identified and discussed more thoroughly here. I am continuing here to espouse the general virtues of triangulation and a strategy of multiple measurement when undertaking comparative research. The weaknesses inherent in any one method can often be compensated for by the strengths of others. Triangulation would appear often (see Figure 4.3) to be an expensive and seemingly wasteful means of undertaking research, but it may be the only means of obtaining a complete picture of some of the research problems in the field.

The principal problem with events data is the very nature of the dependent variable – an event. This assumes that the political world comes in discrete packages, each of which can be labelled an event, an assumption that appears to be difficult to sustain, given the numerous descriptions of political life as being 'incremental' and 'evolutionary' (Hayes, 1991; Lindblom and Woodhouse, 1993). The decision that produced an event may be very different, depending upon which participant in the process is asked, and the exact timing of crucial events may be subject to question. Even when formal decisions are involved, there may be a long lag time between the announcement of a decision and the actual implementation of the decision – when do we say that a complex event actually takes place? The researcher can establish coding rules to eliminate any uncertainty, but the decisions contained in the rules may be suspect, given other theoretical and methodological assumptions. However, if the rules are clear and are made public then they are subject to scrutiny by the scientific community and the appropriate debate can occur.

Another analytic problem with events data is that all events are equal. A regime transition in the former Soviet Union is counted as one event, just as is a regime transition in Burkina Faso. Clearly, the one had a much greater impact on world affairs than did the other, although for the residents of the small African country the proximate event may well be more important. Events could be weighted by the number of people involved, the size of the GNP of a country or the budget of an organisation, or some other appropriate measures. That strategy, however, might violate the whole purpose of the method, for example, counting events. This difficulty appears to justify yet another plea for multiple methods and alternative ways of visualising the same set of occurrences in order to obtain a better picture of the true nature of change.

Another obvious source of potential difficulty in utilising this research method is the definition of time and the application of censorship to events. In some instances, the history of the setting prior to the selected time period is not particularly relevant. In the case of Usui's research discussed above, there were no social insurance adoptions prior to the beginning of the time period so that left censorship was not a real problem. On the other hand, with the Peters and Hogwood research the prior existence of many of the public organisations included as part of the sample could have been a crucial problem, had there been no reliable information on their histories. In this instance, there was such information, and adequate coding of the organisational survival and durability was possible. Some choice of time periods and some censorship appears inevitable in using this research method. The question is whether those restraints seriously damage the generalisability of the research findings.

We should also point out that events analysis *per se* does not provide means for testing hypotheses that provide measures of the relative strength of independent variables. The enumeration of events and the calculation of the rates of survival of the particular 'species' that is being investigated are both very useful for understanding the dynamics of change, but do not provide any sort of test statistics. We have already pointed out that this method can be linked readily with others that do provide more direct measures of the impact of possible variables, but the researcher must be sure that the two-step process yields sufficient added value to justify that additional step.

Political science has as yet encountered some difficulty in defining several of the more important concepts that arise in the extension of the events methodology from simple counting towards population models. For example, one of the most interesting determinants of the viability of organisations in this model is the availability of niches in the environment for them. What types of organisations will the environment support, and does the number and type of organisations that are supportable change over time, and why? For example, most industrialised democracies have experienced the development of 'new social movements' that have some characteristics of political parties and some of interest groups (Duyvendak, 1995; Koopmans, 1996). What has happened in the environment that makes this type of organisation viable, and are they sustainable over a longer period of time? Gray and Lowery (1996) have begun to explicate a concept of niche for interest groups, but their version remains based more upon traditional pluralist interest group theory than on events theory and population ecology models.

Finally, and in some ways most crucially, events history data appear to be, used by themselves, somewhat ill suited to the demands of cross-national comparison. It can be extremely useful in aggregating events across a range of countries, as the examples from Usui, Hannan and Carroll, and Grasoski point out. Likewise, it can be very useful at looking at institutions within a country, as the evidence from Peters and Hogwood research points out. To use this method for comparative analysis will require performing the analysis within several countries and then comparing the results across the countries (see Peters, 1988). That could certainly be done, and would make a definite contribution to comparative analysis, but then entails all the problems of comparability. Is an agency in one country really the same as an agency in another? Can we detect changes in one setting as readily as in others?

Summary

Events history analysis can be extremely useful for comparativists, but as yet the method has been used relatively little. It enables the comparativist to conduct more comparisons across time, and to assemble data-sets that speak to some of the most important aspects of politics, for example, regime change and changes in governments within parliamentary regimes. Further, the method provides a very useful way to look at changes within the political structures of countries – both official structures such as bureaucracies and unofficial political actors such as interest groups and political parties. Many of the interesting questions in comparative politics are concerned with change, and this method enables the researcher to address change directly, albeit change occurring in discrete units.

This may be, in part, as mentioned above, that events history in itself tends not to provide as clear a 'bottom-line' answer about the relative power of explanatory variables as do other methods. There is some evidence that a hypothesis is supported or not, but that evidence is not as readily interpretable as other techniques. It can clearly demonstrate covariation across time, but that does not provide the probabilistic interpretations that most statistical techniques can offer. This may then require performing the research in several stages; though this is not really a severe disadvantage from the perspective of triangulating methods and theory in our research.

9

Statistical Analysis

We have been spending most of our space to this point in the book arguing that case-based analysis and other less formalised research techniques are important components of comparative political analysis. This discussion has been arguing implicitly that, despite its importance in the social sciences, statistical analysis is not everything, and that alternative methodologies do need to be considered and utilised when appropriate. It may not be everything, but statistical analysis is certainly something, and we should examine carefully what conventional statistical analysis can and cannot do to enhance comparative political research. The fundamental question, therefore, is whether comparative political analysis has characteristics that make the use of the conventional modes of statistical analysis less applicable than in other areas of research. Also, if there are impediments to using conventional analysis then are there means of amending the techniques to make them more useful for comparison.

One of the most obvious problems for statistics presented by comparative politics is the reliance on very large and heterogenous units such as nation-states (Teune, 1990). The degree of dispersion existing within these variables makes some of the assumptions of statistical analysis suspect (Janoski and Hicks, 1994; Dogan, 1994b). The use of a single value to characterise a country as diverse as the United States or even the United Kingdom (see Table 9.1) makes potentially questionable any generalisations formed about such a country as an entity. The problem with using a single value for an entire country may be increasingly evident as international migration and growing economic inequality increase the internal diversity of most political systems, as well as changing the political cultures of the countries. Even without that change, our later demonstration of the

Key Text 9.1 Edward Page and Bureaucracy

Bureaucracy is one of the oldest institutions in government. It is also one of the oldest concepts in the comparative analysis of government. Edward Page has demonstrated that this concept still has a great deal of utility for comparative political analysis. He took the 'Ideal-Type' concept of bureaucracy as developed by Max Weber and attempted to determine if the principal administrative system found in the developed democracies displayed the characteristics of that concept. In the course of applying the concept, he also was able to both describe and explain a good deal about these national administrative systems.

Page's study is an extremely good example of the use of the Ideal-Type methodology developed by Weber for his own sociological analyses. The ideal type of the bureaucracy was not intended by Weber to be a representation of reality, but rather was intended to be an intellectual model that could be used to uncover the underlying nature of an administrative system (public or private). Page compared the real-world administrative systems of Britain, France, Germany and the United States to each of the criteria developed by Weber for a bureaucracy. He could then make judgements about the extent to which each system was bureaucratic. These findings could, in turn, be used to compare these systems to each other as well as to the formal model.

While this methodology was useful for Page's study, it does not appear to be a very generalisable approach to comparative politics. The primary impediment to using the approach is the absence of well developed models that can be used as the starting point for the analysis. The Weber model is particularly suitable for this approach given that it specifies clearly a number of components of the model that can then be measured, quantitatively or qualitatively. Further, relatively few models used in the discipline have the range of applicability that Weber's model does. Other models used in political science, for example Lijphart's model of consociationalism (see Key Text 4.2), is perhaps applicable to range of cases but does not have the specificity that Weber's does. Also, models that are generally applicable, for example some models of change and development, have relatively little specificity and hence are difficult to apply in more than an equally general manner.

persistence of different political patterns in France (p. 205) shows that there has always been substantial intra-system diversity.

This chapter will not be a primer on the formal aspects of the statistical models, and will not discuss the calculation of various measures. There is limited space in this volume, and there is a more

TABLE 9.1

Internal diversity in the United States and the United Kingdom (by subnational unit)

	United States			United Kingdom	
High	Low	Average	High	Low	Average
Per capita income					
£8 975 (GL)	5 320 (NI)	7 280	$29 402 (Conn.)	15 838 (Miss.)	21 809
Unemployment					
14.0 (NI)	8.2 (EA)	10.4	10.8 (W. Va.)	2.6 (Nebr.)	6.8
Vote for Left[a]					
50.6 (N)	18.0 (EA)	35.2	53.2 (Ark.)	24.7 (Utah)	43.0

GL = Greater London; NI = Northern Ireland; EA = East Anglia; N = North.
[a] Vote in most recent election; Democrats in United States, Social Democrats in Sweden.

than adequate supply of material of that sort already available (Achen, 1986; Goldberger, 1991; King, 1989). Instead, this discussion will be an assessment of how the statistical techniques do or do not apply in comparative political analysis, and the problems encountered when they are utilised in this research. Some of this will echo arguments in previous chapters. For example, statistical analyses can be no better than the measurements that are fed into the equations, so any discussion of good statistical analysis in comparative politics must first address the issue of adequate measurements and their equivalence across countries. Also, statistical analysis can be no better than the theory used to guide the selection and operationalisation of its variables, and therefore the importance of theoretical questions will also be revisited in this chapter. The one possible exception to this generalisation would be a statistical 'fishing expedition', when there is little theoretical guidance for researching a topic; given the expansion of political analysis over the past several decades, however, it is hard to think of a virgin topic of that sort.

In addition, we will be looking at questions of statistical relationships across time, and how to compensate for the lack of independence of observations across time. Comparative politics is usually thought of as research focusing on questions concerning differences across space rather than across time, but change should also be a crucial question for comparative research. Time-series analysis is a crucial technique through which to address patterns of development and change in comparative politics (Hage *et al.*, 1989; Peters, 1973). In addition, time-series analysis can address questions of causation that would be impossible to address with conventional cross-sectional analysis, given that the temporal sequencing of changes can be established with a time-series but not in a cross-sectional analysis. Causation still cannot be definitively 'proven' with time-series, given that both the presumed independent and dependent variables could be responding to some unmeasured third variable that causes the observed changes in both, albeit at different times.

Despite these advantages, time-series analysis presents some significant pitfalls for the unwary. The observations in one time period are, at least in part, a function of the observations in the previous time periods. A country does not become wealthy overnight, but rather year by year, over decades. This incremental reality of cross-time data violates many fundamental assumptions of statistical analysis, but researchers still must be able to study politics and political change across time. Analysis of events data can carry research across time very much further than has been believed by most researchers in political science, but there are some questions that it simply cannot address effectively. Further, as has already been pointed out, events history analysis does not necessarily provide very useful assessments of the relative effects of candidate independent variables, measures that are needed for developing theory, or at least for rejecting inadequate theories.

Statistical Modes of Explanation in Comparative Politics

We will now return to the fundamental litany with which we previously discussed problems of case selection and measurement:

> **Maximise experimental variance, minimise error variance and control for extraneous variance.**

The statistical mode of explanation and analysis offers a distinctive approach to coping with the issues raised by this litany, just as does the method of case-research. We have been arguing throughout this book that each method has an appropriate place in comparative politics, as indeed the extent of its use would suggest. Bartolini (1993: 137) argues, however, that these modes of research are not really different, as do King *et al.* (1994). Still, for understanding, it seems appropriate to differentiate them, and their relative strengths and weaknesses, before attempting to lump them together. Their appropriate places, however, are different, and the researcher must understand what strengths and weaknesses each basic approach brings with it when it is applied to a research situation.

Whereas the case method, by definition, selects a few cases for intensive analysis, the statistical method (everything else being equal) attempts to cope with error and extraneous variance by both extending the size of the sample and, where feasible, randomising selection of the elements of the sample. Further, the statistical method has the luxury of controlling for extraneous variance through a variety of statistical techniques. Regression analysis, the most common statistical model used in political science, can include a number of hypothesised independent variables and possible control variables. If the correct variables have been identified, then this method can provide estimates of which ones are the 'real' sources of variance observed in the dependent variable.

In particular, the statistical method permits the researcher to assess the impact of each independent variable in the presence of all the others, so that their relative strengths in explaining the dependent variable can be measured. Regression analysis assumes a linear relationship among these variables, with the possibility of also including interaction terms to assess the extent to which some variables may be important only in the presence of certain values of others variables.[1] Regression can therefore cope easily with the roles played by multiple variables, in a manner somewhat similar to

---

[1] The usual additive relationship is

$$Y = a + b_1 X_1 + b_2 X_2 + e$$

With interaction the equation becomes

$$Y = a + b_1 X_1 + b_2 X_2 + b_3 X_1 X_2 + e$$

that of multiplication operator in the Boolean method already discussed.

The important difference is that regression can examine those interactions with continuous variables rather than through simple dichotomies, and thereby can present a more complete picture of their relationships. We pointed out that a researcher will have to dichotomise some inherently continuous variables in order to include them in a Boolean analysis. With the ability to use the continuous variable a researcher can determine if levels of a variable have a systematic relationship with a dependent variable, rather than simply looking at whether the presence or absence of one phenomenon, or a 'high' or 'low' level, is related to the presence or absence of another.

The case method researcher also must deal with just the cases that he or she has, and extract all available information from those cases, knowing all the while that the cases may not be in any way representative of a population of countries – they are generally picked because they are most definitely *not* representative. The statistical method, on the other hand, is attempting to generalise from a 'sample' to a population of political units or individuals. Even when the sample used for the statistical analysis is all relevant countries, the assumption is made that this is still a sample of all countries at all times. One of the fundamental questions for statistics is whether the relationships found in this sample are sufficiently strong to generalise to the entire population. In other words, are the findings sufficiently strong to say that there is little chance of their having occurred merely by chance?

As noted already, when researchers are using statistics with data sources such as population surveys of political attitudes, the practice of testing for generalisability, or for statistical significance, makes a good deal of sense. A random sample of the population is taken as the means of attempting to assure that there is no systematic error introduced through the purposeful selection of the cases. At that stage, the researcher can assess whether the relationships detected between an independent variable, for example, social class, and a dependent variable, for example, partisan preference, are sufficiently strong to justify saying that these relationships probably exist within the total population. Even then, the confidence in those findings remains probabilistic, with some chance that the findings still occurred by chance. These inevitable misses are an occurrence most often seen as 'rogue polls' in the course of a long electoral campaign, with many samples being selected in a short period of time.

The other standard test that is utilised in statistical analyses of this type is the percentage of the variance explained. In other words, the dependent variable has a total amount of variance – the observations each vary throughout a range around the mean and that variance is summed – and we can estimate what percentage of that total variance the independent variable or variables predict accurately. That is, in some techniques the procedure will predict that a case belongs to a certain group – democratic or non-democratic states, for example. What percentage of the time does the predictive model forecast group membership correctly? Or, the model may predict that a government will spend a certain percentage of its gross domestic product on social services. How close, on average, are those predictions coming from the statistical model to the observed values?

Further, statistical tests enable the researcher to obtain measures of the relative effects of each independent variable used to attempt to explain that variation. Most statistical techniques permit determining what effect each variable has in the presence of the other independent variables. In statistical analysis, such as regression, even variables strongly related to the dependent variable in a bivariate analysis may lose their explanatory power once other, more powerfully related variables are included. That test of strength in the presence of other variables is, of course, something that is not possible to obtain through small-*N* research with its limited number of cases. Even with statistical techniques, however, the selection of test and control variables is crucial for any evaluation of causation; if the appropriate test variables are not included in the analysis then their effects cannot be measured, and spurious correlations will be accepted as valid.

Even in fields of enquiry that have available random samples of large populations, many methodologists are now arguing that researchers should do away with the traditional measures of statistical significance and percentage of variance explained. King (1990), for example, argues that one of the most commonly used regression statistics – R^2 – is not as important as a source of validation as it is usually thought to be. R^2, or the square of the correlation coefficient, is a measure of the proportion of variance in the dependent variable 'explained' by the independent variables. King argues instead for the use of unstandardised measures of effect as the means of determining if the presumed independent variables are indeed able to predict changes in the dependent variable, as well as for the use of a variety of regression diagnostics to assess the usefulness of the regression. The fundamental point of this seemingly technical debate is that the purpose of statistical analysis should be to demonstrate causation, rather than simply covariation, and therefore more emphasis should be placed on regression rather than on correlation coefficients.

Thus, although statistical analysis (especially regression) is indeed the backbone of contemporary political science research, there are disagreements about what role each particular technique in the analytic armamentarium plays. Further, there are special techniques that must be considered when certain special conditions are present. For example, conventional regression does not provide unbiased estimates of relationships for dichotomous dependent variables (for example, the dependent variables used in most events history analysis), so that techniques such as discriminant function analysis and logit regression must be used (DeMaris, 1992). Again, these are technical questions about which we need not worry in any detail here, other than to say that once the research question is defined then questions of manipulating data do become central. Rather, we should be more interested in the general characteristics of statistical analysis and the problems that comparative research presents for using these methods.

Statistical analysis is indeed something, and is a crucial weapon in the arsenal of comparative political analysis. It provides a means of assessing the relative effects of a variety of independent variables on each dependent variable, and it also permits looking at the joint effects of the multiple independent variables on the dependent variable. The results of these analyses do not necessarily prove causation, but they certainly do provide a place to start thinking about causation; if there is no association then there can be no causation. Interestingly, therefore, one of the most maligned statistical techniques – factor analysis – can also be of substantial utility theoretically (Rummel, 1995). Factor analysis extracts 'factors', or underlying variables, from the correlation matrices of a number of variables. In most techniques, these factors are orthogonal and therefore unrelated to each other. Rather than theory testing, factor analysis is usually employed as an exploratory technique or as a means of data reduction. By definition, the factors extracted from a set of variables are not related to each other, so the absence of any association can be used as a means of falsifying a theory. Given that there is such an overstock of positive relationships among variables, this has the potential of eliminating some putative causal factors.

The case method consciously attempts to limit the number of countries included in an analysis, and therefore is not affected by some problems of measurement that afflict other approaches to comparative analysis. Using statistical analysis requires the existence of data that are comparable – for example, collected in the same manner, and with the same cultural interpretation – in all settings. This standard is often difficult to meet in broadly comparative research, given that the data quality for industrialised countries is substantially superior to that available for less developed systems. This can be true even for basic aggregate, and can become true when other forms of research are tried. Surveys may produce massive levels of unanswered questions, simply because concepts derived from more 'modern' political settings did not travel well to less developed systems. These interpretative questions will persist, even if the technical question of translation is handled adequately.

These data problems are a more technical manifestation of the travelling problem discussed by Sartori (1970). Even within the more developed world, there are marked differences in data availability among countries. The elemental fact of the relative inadequacy of data for some countries may produce 'samples' of cases that are skewed. That, in turn, will produce findings that, while statistically correct, may ultimately be misleading and inhibit the development of comparative theory. For example, even within the more developed world, the relative dearth of comparable data on the Mediterranean democracies tends to exclude them from many studies, and with that exclude their special form of democracy (Lijphart *et al.*, 1988) from consideration. For instance, although Spain, Portugal and Greece are members of the organisations such as the OECD, the data for them are frequently missing or out of date.

Statistical analysis has few real means to guarantee protection from error variance. Much of the effective protection against the introduction of random error (as opposed to the systematic error discussed as extraneous variance) comes from taking care in measurement. All the problems that can arise in the cross-national measurement of concepts are the principal sources of error variance in comparison. The particular problem that error variance presents is that it is difficult to know when and where it occurs, and therefore to know just what influence it has on the findings of research.

The Question of Time

We have argued above (pp. 23–4) that in addition to cross-system analysis (whether national or subnational), comparative politics should be concerned with cross-time analysis, which has several contributions to make to comparative studies. The first and most fundamental is that if researchers are interested in change and political dynamics then it is difficult to study those phenomena effectively with cross-sectional data (data taken from a single point in time). They may be able to infer dynamics – for example, that if a country becomes wealthier it will begin to devote a larger proportion of GDP to social service expenditure – but that can only be a relatively weak inference from the cross-sectional distribution of data. To test that idea directly requires examining the evidence across time. Although Adolph Wagner argued that the wealthier a country became, the more it would spend through the public sector, that relationship may not be linear when examined over time (Herber, 1983).

Further, time-series analysis may permit the researcher to look more directly at questions of causation than will cross-sectional statistical analysis. When an apparently strong relationship exists between variables *x* and *y* in a cross-sectional analysis, it is not at all clear in every case what is the independent and what is the dependent variable. All we know is that the two variables are associated. Theory and common-sense may tell us that one factor is more likely to cause the other than the other way around, but there is not always such guidance, and the theory could well be inadequate. With time-series analysis, however, we can alter the timing of the variables, lagging one variable by a year or a month, or whatever the appropriate period may be. If lagging some variable *x* improves the relationship between it and another variable *y* then it can be argued that *x* is temporally prior to *y*, thus satisfying one of the classical conditions of causation. A variety of more sophisticated analytic techniques allow researchers to determine the timing of the relationships among variables.

Following from the above discussion, cross-sectional analysis permits us to compare distributions of countries, but we may want to examine developmental patterns across countries. For example, even if two countries have achieved the same level of social spending, or political participation, or whatever the dependent variable may be, they may nevertheless have arrived at that point in different ways and for different reasons. Determining the differences in paths with cross-sectional data would be difficult, but longitudinal analysis would facilitate that comparison. One clear example of this type of comparison can be seen in several developmental studies of the welfare state in Europe.

Finally, longitudinal analysis permits the researcher to determine if there has been a significant discontinuity in the patterns of development across time. There may be a pattern of relationships that appears significant statistically across time, but if the total time-series is broken into smaller time periods, do the same relationships appear? If they do not, and if the time at which the breaking point in the series occurs has theoretical meaning, then the research can say a great deal more about political and social development, and the importance of crucial events, than could cross-sectional analysis. If there is a candidate point at which the series should have changed then there are ways of testing the hypothesis of change, or there are also means for having the statistical technique identify discontinuities in the series.

In addition to the simple virtues of all time-series analysis, interrupted time-series analysis can address questions arising from the quasi-experimental nature of political science. Researchers in political science have little or no capacity to control the 'experimental treatment' that may produce change in the dependent variable. Researchers can, however, identify the time or times of the actions or events, that are hypothesised to have produced a change in the time-series. Campbell and Ross (1968) demonstrated in their classic article how to employ quasi-experimental analysis to test for the significant effects of an intervention. There is now a substantial body of statistical theory (Chatfield, 1989; Freeman, 1983) developing more complex techniques for measuring the impacts of such interventions in a time-series. More complex mathematical models for assessing changes in regression analysis are emerging (Janoski and Hicks, 1994: 38–44), but the fundamental question of determining whether an intervention made a difference for some dependent variable remains constant.

Problems in Time-Series Analysis

Although using time-series analysis provides a number of benefits to the researcher, it also has a number of potential problems. Perhaps the most important of these problems is that time-series can violate some of the important assumptions of statistical analysis, especially regression analysis. For example, if we are attempting to estimate whether there is a meaningful relationship between two variables, the assumption is that the observations used to test that hypothesis are independent. If the observations are not independent, then the value of any relationship found is likely to be inflated by the dependence of cases involved. Unfortunately, across time the value of a variable observed at one point is likely to be influenced by the values observed in the previous time period. If a country is democratic at one time, it is likely to have been democratic the year before that, and the year before that. This is true even for variables that are not simply dichotomies; if a country is rich this year then it is likely to have been about as rich the year before. We have already pointed out (pp. 197–200) that this problem is not unique to time-series, but it does appear to be more prevalent and more potentially harmful in time-series analysis.

For some of the same reasons that autocorrelation is a problem in time-series, so also is multicollinearity, or the intercorrelation of independent variables that can also bias results. Any number of socio-economic and political variables tend to vary together across time, in part as components of generalised processes of socio-economic change. Thus, many of the variables that we would want to include as independent variables in a time series regression are themselves highly intercorrelated, producing biased estimates in the analysis. This may be yet another instance in which theory becomes a crucial component of the research process, informing the researcher which variables are essential for the analysis, and also which can be discarded safely in order to reduce the number of intercorrelated variables.

The Problem of Context

As well as time, the use of statistical analysis in comparative politics must also cope with problems of space. In Chapter 5 (pp. 117–19) we discussed the problem of context from a theoretical perspective, but involving contextual variables also raises a number of analytic and methodological questions. In particular, researchers must be concerned with carefully defining the unit of analysis for comparative research, and with finding ways to make inferences about political behaviour that may bridge those levels of analysis. These demands will force us first to understand the 'unit of analysis' problem and also look at rather classical questions in the social sciences about ecological correlation.

It is crucial in comparative analysis to separate, as Ragin (1987: 8–9) argues, 'observational units' from 'explanatory units'. That is, a researcher may actually be interested in differences among countries in terms of their political culture, but the evidence that is available – the observational units – are the individuals whose political attitudes are recorded through survey analysis. The researcher then must infer across those levels (nation and individual) that country (the presumed explanatory unit) made a difference. This type of inference can be very tricky. There may be differences in observed attitudes by country, but those differences may be a function of the economic or demographic structures of the population as much as any real effect of the country and its culture. Przeworski and Teune (1970) demonstrated rather clearly, for example, that much of the difference observed in the *Civic Culture* study of Almond and Verba (1967; 1980 – and see Key Text 2.1), especially for Mexico, could be attributed to economic structures rather than to differences among the countries. The analytic task therefore is to attempt to separate true influences of the context (for example, a national political culture) from individual level influences.

Attempting to include cross-level inferences into research inevitably runs the risks of the ecological and the individualistic fallacies. In the ecological fallacy, the more common problem in research, the researcher falsely infers relationships among attributes of individuals from the relationships observed in aggregates (Robinson, 1950). This was a particular problem with voting behaviour before the widespread availability of mass survey research, and later exit polling. For example, in the classic example, Robinson noted that in the United States there was a positive correlation between the level of English literacy of an area of the United States and the number of foreign-born residents. Were those foreign-born residents more literate in English than average? The answer was No, but the immigrants (perhaps because of economic opportunities) chose to settle in areas that happened to have high rates of literacy.

Despite the inherent difficulties of ecological correlation, this tradition has produced some very useful research. In particular, the French school of cartographic electoral analysis (Goguel, 1970; Siegfried, 1930 – see Key Text 9.2) generated a much better understanding of voting behaviour in France than would have been possible with other means available at that time. Similarly, the techniques of analysis used by V. O. Key (1949) to examine political factionalism in the American South were essentially ecological, and also extremely effective.

Even after the development of survey research and other individual level techniques ecological correlations can still be useful when survey evidence is not practical or is too expensive. Further, any research that examines individual behaviour in geographical or other groups does not necessarily commit the ecological fallacy. If the hypothesis being tested is phrased in terms of the ecological unit then the findings would not be fallacious, even if they are not the most useful. For example, some of the geographical patterns used by Goguel for elections before World War II persist and can help understand voting in the late twentieth century (see Key Text 9.2).

The individualistic fallacy is the reverse of the ecological fallacy. In this fallacy, the properties of collectivities are assumed on the basis of the observed characteristics of their members. If we return to the study of political culture discussed above (pp. 82–3) the tendency in that body of literature is to infer that certain countries have cultural characteristics because of the findings of attitudinal surveys. Thus, from the basis of Ronald Inglehart's numerous (1977; 1990) attitudinal studies on 'post-materialist values', we might have expected governments in the industrialised democracies to have shifted their attention away from economic issues towards social issues, and then back again. That change does not appear to have occurred, however, and some other collective properties are influential in shaping institutional behaviour.

The two fallacies described above do not exhaust the potential issues concerning cross-level inference and the necessity to include contextual factors in statistical analyses. These issues are both statistical and theoretical, as is usually the case for issues in comparative analysis. The researcher can begin by asking what contextual factors are identified by theory that might be relevant for explaining individual-level behaviours, and conversely what individual factors should be included in any explanations of institutional- or national-level performance? If the theoretical guidance is sufficiently powerful, then the researcher can have a good idea of what cross-level effects to test for, and what variables to include in the analysis. If there is no such theoretical guidance then the researcher is left with a search for empirical regularities that may give clues to the presence and nature of the contextual factors.

As is often the case, the most interesting questions in comparative politics appear to be the most difficult to research effectively. Part of the basic logic of comparative politics is that the context within which politics takes place is important for shaping the behaviour observed. Similarly, the behaviour of aggregates – whether nation-states or institutions – should be closely related to the behaviour of the

Key Text 9.2 François Goguel and André Siegfried and Cartography

Most comparative analysis remains qualitative, with cases studies and similar forms of research continuing to dominate the field. When quantitative data is used for comparison it typically is presented in tables or graphs. There is also an alternative tradition of presenting quantitative data in the form of maps. This tradition has been especially well-developed in France; two of the most important figures for this cartographic school were André Siegfried (1930) and François Goguel (1970). This method was later adopted by V. O. Key to analyse Southern politics in the United States and its changes over time.

Representing political data in map form has several important advantages. The maps can point out the geographical patterns that exist and that geographical proximity may help to understand some aspects of political life. Further, mapping data may make some patterns apparent that might be more difficult to see in other forms of data presentation, especially those that process the data statistically. These patterns are especially interesting when the data is mapped across time and the patterns found at one time persist across years and even decades. For example, Goguel's study of French voting showed that patterns found in the late 19th century still present in the mid-20th century. That persistence might have been uncovered using other methods, but was clearly seen from the maps. Finally, this method can demonstrate these patterns using ranges on the variables, for example 20–30 per cent, rather than exact figures, and hence may uncover patterns that might be lost in more formal statistical analysis.

Like all methods used for political analysis this is not without some problematic aspects. One is that the emergence of the pattern may be dependent upon selecting the correct dividing points – the degreeism problem discussed by Sartori (1991). Further, although the visual evidence can be compelling, there is no formal means of associating the observed patterns on a 'dependent variable' (voting for a particular party) with an 'independent variable' (urbanisation). Finally, many important variables for social research may not be distributed in a spatially concentrated manner, making this form of research difficult or impossible. Still, for a range of issues in comparative politics mapping can be a useful alternative, or supplement, to other means of investigation.

components of those aggregates. Finding the means of making those linkages is not always easy, but must be a part of the ongoing agenda of comparative analysis. Determining the nature of the relationships is all the more difficult given that the levels of analysis (and reality) interact across time, so it is difficult to determine the nature of cause and effect.

Coping with a Small *N*

Most statistical analysis depends upon a relatively large number of observations. The underlying logic is that the larger the sample the less likelihood there is of any observed significant relationship between variables having come about through sheer chance. With large-*N* studies, a researcher can be reasonably sure that if there is an observed significant relationship between an independent and dependent variable then that relationship will have occurred because some relationship exists in the population of all such observations. Therefore, one concern for researchers is to develop ways to increase the size of the sample while maintaining the same quality of measurement.

Bootstrapping

There are a number of ways available to help extend the sample available, or to reduce dependence upon a large sample for effective statistical inference. One of the most common of these methods is referred to as 'bootstrapping' (Mooney, 1996), in which a limited number of existing cases in a sample are extrapolated by multiple resamplings to estimate the parameters within the population. This expansion is not done simply through multiplying the available observations, but rather employs a Monte Carlo simulation technique to estimate the underlying distribution of data. This permits making some reasonable estimates of the underlying population from a limited sample.

Bootstrapping may not be a fully adequate replacement for the large samples usually sought in political science. In the first place, the results of this method are not the parametric statistics – for example, regression statistics or *t*-tests – that are familiar to most political scientists. Further, the technique does involve using a limited amount of evidence to generate a statement about a distribution of data.

Pooled Time Series

Another method for increasing sample size that can be very useful for comparative politics is using pooled time-series data in regression analysis (Stimson, 1984). This method combines time-series analysis with cross-sectional analysis to generate a much larger number of observations for a research question than would be possible through either presentation of the data by itself. The pooling method involves simply taking observations from a number (x) of cases (countries or other political units) across a number (y) of time points (years or whatever) to create a data-set of (xy) observations. This accumulation of evidence can permit the use of statistical techniques that would be very unreliable with a limited sample based only on a single observation per country.

As well as simply adding to the number of cases available to the researcher, pooled time-series data enable the researcher to combine more readily different categories of variables (Hicks, 1994). Some variables, for example, institutional characteristics, are usually relatively constant for each country over time, and hence not usable as explanatory variables. With pooling, variables that can be used to compare countries at a single point in time can be added to more dynamic factors – for example, unemployment rates – within the same analysis. The ability to integrate these two varieties of variables is especially important for comparative analysis, given that some characteristics of political systems that are invariate are central in political theories (Weaver and Rockman, 1993 – see Key Text 5.3; Hicks, 1994: 170–1). Politicians and the public may respond to changes in their economic and social environments, but they must do so within an institutional context. For example, a number of studies of welfare-state expenditure point to differences due to both institutional and short-term factors (Hicks and Swank, 1992; Pampel and Williamson, 1988).

Further, the use of pooled time-series enables comparative researchers to address problems of causation more directly than they might otherwise be able to. Cross-sectional statistical analysis can demonstrate association rather easily, but it cannot deal directly with issues of causation – a relationship among variables exists, but there is little way of determining the cause of that distribution. With the inclusion of time-series data, the causal question can be addressed more directly, albeit still with caveats about the possibility of extraneous causes of relationships across time. That capacity is supplemented by the availability of multiple cross-sections of data, and the ability to look at the stability of distributions.

While pooled time-series analysis helps to solve the problem of a restricted number of cases, and help with other issues of research design, the method may present a number of important statistical problems. The obvious problem is that this compilation of data inherently violates one of the fundamental assumptions of regression analysis, and statistics in general – the independence of the observations. We have already noted this problem for time-series analysis when considered by itself, but the problem becomes somewhat compounded when the observations are pooled. The method in essence involves repeated sampling of the same cases, creating with it perhaps a false sense of security in larger numbers on the part of the unsceptical. Pooled times series also may strain other fundamental assumptions of statistical analysis (Stimson, 1985). There are methods to minimise these problems, and to produce meaningful results from pooled data (Beck and Katz, 1995), but the researcher must be both cognizant of the problems and careful in the analysis.

The problems of using pooled time-series may be more than just statistical. A method that lumps together the observations from a number of countries may quickly make the researcher lose sight of those countries. It is possible to include country as one of the variables in the analysis, but if so it might be more efficient to simply conduct the time-series analysis within countries and then compare the results across countries. We noted above that pooled time-series analysis permits including institutional factors in the analysis, but if we still want to think about real countries then this may not be the best method. Of course, some scholars of comparative politics would argue that we should think less about the proper names of countries and more about the relationships among variables, and pooled time-series analysis is very useful for that purpose.

Secondary Analysis

Yet another means of increasing the available number of cases for comparison is to utilise secondary analysis, or the reanalysis of data collected for other purposes (Hakim, 1982). There is a huge range of primary data available in the social sciences, mostly collected within a single country for the purpose of describing the politics or social conditions within that single country. The trick for comparison then is to aggregate all of that data into a framework and then use them to understand not just the one country but a range of countries. Further, these data can then be used to make more general theoretical statements.

The barriers to this aggregation of data should be rather obvious by this time in the discussion of comparison (Dale *et al.*, 1988). One of the principal issues is that of measurement and the comparability of data gathered across political systems (Dalton, 1996; Kaase and Newton, 1996). Fortunately, some of the questions that interest political scientists are understood in similar or identical fashions in all countries, and therefore travel extremely well. Voting, partisan identification, issue preferences and a whole range of other political questions travel across the developed democracies, and also are familiar in most of the other countries of the world. Even here there may be difficulties. The familiar Left–Right ideological spectrum may be understood widely, yet be very different. Even the left wing of the Democratic Party in the United States is far to the right of social democratic parties in most European systems, so that equivalence becomes difficult to establish. Researchers therefore can address a number of fundamental political issues with some confidence in the comparability of findings.

When we begin to move from the simple political questions to attitudes and values, the problems of comparability accelerate rapidly. Even when the intention of the research is the same in different countries, differences in language, operationalisation and all the other familiar barriers to comparability arise and diminish the utility of the comparisons. A certain degree of difference may be acceptable and produce little real difficulty for analysis. This is especially true if there are time-series data, and comparisons can be made of trends across time within countries. Further, some differences in the operationalisations of variables may actually improve the comparability of the data across systems, given that functional equivalence rather than direct equivalence may be achieved.

Some scholars also argue that the dangers of data that are excessively homogenised are almost as great as those of dangers of data that are incompletely homogenised (Glover, 1996). This problem is sometimes confronted in the data developed by international bodies such as the Organisation for Economic Cooperation and Development (OECD) and the International Labour Organisation (ILO). These data often reflect negotiations and compromises among the statistical systems of the countries that adhere to these organisations. As a result, the definitions may reflect more politics than a clear conception of what the data are meant to be. Those conceptual definitions may have been in the individual national systems, but have become obscured by compromise.

The use of secondary analysis also generates a selection bias of its own into comparative analysis. Given that the researcher using secondary data is dependent upon other people to make the choices about where those data are available, he or she will have little ability to choose cases on the basis of theory. As noted, for a number of variables, data would be available in almost any country, but for other questions there would be data only in those countries having more advanced social science communities. Countries such as Norway and the Netherlands may then take on greater importance in theory development than they might warrant otherwise. In some instances, the availability of data will permit some illumination of concepts and theories without direct testing, but the danger arises when it is assumed that the non-random assortment of countries in which data are present necessarily allows testing of theories.

Summary

The importance of statistical analysis is often overstated in the contemporary social sciences. We have already pointed out that a great deal of comparative research proceeds with little concern about statistical analysis. That said, comparative politics does need statistics, but statistical analysis also needs comparative politics. For many if not most political scientists, the argument that comparative politics can benefit from attention to statistical analysis is unremarkable. The increasing importance of statistics and formal analysis in political science, and the capacity of these forms of analysis to test theory, makes it obvious to many researchers that this is a crucial development for this subfield. That is true even though the descriptive and configurative nature of comparative politics pushes many scholars towards other forms of analysis.

The argument that statistics needs comparative analysis appears to require greater justification. The concentration of statistical analysis on the individual level of analysis tends to leave a number of institutional and structural factors out of the analysis. In addition, statistical analysis conducted within a single national setting is an inadequate basis for developing general political theory. Comparative analysis enables testing the theory in a variety of settings, permitting either confirmation of the propositions or perhaps an elaboration of the theory. We may be able to say that the particular theory works in some settings but not in others, and then establish names for those conditions that go beyond simple names of countries, or subnational units. No matter what the nature of the outcome of the analysis, the results will be more useful for the purposes of building theory than if they had been conducted only within a single setting.

10

The Future of Comparative Politics

Comparative politics should be a central, if not *the* central, concern of political science. For most research in the discipline there is little or no opportunity for experimentation – citizens are not likely to submit to very much experimentation on matters as crucial as the selection and management of their governments. Even were more experimentation possible for political situations, it is not at all clear that the results would be as beneficial for comparative political research as they might be for other parts of the discipline. Comparative scholars generally can be more productive when attempting to understand political behaviour within its natural context than when trying to analyse it in the artificial settings characteristic of social experimentation. This assumes that, contrary to Przeworski and Teune's (1970) ideas about most different systems designs, there are structural properties of systems that are important for explanation. Occasionally, governments do conduct what are in essence natural experiments, for example New Zealand and Japan changing their systems of voting, but those opportunities for testing theory are extremely rare. Given the importance of comparative analysis for the development of empirical political theory, this book has focused on the numerous dangers to valid comparative research, and on the ways in which the analysis can be improved.

There are no magic bullets to solve most of the problems in comparative politics. Therefore, most of what we have been providing in this book has been a set of warnings about the potential problems in research, and caveats about excessively ambitious claims for the results. Most comparative research involves a series of trade-offs

Key Text 10.1 Gosta Esping-Anderson and the Welfare State

Most comparative analysis in political science concentrates on the institutions of government, or on the individual behaviour of citizens (voting and other forms of participation). An alternative strategy is to understand political systems through what they do, and the decisions that they make about what programmes to provide for their citizens. The argument of a policy approach is that all the institutional differences are certainly interesting, but what really matters most is what government does. The differences among public programmes are often subtle, and therefore comparison may be difficult. Those subtle differences are, however, significant for what happens to citizens.

Gosta Esping-Anderson approached his comparison of the industrialised democracies by examining their social policies. All of these countries provide pensions, unemployment insurance, social assistance and a range of other programmes. but there are still marked differences in the way in which they are delivered. For example, characteristics such as the relationship of benefits to contributions and the extent of means-testing of benefits were crucial for understanding the true nature of the programmes.

Esping-Anderson argued that these decisions about social policy provided an excellent window on the politics of these countries. He argued that despite the many specific differences among programmes there were in essence three types of social welfare systems: *conservative* (typified by Germany), *liberal* (United Kingdom), and *socialist* (Sweden). These patterns could be found in a number of social programmes including pensions, unemployment insurance, and labour market policy. In his view of the welfare state these three patterns were based primarily on the degree of de-commodification of labour in these countries.

In addition to the use of the outputs as a means of understanding politics within individual countries this study indicates several other points about strategy in comparative political research. One of these is the importance of mid-range theory for developing broader theories. Esping-Anderson is concerned only with the industrialised democracies, but the logic of the analysis could be used for the growing number of countries forced to think about increased provision of social services to their populations. In addition, the research demonstrates how quantitative data can be used to isolate groupings within a set of countries, and how those groupings can in turn be used for further quantitative analysis. There has been a good deal of research on comparative public policy, but Esping-Anderson has provided research that corresponds to the contemporary canons of social science research, and has helped to reinvigorate research in this field.

and difficult decisions. If a project maximises internal validity then it is almost certain to sacrifice external validity. If a project is able to find important similarities in a range of national experiences then it is less likely to be able to make any definitive points about the individual cases. The fundamental point of these warnings therefore remains that the researcher must be aware of the choices he or she faces, and also be cognizant of the implications of those choices. The trade-offs cannot be avoided; they can only be better understood so that wise choices can be made.

The future of comparative politics is important for the future of the discipline of political science, but comparative analysis faces a number of challenges. Some of those challenges are intellectual, and are concerned with the relationship of theories and methods to the 'facts' of national and subnational politics. Many of these problems are reflected in the trade-offs described above. If the future of the subdiscipline is conceptualised as a business then there are a number of investment decisions that must be made. Is it best to invest our scarce academic resources in more traditional monographic studies of one or a limited number of cases? Or should our capital be used for more large-scale, directly comparative, and probably quantitative studies? We need to do some of both, but what is the best mix? The answer to that question will in part depend upon what we think the goals of comparison should be – finding important similarities in political behaviour or careful descriptions of individual political systems.

The challenges to comparative politics also reflect changes in the real world of government and politics. There are significant changes in politics that require rethinking our theories and even our facts. The fall of communism and the attempts at democratic consolidation in Central and Eastern Europe have opened a whole new locale for research. Likewise the development of regional bodies such the European Union, the North American Free Trade Agreement, and ASEAN raise important questions about the relationship of comparative politics and international relations (Sbragia, 1992). The linkage between international politics and comparative politics may be strengthened further by the increasing importance of the global marketplace for national economies, with the subsequent argument that governments can no longer govern in the ways to which they had been accustomed for decades (Strange, 1996; but see Hirst and Thompson, 1996).

Key Text 10.2 Giovanni Sartori and Party Systems

The history of political science has seen a number of attempts to categorise and understand political parties and the systems of parties found in different political systems. One of the most important of these efforts was Maurice Duverger's *Political Parties* (originally *Les partis politiques*) published in 1951. Duverger argued that all the differences in democratic party systems could be resolved into the fundamental difference between two-party and multi-party systems.

Giovanni Sartori argued that party systems were more complex and that there were three basic types: two-party, moderate multi-party, and extreme multi-party systems. Sartori argued that in many ways the moderate multi-party and the two-party systems are more similar than the two types of multi-party systems. In a moderate multi-party system, such as that found in Sweden and Norway, although a number of parties may compete for office there are in essence two blocs. Those two blocs, usually defined along a basic left–right dimension, may experience substantial movement of voters among the constituent parties but much less movement between the blocs. They are, in practice, two parties rather than many in these systems.

Sartori also spends a good deal of time explaining the possible sources of division in extreme multi-party systems. He points out that in Fourth Republic France and Italy there are a number of cleavages that divide the political families. In addition to the usual economic cleavages there are issues such as clericalism, monarchicalism, statism and others that cut across each other. This showed not only that there were numerous issues that divided the public in those countries but also that many of those issues were not bargainable in the way that economic issues might be.

Sartori's analysis helped to move the study of political parties beyond the simple dichotomy put forward by Duverger and others. This work helped to clarify the concept of multi-partyism in European politics and also to identify the sources of tensions within those systems. The multiple and incommensurable cleavages that appeared in multi-party systems helped to make their instability and seeming difficulty in policy-making more comprehensible. It is also important to remember that although this contribution focused on European political parties it was written in a developmental framework, so that there was some assumption of transition towards more moderate politics, perhaps even in the most divided political systems.

What follows in this chapter is a discussion of a number of the challenges and trade-offs that researchers in comparative politics currently must face. These issues are phrased in terms of challenges, but they also constitute genuine opportunities for the development of the field, and for the development of political theory considered more broadly. Fortunately, probably not all scholars will choose the same ways in which to address these challenges, and the lively pluralism that has characterised the subdiscipline will continue. The choices that researchers must make will, however, help define the directions in which political science develops in the future.

Territory or Function: Choices in Comparison

We have been discussing the possibility of organising comparisons in a variety of different ways, ranging from single-country studies to global juxtapositions using data from virtually all available political systems. We have argued throughout that developing middle-range theories may be a useful compromise position between the excessive generalisation of the global studies and the excessive particularism of the single country study (LaPalombara, 1968; Macridis, 1986). Developing these middle-range approaches permits focusing attention upon particular cases, but it also provides the researcher with the material necessary to make limited generalisations about politics. The resulting more limited theories can perhaps then serve as a means of subsequently building even broader theories.

Even if developing middle-range theory is the accepted strategy for comparison, there are still research questions that must be addressed. Within the category of middle-range theory itself, there is still a choice to be made between theories focusing attention on particular institutions and theories concentrating on groups of countries. To the extent that a theoretical approach can explain how an institution functions, it appears less capable of saying anything very useful about differences among countries as entities in themselves. Likewise, if a theory is effective at explaining the whole-system behaviour of countries then it is able to say substantially less about individual institutions within those systems.

We should not expect any one theory to solve all our analytic problems in comparative politics. There is sufficient room in the comparative study of politics for both types of approaches, and the one should inform the other. For example, a number of studies

(Mackie and Franklin, 1984; Laver and Shepsle, 1996; Strom, 1990) of cabinet government and cabinet duration have developed a much better understanding of the factors that affect the survival of cabinets in parliamentary governments. Many of those studies have been much less concerned with individual countries than with general patterns. Their findings should then be brought to bear on individual countries or categories of countries (majoritarian versus consensual democracies, for example). There is some evidence of developments in this direction (Budge and Keman, 1990; Budge and Laver, 1992), and there are now numerous studies of the rise and fall of cabinets in individual countries (Strom, 1990; Pridham, 1986). There is still a good distance to go, however, in linking institutionally and geographically based studies of the same phenomenon, even one as clearly identifiable as changes in governing coalitions.

One possible way of linking institutional analysis and geographically based analysis is to focus on processes rather than on more static phenomena, whether institutions or systems. As Alexander George (1979) has argued about the development of case studies, a concentration on how decisions move through a system forces an integration of a variety of different perspectives. Process-chasing requires some knowledge not only about institutions, but also about the nature of the political system more generally. The bad news, however, is that the study of political processes comparatively is probably less developed than the study of either institutions or certainly the study of entire political systems.

We have, for example, reasonably good studies of legislatures across a range of countries. We also have a large number of good studies of cabinets and political executives. What we tend to have less of are good studies of the processes of making legislation or, phrased in structural-functional terms, of rule-making. To be useful theoretically, this research would have to go well beyond the old 'how a bill becomes a law' studies (Bailey, 1952; James, 1997) , but process-oriented research of that type can rarely be found. There are an increasing number of studies of particular components of the legislative process – for example, agenda-setting – but there are few if any that provide a thorough comparative analysis of policy-making.

Interestingly, one area in which there are a number of studies of process drawn from experiences in several varied countries (Grindle, 1980; Hanf and Toonen, 1985; Barrett and Fudge, 1981) is in the study of policy implementation. The process of translating legislation into working programmes appears sufficiently similar across a wide range of political systems to be amenable to comparative analysis. As noted above (pp. 123–4) bureaucratic structures and bureaucratic processes tend to be somewhat more comparable across countries than other political institutions and processes. Thus, the same barriers that afflict attempts to implement in the industrialised countries (Hood, 1978; Pressman and Wildavsky, 1976) also afflict less developed political systems, so that the comparison of process can be made directly, without having to discount heavily for the structural and task differences across the systems.

Theory and the Restriction of Perspective

We have been utilising theory as one of the principal heroes of this book. When there is a problem of interpreting evidence, and a need for identifying possible independent variables, we always turn to available theories. This is a very valid perspective on the role of theory, and the enterprise of research enterprise should be conducted by constantly interacting theory and data. Theory does provide us with a set of guideposts about where to look for assistance, and it also provides researchers a way to visualise the political world. Without that collection of theoretical ideas about the world, the researcher is at sea, not knowing where to turn for guidance. This may force research into pure description, or into fishing expeditions for variables that might help explain the dependent variable.

Despite all the positive virtues of theories in comparative research, they are also tragic heroes, with some important flaws. Theory can be a strait-jacket as much as a life-jacket for the researcher. Theories do provide a set of tools for understanding the complexity of the political world, but they can also function to limit that vision as well. Theories provide a 'trained incapacity' to see the world in other than particular ways. Therefore, if that received vision is incorrect and inadequate, it becomes very difficult to alter the conception. Political science has had relatively few 'strong theories', or paradigms, that can so restrict vision, but even our relatively more open versions of theory do place a limited set of blinkers on researchers. Further, the increasing use of rational choice analysis in comparative politics does bring a much stronger version of theory into the discipline.

In some ways, comparative politics is better situated to defend itself against an excessively narrow vision of politics offered by theories than are other parts of the discipline. Although the American components of the discipline have tended to exert an exceedingly strong influence around the world, there are other national styles that put forward very different questions and provide very different answers. Even within the English-speaking world, there are marked differences between American and British political science (see p. 7), and certainly also the Canadian and Australian (Uhr, 1992) versions of the discipline. When we venture somewhat further afield and look at French or German versions of political science, much less those found in Latin America or Asia, the differences in approach and the fundamental puzzles addressed by researchers are very clear. As well as the interactions with those different intellectual traditions, comparative politics must interact with marked differences in the real world. These interactions force a more consistent reappraisal of the pattern of thought in comparative politics than would necessarily be true in those other parts of political science that can look at a narrower slice of the political world.

Finally, we should point out the dangers of theory pushing towards a single, uniform explanation of complex phenomena. Theories tend to create advocates, and those advocates argue that their favourite approach is *the* way to understand the dependent phenomenon. The problem is that most interesting political phenomena reflect a number of institutional and behavioural features. Any artificial limitation of the range of explanations utilised, or any lack of recognition of the complex interactions among different causes of the observed phenomena, is unlikely to produce an adequate understanding of those events. At present rational choice theory appears to be the approach that is offered as the cure for all the ills of the discipline (see Budge, 1993), with institutionalism of various sorts being the principal competitor. Useful as these two theoretical approaches may be, each has its own flaws and hence each may require some tempering from other perspectives.

Methods and the Restriction of Vision

It is not only theory that restricts the vision of researchers and can predetermine the outcomes of an analysis. The choice of the methodology for a research project can also produce much of the same restriction of scope and narrowing of evidence that are deemed relevant to answering the question under investigation. For example, if a researcher is interested in statistical analysis then he or she will inevitably focus on issues and variables that are relatively amenable to quantification and to inclusion in available statistical techniques. This dominance of statistics and the readily quantifiable has been criticised in a number of places (Dogan, 1994b), but such methods remain a prevalent form of research, if not *the* prevalent one.

Similarly, a researcher who relies on case-study techniques will have a somewhat limited array of possible explanations and findings. Beginning with this form of research will tend to produce explanations that focus on internal processes and cultural factors. Case studies are also likely to exclude possible macro-level explanations for changes observed in the 'dependent variable', given that it is difficult to identify those when one is paying almost all one's attention to the details of a particular case. A researcher can hardly identify macro-level forces from the evidence that can be gained from a single case. The evidence from several cases that do not conform to expectations based on internal dynamics could lead to the assumption of external forces, but even then the tendency may be to assume that the differences were functions of other endogenous sources of variance.

There is also a very strong interaction between theory and methodology, with some potential reinforcement of the biases contained in each. Theories that assume that political events and behaviours are a function of external forces (economic change, social change, and so on) are almost inevitably going to have to collect large samples of evidence and then apply statistical analysis. There is some room for more case-based research (see Bennett, 1992; Foley, 1993), including some of the most influential examples of this research (Skocpol, 1979; Bendix, 1964), but the dominant mode of analysis will remain statistical. Likewise, theories that argue for the importance of endogenous forces – leadership, group dynamics, and so on – will tend to almost always depend upon case-based research, although the availability of both meta-analytic and Boolean techniques (see Chapter 6) can push this research towards the more statistical camp.

The selection of particular methods also shapes the validity questions that the research can address. Case method research tends to be very strong on external validity, and any findings from that style of research are likely to be well connected with the real world of politics, given that the researcher will have been collecting data in a natural setting. In contrast, research based on social experiments (rare in comparative politics), or on formal models (an increasingly common form of 'mind experiment' in the field), may have extremely high degree of internal logic and/or internal validity, but may also have relatively little connection to the 'real world' of politics. Unfortunately, relatively few works attempt to integrate these several research traditions to strengthen both fundamental strands of validity (for an exception, see Tsebelis, 1994).

In short, any choice of method or of theory will necessarily exclude other options for explanation. By that very exclusion, choosing any approach always has some tendency to predetermine the outcomes of the research; the theory tells the researcher what evidence is relevant and what can, and should, be excluded. The difficulty then becomes how to use theory and methodologies without being used by them. Again, there are no magic formulas that enable the researcher to ascertain how much of his or her work has been predetermined by the particular method and theory used, and most scholars have a difficult time standing apart from their own research tradition to judge it, and its results, with any objectivity. Thus, paradoxically, doing scientific research is virtually impossible without the availability of theories and methods, but those theories and methods make change and self-evaluation of the theories more difficult, and may, in some ways, hamper the further development of theory.

The Exceptional and the Ordinary: What Can We Learn from Each?

Most comparative political scientists could be said to behave very much like magpies. These birds are famed for amassing collections of shiny objects. These have no real use and have little or no connection with each other, but they please the magpie. This somewhat unflattering (self-) characterisation is meant to represent the tendency to concentrate attention on the exceptional and the extraordinary, while the bulk of what defines a political system is really very ordinary. The tendency, in choosing cases for comparative analysis, is to select the extreme example or the unusual case. For example, when studying public policy there has been a tendency to look at large-scale policy failures (Bovens and t'Hart, 1996) or at dramatic implementation failures (Pressman and Wildavsky, 1976). These cases are rarely compared with successes, or even with more typical cases that have more mixed outcomes. Despite the claims of the critics of government, there are probably many more successes than dramatic failures, and some of those success are themselves quite dramatic – putting a man on the moon is an obvious example. Despite a more frequent occurrence is often than admitted, the successes do make much less interesting reading. Likewise, when writing about parliamentary government, there is a tendency to focus on the dissolution of cabinets and the politics surrounding the formation of new governments. This research strategy ignores most of what these governments do, and what are arguably the most important parts of governing for average citizens – for example, making policy.

Similarly, we have a tendency to characterise national politics by the extreme and the unusual. British politics can be observed through events such as the Falklands War (Freedman, 1988), or Japanese politics through somewhat atypical decisions concerning taxes (Kato, 1994). These are certainly important cases, but do not capture the reality of day-to-day affairs in these systems. Those more mundane events are crucial for understanding politics in such countries, but are difficult to write into an appealing story that will capture the attention of the scholarly community, much less the popular one. How the more mundane can be included more readily into the ongoing discourse of political science is a crucial question for comparative analysis. Further, how do we categorise those events, and generate reliable descriptions of systems based on those data?

While the propensity to focus on the exceptional tends to ignore a great deal of the political world, it can also serve an important theoretical purpose. If these examples are selected for purposes of identifying the extreme conditions at which a hypothesis is valid, or finding the cases that can disprove a hypothesis or theory, they help to establish the validity of theory. Thus, the question of case selection points to yet another trade-off apparent in the study of comparative politics. On the one hand, scholars need to use comparative politics to describe different political systems, and to find out what really characterises the particular cases and their behaviour. On the other, they also want to test general theories that may have some applicability outside one system, and to be able to make general statements about politics. To the extent that we focus on the unusual, and the extreme, our research can reject general propositions, or provide them the strongest possible support.

Modesty But Hope

This volume, I hope, points to some major accomplishments in the field of comparative political analysis. While far from perfect, the field has made significant advances beyond the position it held during the 1930s, or even the 1960s. The battles to redefine the field during the 1950s and 1960s may now appear outdated, excessively strident, and even a bit quaint, but they were crucial for the advancement of the discipline. They were also important for creating greater self-awareness among researchers about what constituted adequate comparative analysis. The developments in comparative politics have been in part methodological – the political scientist now has many more tools available with which to address research questions – but the advancements have not been entirely technical. Many of the developments have also been theoretical, and if nothing else the recognition of the numerous useful and appropriate ways to study comparative politics now available to the scholar has been a positive development in the field.

We have pointed to the weaknesses of many of the studies, in part to demonstrate what challenges lie ahead. Despite the advances that have been made, there are still a number of questions that continue to plague the study of comparative politics. There are no quick methodological or theoretical fixes for these; indeed, as we have been arguing throughout, most attempts to solve theoretical or analytic problems with quick fixes may make them more difficult, in part by masking their true nature. The arguments on behalf of multiple measures, multiple theories, and 'triangulation' that have appeared in a number of places in this volume also reflect the need to make modest claims on behalf of what we already know. We know largely only what a particular theory or a particular method enables us to know, and without some broader conception of the issues we may well miss some very fundamental parts of the puzzle of comparative politics.

Despite the problems we have identified, and the modesty of the claims that now can be made about comparative political research, there is also a great deal of hope for the future. The events in the real world over the past decade have made the need for a better comparative understanding of the political process all the more important. Democratisation and rapid political change in the former communist countries, and in many other formerly authoritarian ones, have emphasised the need to understand better how democracy actually functions, and how democratic political change can be implemented and sustained. In addition, the attempt to create a new political entity in the shape of the European Union (Sbragia, 1992; Wallace and Wallace, 1996) represents another major challenge to our collective knowledge about institutional design. The industrialised democracies are also undergoing massive reform processes that are producing very different administrative and policy systems. In short, wherever we look in the political world there are changes that require interpretation and inclusion into the ongoing work of comparative analysis.

The Future of Comparative Politics

The above discussion of the changes in the political world leads us to a final point about comparative politics. Speculating about the future, either of politics or even of an academic pursuit is always a risky undertaking. Still, there are some trends that appear well enough institutionalised for us to be able to discuss them with some confidence. One of these is globalisation. This trend can be seen most clearly in economics, but it also has important political manifestations. Indeed, the increasingly international nature of the economy is argued to require that governments also adapt and become increasingly similar across national boundaries. This adaptation may be manifested in part through regional organisations such as the European Union, the Andean Pact, and the North American Free Trade Association. These organisations are all attempts to use political agreements as a means of structuring some protection against the pressures of the global free market.

Another of the political propensities that appears to be spreading around the world is democratisation. Many of the countries of Latin America that had been governed by military–authoritarian regimes for years have adopted more democratic forms of government, and these democracies appear to be enduring in many systems, despite numerous economic and social challenges. The transformations in Eastern and Central Europe have been even more dramatic, with functioning democracies being created, albeit painfully in some cases, in countries with little or no history of this manner of governance. Even countries that have been nominally democratic are attempting to find ways to further involve their publics in the process of making and implementing policy, with the concept of 'empowerment' being as important in Ottawa as in Montevideo.

Not all the political trends that can be identified in the world today are so congenial. One of these is the increase in subnational ethnicity and the expanded possibility of ethnic conflict. The most obvious cases are the breakup of the former Yugoslavia, ethnic conflicts in the former Soviet Union and continuing ethnic wars in Sri Lanka and Africa. Even if there is no overt ethnic conflict, there are tensions, and political mobilisations, around ethnic issues. Some of these conflicts are a function of the increasing rates of international migration, as tensions are created by movement of population (Cornelius *et al.*, 1994; Castles and Miller, 1993). These ethnic tensions will require some rethinking of the manner in which governments perform their tasks, and how they cope with their internal tensions.

The common, homogenising trends influencing so many of the world's governments will make comparative politics both more profitable intellectually, and more difficult. The common trends observable in the environment of politics can be conceptualised as providing common stimuli to which different countries will respond in their own particular way. On the other hand, the common nature of these trends is making comparison more difficult, given the diffusion of political styles and political practices. This is a clear case of Galton's problem (pp. 41–2), in which there is so much in common that it is difficult to determine what is a product of indigenous decisions and what a product of diffusion. While countries may not have evolved in certain ways without the exogenous stimuli, the manner in which they do respond does demonstrate a good deal about their political style.

Comparative politics should be a growth industry within political science. The rapidly increasing availability of information through a variety of media is making comparative data available to scholars at an almost frightening pace. The availability of mounds of data does not, however, eliminate the need for effective theorisation and conceptualisation. Those ideational issues remain the basic tasks for the discipline, with the development of statistical and other technical methods important auxiliaries to the more fundamental tasks of developing concepts with which to classify the data. This book should have pointed to the crucial role that designing research and measuring concepts plays in the enterprise of comparative political research. Without those methodological skills, and an awareness of the numerous pitfalls that await the unwary researcher, comparative politics is always in danger of providing a false certainty about the political world.

Most political scientists are experts in their own national systems. Living in one country can exaggerate the importance of that country in the eyes of the scholar, and the availability of information in sources ranging from the morning newspaper through government documents and interviews with government officials makes conducting research at home substantially easier. Further, doing research in the one system eliminates most theoretical and conceptual travelling problems, as well as the more practical problems of personal travel. The difficulty is that research in the one system, no matter how thorough and sophisticated it may be, is no substitute for comparison, for understanding politics and for creating generalisations about the world of politics.

References

Abbott, A. (1983) 'Sequences of Social Events: Concepts and Methods for the Analysis of Order in Social Process', *Historical Methods* 16, 129–47.
Abbott, A. (1992) 'An Old Institutionalist Reads the New Institutionalism, *Contemporary Sociology* 21, 754–6.
Aberbach, J. D., R. D. Putnam and B. A. Rockman (1981) *Politicians and Bureaucrats in Western Countries* (Cambridge, MA: Harvard University Press).
Abramson, P. R. and R. Inglehart (1995) *Value Change in Global Perspective* (Ann Arbor: University of Michigan Press).
Achen, C. H. (1986) *Statistical Analysis of Quasi-Experiments* (Berkeley: University of California Press).
Achen, C. H. and W. P. Shively (1995) *Cross-Level Inference* (University of Chicago Press).
Agh, A. (1994) *The First Steps: The Emergence of East Central European Parliaments* (Budapest: Hungarian Centre for Democratic Studies).
Agnew, J. (1996) 'Mapping Politics: How Context Counts in Electoral Geography', *Political Geography* 15, 129–46.
Alford, R. (1963) *Party and Society: The Anglo-American Democracies* (Chicago: Rand-McNally).
Allison, G. T. (1971) *The Essence of Decision* (Boston: Little, Brown).
Allison, P. D. (1984) *Events History Analysis: Regression for Longitudinal Data Analysis* (Newbury Park, CA: Sage).
Almond, G. A. (1956) 'Comparative Political Systems', *Journal of Politics* 18, 371–409.
Almond, G. A. (1980) 'The Intellectual History of the Civic Culture Concept', in Almond and S. Verba, *The Civic Culture Revisited* (Boston: Little, Brown).
Almond, G. A. and J. S. Coleman (1960) *Politics in Developing Countries* (Princeton: Princeton University Press).
Almond, G. A., S. C. Flanagan and R. J. Mundt (1973) *Crisis, Choice and Change: Historical Studies of Political Development* (Boston: Little, Brown).
Almond, G. A. and H. D. Lasswell (1934) 'Aggressive Behavior of Clients Toward Public Relief Workers', *American Political Science Review* 28, 643–55.
Almond, G. A. and G. B. Powell (1966) *Comparative Politics: A Developmental Approach* (Boston: Little, Brown).
Almond, G. A. and G. B. Powell (1978) *Comparative Politics: System, Process and Policy* (Boston: Little, Brown).
Almond, G. A. and S. Verba (1967) *The Civic Culture* (Boston: Little, Brown).
Almond, G. A. and S. Verba (1980) *The Civic Culture Revisited* (Boston: Little, Brown).

Alt, J. E. (1971) 'Some Social and Political Correlates of County Borough Expenditures', *British Journal of Political Science* 1, 49–62.

Alt, J. E. and G. King (1994) 'Transitions of Governmental Power: The Meaning of Time Dependence', *Comparative Political Studies* 27, 190–210.

Alten, F. von (1995) *The Role of Government in the Singapore Economy* (Frankfurt: Peter Lang).

Alter, K.J. and S. Meunier-Aitsahalia (1994) 'Judicial Politics in the European Community–European Integration and the Pathbreaking *Cassis de Dijon* Decision', *Comparative Political Studies* 26, 535–61.

Alvarez, R., G. Garrett and P. Lange (1991) 'Government Partisanship, Labor Organization and Macro-Economic Performance, 1967–1984', *American Political Science Review* 86, 539–56.

Ames, B. (1987) *Political Survival: Politicians and Public Policy in Latin America* (Berkeley: University of California Press).

Ames, B. (1996) *Soft Theory, Hard Evidence: Rational Choice and Empirical Investigation in Brazil* (Washington, DC: Woodrow Wilson Center).

Anderson, C. (1995) *Blaming the Government: Citizens and the Economy in Five European Democracies* (Armonok, NY: M.E. Sharpe).

Anderson, L. and M. A. Seligson (1994) 'Reformism and Radicalism Among Peasants: An Empirical Test of Paige's *Agrarian Revolution*', *American Journal of Political Science* 38, 944–72.

Anderson, T. P. (1982) *Politics in Central America* (New York: Praeger).

Asher, H. B. (1983) *Causal Modeling*, rev. edn (Beverly Hills, CA; Sage).

Ashford, D. E. (1981) *Policy and Politics in Britain: The Limits of Consensus* (Philadelphia, PA: Temple University Press).

Ashford, D. E. (1982) *Policy and Politics in France: Living with Uncertainty* (Philadelphia, PA: Temple University Press).

Atkinson, M. and W. B. Coleman (1988) 'Strong States and Weak States: Sectoral Policy Networks in Advanced Capitalist Economies', *British Journal of Political Science* 19, 47–67.

Aucoin, P. (1995) *The New Public Management: Canada in Comparative Perspective* (Montreal: Institute for Research on Public Policy).

Bailey, S. K. (1950) *Congress Makes a Law: The Story Behind the Employment Act of 1946* (New York: Columbia University Press).

Banfield, E. (1958) *The Moral Basis of Backward Society* (Glencoe, IL: Free Press)

Banks, A. S. (1971) *Cross-Polity Time Series* (Cambridge, MA: MIT Press).

Banks, A. S. and R. B. Textor (1963) *A Cross-Polity Survey* (Cambridge, MA: MIT Press).

Barghoorn, F. C. and T. F. Remington (1986) *Politics in the USSR*, 3rd edn (Boston: Little, Brown).

Barrett, S. and C. Fudge (1981) *Policy and Action* (London: Methuen).

Bartolini, S. (1993) 'On Time and Comparative Research', *Journal of Theoretical Politics* 5, 131–67.

Bates, R. (1988) *Toward A Political Economy of Development: A Rational Choice Perspective* (Berkeley: University of California Press).

Bebler, A. and J. Seroka (1990) *Contemporary Political Systems: Classifications and Typologies* (Boulder, CO: Lynne Rienner).

Beck, N. and J. N. Katz (1995) 'What to Do (and Not to Do) With Time-Series-Cross-Section Data in Comparative Politics', *American Political Science Review* 89, 634–47.

Beckerman, W. (1968) *An Introduction to National Income Analysis* (London: Weidenfeld and Nicolson).

Beer, S. H. (1982) *Britain Against Itself: The Contradictions of Collectivism* (London: Faber).

Bendix, R. (1964) *Nation-Building and Citizenship: Studies of our Changing Social Order* (New York: Wiley).

Bendor, J. and T. Hammond (1992) 'Rethinking Allison's Models', *American Political Science Review* 86, 301–22.

Bennett, C. (1991) 'What is Policy Convergence and What Causes It?', *British Journal of Political Science* 21, 215–33.

Bennett, V. (1992) 'The Evolution of Urban Popular Movements in Mexico Between 1968 and 1988', in A. Escobar and S. E. Alvarez', *The Making of Social Movements in Latin America* (Boulder, CO: Westview).

Berg-Schlosser, D. (1984) 'African Political Systems: Typology and Performance', *Comparative Political Studies* 17, 121–51.

Berg-Schlosser, D. (1985) 'Elements of Consociationalism in Kenya', *European Journal of Political Research* 13, 95–109.

Berg-Schlosser, D. and G. De Meur (1994) 'Conditions of Democracy in Interwar Europe: A Boolean Test of Major Hypotheses', *Comparative Politics* 26, 253–80.

Berg-Schlosser, D. and R. Rytlewski (1993) *Political Culture in Germany* (Basingstoke: Macmillan).

Bermeo, N. (1991) 'Liberalization and Democratization in the Soviet Union and Eastern Europe, Special Issue of *World Politics* 44, 1.

Beyme, K. von (1981) 'Der liberale Korporatismus als Mittel gegen die Unregierbarkeit', in U. von Alemann (ed.), *Neokorporatismus* (Frankfurt: Campus).

Blackmer, D. L. M. and S. Tarrow (1975) *Communism and Italy and France* (Princeton University Press).

Blalock, H. (1964) *Causal Inference in Nonexperimental Research* (Chapel Hill: University of North Carolina Press).

Blalock, H. (1984) *Basic Dilemmas in the Social Sciences* (Beverly Hills: Sage).

Blondel, J. (1980) *World Leaders* (London: Sage).

Blondel, J. (1982) *The Organization of Government* (London: Sage).

Blondel, J. (1985) *Government Ministers in the World Today* (London: Sage).

Blondel, J. and F. Müller-Rommel (1988) *Cabinets in Western Europe* (Basingstoke: Macmillan).

Blondel, J. and F. Müller-Rommel (1993) *Governing Together: The Extent and Limits of Joint Decision-Making in Western European Cabinets* (Basingstoke: Macmillan).

Bobrow, D. B., S. Chan and S. Reich (1996) 'Southeast Asian Prospects and Realities: American Hopes and Fears', *Pacific Review* 9, 1–30.

Bodiguel, J.-L. and L. Rouban (1991) *Le Fonctionaire Detrône* (Paris: Presses de la Fondation nationale des Sciences Politiques).

Bollen, K. A. (1980) 'Issues in the Comparative Measurement of Political Democracy', *American Sociological Review* 45, 370–90.

Bollen, K. A. (1990) 'Political Democracy: Conceptual and Measurement Traps', *Studies in Comparative International Development.*

Booth, J. A. and M. A. Seligson (1989) *Elections and Democracy in Central America* (Chapel Hill, NC: University of North Carolina Press).

Borre, O. and E. Scarborough (1995) *The Scope of Government* (Oxford: Oxford University Press).

Boston, J. (1996) *Public Management: The New Zealand Model* (Auckland: Oxford University Press).

Bova, R. (1991) 'Political Dynamics of the Post-Communist Transition: A Comparative Perspective', *World Politics* 44, 113–38.

Bovens, M. and P. t'Hart (1996) *Policy Fiascoes* (New Brunswick, NJ: Transaction).

Bowie, R. R. (1974) *Suez, 1956* (London: Oxford University Press).

Brace, P. (1993) *State Government and Economic Performance* (Baltimore: Johns Hopkins University Press).

Braibanti, R. J. D. (1966) *Asian Bureaucratic Systems Emergent from the British Imperial Tradition* (Durham, NC: Duke University Press.

Brewer, J. and A. Hunter (1989) *Multimethod Research: A Synthesis of Styles* (Newbury Park, CA: Sage).

Budge, I. (1993) 'Rational Choice as Comparative Theory: Beyond Economic Self Interest', in H. Keman (ed.), *Comparative Politics* (Amsterdam: VU Press).

Budge, I. and H. Keman (1990) *Parties and Democracy: Coalition Formation and Government Functioning in Twenty Democracies* (Oxford University Press).

Budge, I. and M. Laver (1992) *Party Policy and Government Coalition* (Basingstoke: Macmillan).

Bunce, V. (1981) *Do New Leaders Make a Difference?: Executive Succession and Public Policy Under Capitalism and Socialism* (Princeton: Princeton University Press).

Bunce, V. (1984) *Do New Leaders Make a Difference?* (Princeton University Press).

Bunce, V. (1995) 'Comparing East and South', *Journal of Democracy* 6, 87–100.

Burton, M. G. and J. Higley (1987) *Elite Settlements* (Austin, TX: Institute of Latin American Studies, University of Texas).

Butler, D. and D. Kavanagh (1992) *The British General Election of 1992* (New York: St. Martin's).

Butler, D., H. Penniman and A. Ranney (1981) *Democracy at the Polls* (Washington, DC: American Enterprise Institute).

Butler, D. and D. Stokes (1970) *Political Change In Britain: Forces Shaping Electoral Choice* (London: Macmillan).

Calvert, S. and P. Calvert (1989) *Argentina: Political Culture and Instability* (Basingstoke: Macmillan).

Campbell, A., P. Converse, W. Miller and D. Stokes (1960) *The American Voter* (New York: Wiley).

Campbell, D. T. and D. W. Fiske (1959) 'Convergent and Discriminant Validation by the Multitrait-Multimethod Matrix', *Psychological Bulletin* 56, 81–105.

Campbell, J. L. and O. K. Pedersen (1996) 'Theories of Institutional Change in the Postcommunist Context', in Campbell and Pedersen (eds), *Legacies of Change* (Hawthorne, NY: Aldine de Gruyter).

Campbell, D. T. and H. L. Ross (1968) 'The Connecticut Crackdown on Speeding: Time-Series Data and Quasi-Experimental Analysis', *Law and Society Review* 3, 33–53.

Campbell, D. T. and J. C. Stanley (1967) *Experimental and Quasi-Experimental Design for Research* (Chicago: Rand-McNally).

Cappelletti, M. (1989) *The Judicial Process in Comparative Perspective* Oxford: Clarendon).

Cardozo, F. H. and E. Faletto (1979) *Dependency and Development in Latin America* (Berkeley: University of California Press).

Carroll, G. R. (1987) *Publish and Perish: The Organizational Ecology of the Newspaper Industries* (Greenwich, CT: JAI Press).

Casamayou, M. H. (1993) *Bureaucracy in Crisis: Three Mile Island, the Shuttle Challenger, and Risk Assessment* (Boulder, CO: Westview).

Casstevens, T. W. (1984) 'The Population Dynamics of Government Bureaus', *UMAP Journal* 5, 178–99.

Castles, F. G. (1993) *Families of Nations: Patterns of Public Policy in Western Democracies* (Aldershot: Dartmouth).

Castles, S. and M. Miller (1993) *The Age of Migration: International Population Movements in the Modern World* (Basingstoke: Macmillan).

Castles, F. G. and D. Mitchell (1993) 'Worlds of Welfare and Families of Nations', in Castles (ed.), *Families of Nations: Patterns of Public Policy in Western Democracies* (Aldershot: Dartmouth).

Castles, F. G. and R. Wildenmann (1986) *Visions and Realities of Party Government* (Berlin: de Gruyter).

Cawson, A. (1986) *Corporatism and Political Theory* (Oxford: Blackwell).

Chatfield, C. (1989) *The Analysis of Time Series: Theory and Practice*, 4th edn (London: Chapman & Hall).

Clifford, M. E. (1994) *Troubled Tiger: Businessmen, Bureaucrats and Generals* (Armonok, NY: M.E. Sharpe).

Cnudde, C. F. and D. E. Neubauer (1969) *Empirical Democratic Theory* (Chicago: Markham).

Collier, D. (1995) 'Translating Quantitative Methods for Qualitative Researchers: The Case of Selection Bias', *American Political Science Review* 89, 461–6.

Collier, R. B. (1993) 'Combining Alternative Perspectives: Internal Trajectories versus External Influences as Explanations of Latin American Politics in the 1940s', *Comparative Politics* 26, 1–30.

Collier, R. B. and D. Collier (1991) *Shaping the Political Arena: Critical Junctures, the Labor Movement, and Regime Dynamics in Latin America* (Princeton: Princeton University Press).

Collier, D. and J. E. Mahon (1993) 'Conceptual "Stretching" Revisited: Adapting Categories in Comparative Analysis', *American Political Science Review* 87, 845–55.

Collier, D. and R. Messick (1975) 'Prerequisites Versus Diffusion: Testing Alternative Explanations for Social Security Adoption', *American Political Science Review* 69, 1299–1315.

Conradt, D. P. (1995) 'The 1994 Campaign and Election: An Overview', in Conradt (ed.), *Germany's New Politics* (Providence, RI: Berghahn).
Constas, H. (1958) 'Max Weber's Two Conceptions of Bureaucracy', *American Journal of Sociology* 63, 400–9.
Cook, T. D. *et al.* (1992) *Meta-Analysis for Explanation* (New York: Russell Sage).
Cook, T. D. and D. T, Campbell (1979) *Quasi-Experimentation: Design and Analysis for Field Situations* (Chicago: Rand-McNally).
Cornelius, W. A., P. L. Martin and J. F. Hollifield (1994) *Controlling Immigration: A Global Perspective* (Stanford University Press).
Crepaz, M. M. L. (1996) 'Consensus Versus Majoritarian Democracy: Political Institutions and Their Impact on Macroeconomic Performance and Industrial Disputes', *Comparative Political Studies*, 29, 4–26.
Dahl, R. A. (1961) 'The Behavioral Approach in Political Science: Epitaph for a Monument for a Successful Revolution', *American Political Science Review* 55, 763–72.
Dahl, R. A. (1966) *Political Oppositions in Western Democracies* (New Haven, CT: Yale University Press).
Dahl, R. A. (1971) *Polyarchy* (New Haven, CT: Yale University Press).
Dahl, R. A. (1980) 'Pluralism Revisited', in S. Ehrlich and G. Wootton (eds), *The Three Faces of Pluralism* (Westmead: Gower).
Dahl, R. A. (1982) *Dilemmas of Pluralist Democracies* (New Haven, CT: Yale University Press).
Dale, A., S. Arber and M. Procter (1988) *Doing Secondary Analysis* (London: Unwin Hyman).
Dalton, R. J. (1996) *Citizen Politics in Western Democracies: Public Opinion and Political Parties in the United States, Great Britain, West Germany and France*, 2nd edn (Chatham, NJ: Chatham House).
Dalton, R. J., S. Flanigan and P. A. Beck (1984) *Electoral Change in Advanced Industrial Democracies* (Princeton University Press).
De Meur, G. and D. Berg-Schlosser (1994) 'Comparing Political Systems: Establishing Similarities and Dissimilarities', *European Journal of Political Research* 26, 193–219.
De Meur, G. and D. Berg-Schlosser (1996) 'Conditions of Authoritarianism, Fascism and Democracy in Interwar Europe: Systematic Matching and Contrasting of Cases for "Small N" Analyses', *Comparative Political Studies* 29, 423–68.
De Winter, L., D. Della Porta and K. Deschouwer (1996) 'Comparing Similar Countries: Italy and Belgium', *Res Publica* 38, 215–35.
DeFelice, E. G. (1980) 'Comparison Misconceived: Common Nonsense in Comparative Politics', *Comparative Politics* 13, 119–26.
DeMaris, A. (1992) *Logit Modeling: Practical Applications* (Newbury Park, CA: Sage).
Denzin, N. (1978) *The Research Act*, 2nd edn (New York: McGraw-Hill).
Derlien, H-U. and G. Szablowski (1993) *Regime Transitions, Elites and Bureaucrats in Eastern Europe* (Oxford: Blackwell).
Desrosieres, A. (1996) 'Statistical Traditions: An Obstacle to International Comparisons?', in L. Hantrais and S. Mangen (eds), *Cross-National Research Methods in the Social Sciences* (London: Pinter).

Dessler, D. (1989) 'What's at Stake in the Agent-Structure Debate', *International Organization* 43, 441–73.
Deutsch, K. (1963) *The Nerves of Government: Models of Political Communication and Control* (Glencoe, IL: Free Press).
Deutsch, K. (1966) *Nationalism and Social Communications* (Cambridge, MA: MIT Press).
Diamant, A. (1962) 'The Bureaucratic Model: Max Weber Rejected, Rediscovered, Reformed', in F. Heady and S. L. Stokes (eds), *Papers in Comparative Public Administration* (Ann Arbor, MI: Institute of Public Administration).
Dix, R. H. (1980) 'Consociational Democracy: The Case of Colombia', *Comparative Politics* 12, 303–21.
Dogan, M. (1975) *The Mandarins of Western Europe* (New York: Wiley).
Dogan, M. (1994a) 'The Decline of Nationalism in Western Europe', *Comparative Politics* 26, 281–305.
Dogan, M. (1994b) 'Use and Misuse of Statistics in Comparative Research', in M. Dogan and A. Kazancigil (eds), *Comparing Nations* (Oxford: Blackwell).
Dogan, M. and D. Pelassy (1984) *How to Compare Nations: Strategies in Comparative Politics* (Chatham, NJ: Chatham House)
Dogan. M. and D. Pelassy (1990) *How to Compare Nations: Strategies in Comparative Politics*, 2nd edn (Chatham, NJ: Chatham House).
Dolowitz, D. and D. Marsh (1996) 'Who Learns What from Whom: A Review of the Policy Transfer Literature', *Political Studies* 44, 343–57.
Dominiguez, J. I. and J. A. McCann (1996) *Democratizing Mexico: Public Opinion and Electoral Choices* (Baltimore, MD: Johns Hopkins University Press).
Douglas, M. (1982) *In the Active Voice* (Boston: Routledge & Kegan Paul).
Dunleavy, P. (1991) *Democracy, Bureaucracy and Public Choice* (Englewood Cliffs, NJ: Prentice-Hall).
Dunleavy, P. and B. O'Leary (1987) *Theories of the State: The Politics of Liberal Democracy* (London: Macmillan).
Duverger, M. (1954) *Political Parties: Their Organization and Activity in the Modern State* (London: Methuen).
Duyvendak, W. (1995) *The Power of Politics: New Social Movements in France* (Boulder: Westview Press).
Dye, T. (1966) *Politics, Economics and the Public: Policy Outcomes in the American States* (Chicago: Rand McNally).
Dyson, K. H. F. (1980) *The State Tradition in Western Europe* (Oxford: Martin Robertson).
Easton, D. (1965) *A Framework for Political Analysis* (Englewood Cliffs, NJ: Prentice-Hall).
Easton, D. (1979) *A Systems Analysis of Political Life* (University of Chicago Press).
Eckstein, H. (1963) 'A Perspective on Comparative Politics, Past and Present', in Eckstein and D. Apter (eds), *Comparative Politics* (New York: Free Press).
Eckstein, H. (1966) *Divison and Cohesion in Democracy* (Princeton University Press).

Eckstein, H. (1975) 'Case Study and Theory in Political Science', in F.I. Greenstein and N.W. Polsby (eds), *Handbook of Political Science*, vol. 7 (Reading, MA: Addison-Wesley).
Edinger, L.J. (1977) *Politics in Germany*, 2nd edn (Boston: Little, Brown).
Ehrmann, H.W. (1992) *Politics in France*, 5th edn (New York: Harper/Collins).
Eisenstadt, S.N. (1962) *The Political Systems of Empires* (New York: Free Press).
Elazar, D. (1987) *Exploring Federalism* (Tuscaloosa: University of Alabama Press).
Elazar, D. (1996) 'From Statism to Federalism: A Paradigm Shift', *International Political Science Review* 17, 417–29.
Elder, N., A.H. Thomas and D. Arter (1988) *The Consensual Democracies?: Government and Politics of the Scandinavian States*, rev. edn (Oxford: Blackwell).
Elkins, D.J. and R.E.B. Simeon (1979) 'A Cause in Search of an Effect: Or What Does Political Culture Explain?', *Comparative Politics* 11, 117–46.
Esping-Anderson, G. (1990) *The Three Worlds of Welfare Capitalism* (Princeton University Press).
Eulau, H. (1963) *The Behavioral Persuasion in Politics* (New York: Random House).
Eulau, H. (1994) 'Electoral Survey Data and the Temporal Dimension', in M.K. Jennings and T.E. Mann (eds), *Elections at Home and Abroad* (Ann Arbor: University of Michigan Press).
Evans, P. (1995) *Embedded Autonomy: States and Industrial Transformations* (Princeton University Press).
Farazmand, A. (1989) *The State, Bureaucracy and Revolution in Modern Iran* (New York: Praeger).
Faure, A.M. (1994) 'Some Methodological Problems in Comparative Politics', *Journal of Theoretical Politics* 6, 307–22.
Fearon, J.D. (1990) 'Counterfactuals and Hypothesis Testing in Political Science', *World Politics* 43, 169–95.
Finkle, J.L. and R.W. Gable (1971) *Political Development and Social Change*, 2nd edn (New York: Wiley).
Fiorina, M.P. (1991) 'Coalition Governments, Divided Government and Electoral Theory', *Governance* 4, 236–49.
Fitzmaurice, J. (1981) *Politics in Denmark* (London: Hurst).
Fitzmaurice, J. (1988) *The Politics of Belgium: Crisis and Compromise in a Plural Society* (London: Hurst).
Fitzmaurice, J. (1996) *The Politics of Belgium: A Unique Federalism* (Boulder, CO: Westview).
Flanigan, W.H. and N. Zingale (1985) 'Alchemist's Gold: Inferring Individual Relationships from Aggregate Data', *Social Science History* 9, 71–92.
Flora, P. and A.J. Heidenheimer (1981) *The Development of Welfare States in Europe and America* (New Brunswick, NJ: Transaction).
Foley, M.W. (1993) 'Organizing, Ideology, and Moral Suasion: Political Discourse and Action in a Mexican Town', in D. Levine (ed.), *Constructing Political Culture and Power in Latin America* (Ann Arbor: University of Michigan Press).

Fortes, M. and E. E. Evans-Pritchard (1940) *African Political Systems* (London: Oxford University Press).

Freedman, L. (1988) *Britain and the Falklands War* (Oxford: Blackwell).

Freeman, J. (1983) 'Granger Causality and the Time Series Analysis of Political Relationships', *American Journal of Political Science* 27, 327–58.

Frendreis, J. P. (1983) 'Explanation of Variation and Detection of Covariation: The Purpose and Logic of Comparative Analysis', *Comparative Political Studies* 16, 255–73.

Fried, R. C. (1976) 'Party and Policy in West German Cities', *American Political Science Review* 70, 11–24.

Friedman, J. (1996) *The Rational Choice Controversy* (Cambridge University Press).

Friedrich, C. and Z. K. Brzezinski (1956) *Totalitarian Dictatorship and Autocracy* (Cambridge, MA: Harvard University Press).

Fukuyama, F. (1995) *Trust: The Social Conditions for the Creation of Prosperity* (London: Hamish Hamilton).

Gaffney, J. and E. Kolinsky (1991) *Political Culture in France and Germany* (London: Routledge).

Gasiorowski, M. J. (1995) 'Economic Crisis and Political Regime Change: An Events History Analysis', *American Political Science Review* 89, 882–97.

Gauger, J. D. and K. Weigelt (1993) *Foederalismus in Deutschland und Europa* (Cologne: Wissenschaft und Politik).

Geddes, B. (1991) 'A Game Theoretic Model of Reform in Latin American Democracies', *American Political Science Review* 85.

Geertz, C. (1973) 'Thick Description: Toward an Interpretative Theory of Culture', in Geertz', *Interpretation of Cultures* (New York: Basic Books).

George, A. (1979) 'Case Studies and Theory Development: The Method of Structured, Focused Comparisons', in P. G. Lauren (ed.), *Diplomacy: New Approaches in History, Theory and Policy* (New York).

George, S. (1992) *Britain and the European Community: The Politics of Semi-Detachment* (Oxford: Clarendon).

Gerth, H. H. and C. W. Mills (1958) *From Max Weber: Essays in Sociology* (Oxford University Press).

Gibney, F. (1992) *Korea's Quiet Revolution: From Garrison State to Democracy* (New York: Walker).

Gilbert, M. (1995) *The Italian Revolution: The End of Politics, Italian Style* (Boulder, CO: Westview).

Glass, G. V., B. McGaw and M. L. Smith (1981) *Meta-Analysis in Social Research* (Beverly Hills: Sage).

Glover, J. (1996) 'Epistomological and Methodological Considerations in Secondary Analysis', in L. Hantrais and S. Mangen (eds), *Cross-National Research Methods in the Social Sciences* (London: Pinter).

Goertz, G. (1994) *Contexts of International Politics* (Cambridge University Press).

Goguel, F. (1970) *Geographie des elections francaises sous la troisième and quatrième République* (Paris: Armand Colin).

Goldberger, A. (1991) *A Course in Econometrics* (Cambridge, MA: Harvard University Press).

Goodsell, C.T. (1976) 'Cross-Cultural Comparison of Behavior of Postal Clerks Toward Clients', *Administrative Science Quarterly* 21, 104–40.

Goodsell, C.T. (1995) *The Case for Bureaucracy*, 3rd edn (Chatham, NJ: Chatham House).

Gourevitch, P.A. (1986) *Politics in Hard Times: Comparative Responses to International Economic Crises* (Ithaca, NY: Cornell University Press).

Grafton, C. (1984) 'Responses to Change: Creation and Reorganization of Federal Agencies', in R. Miewald and M. Steinman (eds), *Problems in Administrative Reform* (Chicago: Nelson-Hall).

Gray, V. and D. Lowery (1996) 'A Niche Theory of Interest Representation', *Journal of Politics* 58, 91–111.

Green, D.P. and I. Shapiro (1994) *Pathologies of Rational Choice Theory* (Cambridge University Press).

Grindle, M.S. (1980) *Politics and Policy Implementation in the Third World* (Princeton University Press).

Gunnell, J.G. (1996) 'The Genealogy of American Pluralism: From Madison to Behavioralism', *International Political Science Review* 17, 253–65

Gyimah-Boadi, E. (1996) 'Civil Society in Africa', *Journal of Democracy* 7, 118–32.

Hage, J., R. Hanneman and E. Gargan (1989) *State Responsiveness and State Action* (London: Unwin Hyman).

Haggard, S. and C-I. Moon (1995) 'The South Korean State in International Development: Liberal, Dependent or Mercantile?', in J. Frieden and D. Lake', *International Political Economy*, 3rd edn (New York: St Martin's).

Hagopian, F. (1990) 'Democracy by Undemocratic Means? Elites, Political Pacts and Regime Transition in Brazil', *Comparative Politics* 23, 147–70.

Hague, R., M. Harrop and S. Breslin (1992) *Comparative Government and Politics: An Introduction*, 3rd edn (Basingstoke: Macmillan).

Hahm, S.D., M.S. Kamlet and D.C. Mowery (1996) 'The Political Economy of Deficit Spending in Nine Industrialized Parliamentary Democracies', *Comparative Political Studies* 29, 52–77.

Hakim, C. (1982) *Secondary Analysis in Social Research* (London: Allen & Unwin).

Hall, P. (1973) *Great Planning Disasters* (Berkeley: University of California Press).

Hall, T. (1996) 'NZ set to have new government today', *Financial Times*, 10 December.

Halperin, S. (1997) *In the Mirror of the Third World: Capitalist Development in Modern Europe* (Ithaca, NY: Cornell University Press).

Hammergren, L. (1983) *Administration Reform: Lessons from Latin America* (Boulder: Westview).

Hanf, K. and T.A.J. Toonen (1985) *Policy Implementation in Federal and Unitary Systems* (Dordrecht: Kluwer).

Hannan, M.T. (1979) 'The Dynamics of Ethnic Boundaries in Modern States', in J. Meyer and M.T. Hannan (eds), *National Development and the World System* (University of Chicago Press).

Hannan, M.T. (1991) *Aggregation and Disaggregation in the Social Sciences*, rev. edn (Lexington, MA: Lexington Books).

Hannan, M. T. and G. R. Carroll (1981) 'The Dynamics of Formal Political Structure: An Events History Analysis', *American Sociological Review* 46, 19–35.

Hannan, M. T. and G. R. Carroll (1992) *Dynamics of Organizational Populations* (New York: Oxford University Press).

Hansen, S. B. (1989) 'Industrial Policy and Corporatism in the American States', *Governance* 2, 172–97.

Harbeson, J. W., D. Rothchild and N. Chazan (1994) *Civil Society and the State in Africa* (Boulder, CO: Lynne Rienner).

Hardin, G. and J. Baden (1977) *Managing the Commons* (San Francisco: W. H. Freeman).

Hay, C. (1995) 'Structure and Agency', in D. Marsh and G. Stoker (eds), *Theory and Method in Political Science* (New York: St Martin's).

Hayes, M. T. (1991) *Incrementalism and Public Policy* (New York: Longman).

Heady, F. (1996) *Public Administration: A Comparative Perspective* (New York: Marcel Dekker).

Heclo, H. and H. Madsen (1987) *Policy and Politics in Sweden* (Philadelphia, PA: Temple University Press).

Heidenheimer, A. J. (1985) 'Comparative Public Policy at the Crossroads', *Journal of Public Policy* 5, 441–65.

Heidenheimer, A. J., H. Heclo and C. T. Adams (1990) *Comparative Public Policy: The Politics of Social Choice in America, Europe and Japan* (New York: St Martin's).

Heisler, M. O. (1974) 'Patterns of European Politics: The European Polity Model', in Heisler (ed.), *Politics in Europe* (New York: David Mckay).

Heisler, M. O. (1979) 'Corporate Pluralism: Where is the Theory?', *Scandinavian Political Studies* 2 (n.s.), 277–89.

Hellman, J. A. (1992) 'The Study of New Social Movements in Latin America and the Question of Autonomy', in A. Escobar and S. E. Alvarez (eds), *The Making of Social Movements in Latin America* (Boulder, CO: Westview).

Helms, L. (1996) 'Executive Leadership in Parliamentary Democracies: The British Prime Minister and the German Chancellor Compared', *German Politics* 5, 101–20.

Heper, M. (1991) 'Transitions to Democracy Reconsidered', in D. A. Rustow and K. P. Erickson (eds), *Comparative Political Dynamics* (New York: HarperCollins).

Herber, B. P. (1983) *Modern Public Finance*, 5th edn (Homewood, IL: R. D. Irwin).

Hicks, A. M. (1994) 'Introduction to Pooling', in T. Janaoski and A. M. Hicks (eds), *The Comparative Political Economy of the Welfare State* (Cambridge University Press).

Hicks, A. M. and D. Swank (1992) 'Politics, Institutions and Welfare Policy in Industrialized Democracies, 1960–82', *American Political Science Review* 86, 658–74.

Higgott, R. A. (1983) *Political Development Theory: The Contemporary Debate* (New York: St Martin's).

Higley, J. and Gunther, R. (1992) *Elites and Democratic Consolidation in Latin America and Southern Europe* (Cambridge University Press).

Hine, D. (1993) *Governing Italy: The Politics of Bargained Pluralism* (Oxford: Clarendon).
Hirst, P. and G. Thompson (1996) *Globalization in Question* (Oxford: Blackwell).
Hogwood, B. W. (1996) 'Changes in Regulatory Agencies in British Government', paper presented at Conference on Regulatory Organizations, University of Exeter.
Hogwood, B. W. and B. G. Peters (1985) *Policy Dynamics* (Brighton: Wheatsheaf).
Hood, C. (1978) *The Limits of Administration* (New York: Wiley).
Hood, C. (1991) 'A Public Management for All Seasons?', *Public Administration* 69, 3–19.
Hopkins, T. K. and I. Wallerstein (1980) *Processes of the World System* (Beverly Hills, CA: Sage).
Houghton, D. P. (1996) 'Analogical Reasoning in Policymaking, PhD dissertation, Department of Political Science, University of Pittsburgh.
Hudson, M. C. (1969) 'Democracy and Social Mobilization in Lebanese Politics', *Comparative Politics* 1, 245–63.
Hughes, J. T. R. (1993) *The Governmental Habit Redux: Economic Controls from Colonial Times to the Present* (Princeton University Press).
Hunter, J. E. and F. L. Schmidt (1990) *Methods of Meta-Analysis: Correcting Error and Bias in Research Findings* (Newbury Park, CA: Sage).
Hydén, G. and M. Bratton (1992) *Governance and Politics in Africa* (Boulder, CO: Lynne Rienner).
Inglehart, R. (1977) *The Silent Revolution: Changing Values and Political Styles Among Western Publics* (Princteon University Press).
Inglehart, R. (1990) *Culture Shift in Advanced Industrial Society* (Princeton University Press).
Inglehart, R. (1997) *Modernization and Postmodernization: Cultural, Economic and Political Change in 43 Societies* (Princeton University Press).
Ingram, H. and A. B. Schneider (1988) 'Systematically Pinching Ideas: A Comparative Approach to Policy Design', *Journal of Public Policy* 8, 61–80.
Jackman, R. W. (1987) 'Political Institutions and Voter Turnout in Industrial Democracies', *American Political Science Review* 18, 405–23.
Jackman, R. W. and R. A. Miller (1995) 'Voter Turnout in the Industrial Democracies in the 1980s', *Comparative Political Studies* 27, 467–92.
James, S. (1997) *British Government: A Reader in Policymaking* (London: Routledge)
Janoski, T. and A. M. Hicks (1994) *The Comparative Political Economy of the Welfare State* (Cambridge University Press).
Janssen, J. H. (1991) 'Postmaterialism, Cognitive Mobilization and Public Support for European Integration', *British Journal of Political Science* 21, 443–68.
Johnston, R., C. Pattie and A. Russell (1992) 'Dealignment, Spatial Polarisation and Economic Voting: An Exploration of Recent Trends in British Voting Behaviour', *European Journal of Political Research* 23, 67–90.
Jones, C. O. (1984) *An Introduction to the Study of Public Policy*, 2nd edn (Monterey, CA: Brooks/Cole).

Jones, R. E. (1967) *The Functional Analysis of Politics* (London: Routledge & Kegan Paul).

Jordan, A. G. and J. J. Richardson (1987) *British Politics and the Policy Process: An Arena Approach* (London: Allen & Unwin).

Kaase, M. and K. Newton (1995) *Beliefs in Government* (Oxford University Press).

Kahneman, D. (1995) 'Varieties of Counterfactual Thinking', in N. J. Roese and J. M. Olson (eds), *The Social Psychology of Counterfactual Thinking* (Mahwah, NJ: Erlbaum).

Kalleberg, A. I. (1966) 'The Logic of Comparison: A Methodological Note on the Comparative Study of Political Systems', *World Politics* 19, 69–82.

Kaplan, A. (1964) *The Conduct of Inquiry* (San Francisco: Chandler).

Kariel, H. (1961) *The Decline of American Pluralism* (Stanford University Press).

Karl, T. L. (1990) 'Dilemmas of Democratization in Latin America', *Comparative Politics* 23, 1–22.

Kato, J. (1994) *The Problem of Bureaucratic Rationality: Tax Politics in Japan* (Princeton University Press).

Katz, D., B. A. Gutek, R. L. Kahn and E. Barton (1975) *Bureaucratic Encounters* (Ann Arbor, MI: Institute for Social Research, University of Michigan).

Katz, R. S. (1987) *The Future of Party Government* (Berlin: deGruyter).

Katzenstein, P. J. (1984) *Corporatism and Change: Austria, Switzerland and the Politics of Industry* (Ithaca, NY: Cornell University Press).

Katzenstein, P. J. (1985) *Small States in World Markets: Industrial Policy in Europe* (Ithaca, NY: Cornell University Press).

Kaufman, H. A. (1976) *Are Government Organizations Immortal?* (Washington, DC: Brookings Institution).

Kaufman, H. A. (1991) *Time, Chance and Organizations*, 2nd edn (Chatham, NJ: Chatham House).

Kaufmann, C. D. (1994) 'Out of the Lab and into the Archives: A Method of Testing Psychological Explanations of Political Decision Making', *International Studies Quarterly* 38, 557–86.

Kazancigil, A. (1994) 'The Deviant Case in Comparative Analysis', in M. Dogan and A. Kazancigil (eds), *Comparing Nations: Concepts, Strategies, Substance* (Oxford: Blackwell).

Kedourie, E. (1992) *Democracy and Arab Political Culture* (Washington, DC: Institute for Near East Policy).

Kerwin, C. M. (1994) *How Government Agencies Write Law and Make Policy* (Washington, DC: CQ Press).

Key, V. O. (1949) *Southern Politics in State and Nation* (New York: Random House).

Key, V. O. (1950) *Southern Politics in State and Nation* (New York: Knopf).

Kholi, A. (1995) Conclusion in 'The Role of Theory in Comparative Politics: A Symposium', *World Politics* 48, 46–9.

Khong, Y. F. (1992) *Analogies of War: Korea, Munich, Dien Bien Phu and the Vietnam Decision of 1965* (Princeton University Press).

Kim, P. S. (1992) 'Who Serves the People? Educational Backgrounds of South Korean and Japanese Bureaucrats', *American Review of Public Administration* 20, 119–36.

Kincaid, J. (1990) *American Federalism: The Third Century* (Newbury Park, CA: Sage).

King, D. S. (1995) *Actively Seeking Work* (University of Chicago Press).

King, G. (1989) *Unifying Political Methodology* (Cambridge University Press).

King, G. (1990) 'When Not to Use R2', *Political Methodologist* 3, 11–14.

King, G., J. E. Alt, N. Burns and M. Laver (1990) 'A Unified Model of Cabinet Dissolution in Parliamentary Democracies', *European Journal of Political Research*, 38, 846–71.

King, G., R. O. Keohane and S. Verba (1994) *Designing Social Inquiry: Scientific Inference in Qualitative Research* (Princeton University Press).

Kitschelt, H. (1994) *The Transformation of European Social Democracy* (Cambridge University Press).

Klecka, W. R. (1980) *Discriminant Analysis* (London: Sage).

Klingman, D. C. (1980) 'Temporal and Spatial Diffusion in the Comparative Analysis of Social Change', *American Political Science Review* 74, 123–37.

Kooiman, J. (1993) 'Socio-Political Governance: An Introduction', in Kooiman (ed.), *Modern Governance: New Government-Society Interactions* (London: Sage).

Koopmans, R. (1996) 'New Social Movements and Changes in Political Participation in Western Europe', *West European Politics* 19, 28–50.

Kornberg, A. and H. D. Clarke (1992) *Citizens and Community: Political Support for Representative Democracy* (Cambridge University Press).

Kornberg, A. and L. D. Muslof (1970) *Legislatures in Developmental Perspective* (Durham, NC: Duke University Press).

Kothari, R. (1970) *Politics in India* (Boston: Little, Brown).

Krasner, S. (1984) 'Approaches to the State: Alternative Conceptions and Historical Dynamics', *Comparative Politics* 16, 223–46.

Kravis, I., A. Heston and R. Summers (1975) *A System of International Comparisons of Gross Product and Purchasing Power* (Baltimore, MD: Johns Hopkins University Press).

Kritzer, H. M. (1996) 'The Data Puzzle: The Nature of Interpretation in Quantitative Research', *American Journal of Political Science* 40, 1–32.

Kudrle, R. T. and T. R. Marmor (1981) 'The Development of the Welfare State in North America in P. Flora and A. J. Heidenheimer (eds), *The Devlopment of Welfare States in Europe and America* (New Brunswick, NJ: Transaction).

Kuhn, T. (1970) *The Structure of Scientific Revolutions*, 2nd edn (University of Chicago Press).

Laegreid, P. and O. K. Pedersen (1994) *Forvaltningspolitiken i Norden* (Copenhagen: Jurist og Økonomforbundet).

Laitin, D. (1995) 'The Civic Culture at 30', *American Political Science Review* 89, 168–73.

Lal, B. V. (1986) *Politics in Fiji* (Sydney: Allen & Unwin).

Lane, J-E. and S. Ersson (1990) 'Micro and Macro Understanding', *European Journal of Political Research* 18, 457–68.

Lane, R. (1994) 'Structural-Functionalsim Reconsidered: A Proposed Research Model', *Comparative Politics* 26, 461–77.

Lane, J. E. and S. Ersson (1994a) *Politics and Society in Western Europe*, 3rd edn (London: Sage).

Lane, J. E. and S. Ersson (1994b) *Comparative Politics: An Introduction and a New Approach* (Oxford: Polity Press).
Lange, P. and G. Garrett (1985) 'The Politics of Growth: Strategic Interaction and Economic Performance in Advanced Industrial Democracies, 1974–1980', *Journal of Politics* 47, 792–827.
LaPalombara, J. (1968) 'Macro-theories and Micro-applications: A Widening Chasm', *Comparative Politics* 1, 52–78.
LaPalombara, J. (1970) 'Parsimony and Empiricism in Comparative Politics', in R. Holt and J. Turner (eds), *The Methodology of Comparative Research* (New York: Free Press).
LaPalombara, J. and M. Weiner (1966) *Political Parties and Political Development* (Princeton University Press).
Laponce, J. and W. Safran (1996) *Ethnicity and Citizenship: The Canadian Case* (Ilford: Frank Cass).
Lasswell, H. D. (1950) *National Security and Individual Freedom* (New York: McGraw-Hill).
Laurin, U. (1986) *På Heder och Samveter* (Stockholm: P. A. Norstedts).
Laver, M. and K. A. Shepsle (1996) *Making and Breaking Governments: Cabinets and Legislatures in Parliamentary Democracies* (Cambridge University Press).
Lawless, J. F. (1982) *Statistical Models and Methods for Lifetime Data* (New York: Wiley).
Lawson, K. (1994) *How Political Parties Work: Perspectives from Within* (Westport, CT: Praeger).
Lawson, K. and P. Merkl (1988) *When Parties Fail* (Princeton University Press).
Leibfried, S. and P. Pierson (1995) *European Social Policy: Between Fragmentation and Integration* (Washington, DC: Brookings Institution).
Lesquesne, C. (1994) *Paris-Bruxelles: comment se fait la politique européenne de la France* (Paris: Presses de la Fondation nationale de science politique).
Levy, M. J. (1966) *Modernization and the Structure of Societies* (Princeton University Press).
Lewis, A. (1975) *Saints and Samurais: The Political Culture of American and Japanese Elites* (New Haven, CT: Yale University Press).
Lewis-Beck, M. (1988) *Economics and Elections: The Major Western Democracies* (Ann Arbor, MI: University of Michigan Press).
Lewis-Beck, M. (1994) *Factor Analysis and Related Topics* (London: Sage).
Lieberson, S. (1991) 'Small N's and Big Conclusions: An Examination of the Reasoning in Comparative Studies Based on a Small Number of Cases', *Social Forces* 70, 307–20.
Liebert, U. and M. Cotta (1990) *Parliament and Democratic Consolidation in Southern Europe* (London: Pinter).
Lijphart, A. (1968) 'Typologies of Democratic Systems', *Comparative Political Studies* 1, 3–44.
Lijphart, A. (1971) 'Comparative Politics and the Comparative Method', *American Political Science Review* 65, 682–93.
Lijphart, A. (1975a) *The Politics of Accomodation: Pluralism and Democracy in the Netherlands*, 2nd edn (Berkeley, CA: University of California Press).
Lijphart, A. (1975b) 'The Comparable Cases Strategy in Comparative Research', *Comparative Political Studies*, 8, 158–77.

Lijphart, A. (1984) *Democracies: Patterns of Majoritarian and Consensus Government in Twenty-One Countries* (New Haven, CT: Yale University Press).

Lijphart, A. (1990) 'Democratic Political Systems', in A. Bebler and J. Seroka (eds), *Contemporary Political Systems: Classifications and Typologies* (Boulder, CO: Lynne Rienner).

Lijphart, A. (1997) 'The Puzzle of Indian Democracy: A Consociational Interpretation', *American Political Science Review* 90, 258–68.

Lijphart, A., T. C. Bruneau, P. N. Diamandouros and R. Gunther (1988) 'A Mediterranean Model of Democracy? The Southern European Democracies in Comparative Perspective', *West European Politics* 11, 7–25.

Lindblom, C. E. and E. J. Woodhouse (1993) *The Policy-Making Process*, 3rd edn (Englewood Cliffs, NJ: Prentice-Hall).

Linz, J. J. (1988) 'Legitimacy of Democracy and the Socioeconomic System', in M. Dogan (ed.), *Comparing Pluralist Democracies* (Boulder, CO: Westview).

Linz, J. J. and A. C. Stepan (1978a) *The Breakdown of Democratic Regimes* (Baltimore: Johns Hopkins University Press).

Linz, J. J. and A. C. Stepan (1978b) *The Breakdown of Democratic Regimes, Latin America* (Baltimore: Johns Hopkins University Press).

Lipset, S. M. (1959) 'Some Social Requisites of Democracy: Economic Development and Political Legitimacy', *American Political Science Review* 53, 69–105.

Lipset, S. M. (1963) *The First New Nation: The United States in Historical and Comparative Perspective* (New York: Basic Books).

Lipset, S. M. (1990) *Continental Divide: The Values and Institutions of the United States and Canada* (New York: Routledge).

Lipset, S. M. (1994) 'American Exceptionalism–Japanese Uniqueness', in M. Dogan and A. Kazancigil (eds), *Comparing Nations: Concepts, Strategies, Substance* (Oxford: Blackwell).

Lipset, S. M. and S. Rokkan (1967) *Party Systems and Voter Alignments* (New York: Free Press).

Listhaug, O. and A. H. Miller (1985) 'Public Support for Tax Evasion: Self-Interest of Symbolic Politics', *European Journal of Political Research* 13, 265–82.

Lopez, J. J. (1992) 'Theory Choice in Comparative Social Inquiry', *Polity* 25, 267–82.

Lorwin, V. (1971) 'Segmented Pluralism: Ideological Cleavages and Political Cohesion in Smaller European Democracies', *Comparative Politics*, 3, 141–75.

Lowery, D. and V. Gray (1995) 'The Population Ecology of Gucci Gulch, or the Natural Regulation of Interest Group Numbers', *American Journal of Political Science* 39, 1–29.

Lucas, S. (1996) *Britain and Suez; The Lion's Last Roar* (Manchester University Press).

Lundquist, L. and K. Ståhlberg (1983) *Byråkrati i Norden* (Åbo: Åbo Akademi Press).

MacIntyre, A. C. (1978) 'Is a Science of Comparative Politics Possible?', in P. G. Lewis (ed.), *The Practice of Comparative Politics* (London: Methuen).

Mackie, T. T. and M. N. Franklin (1984) 'Reassessing the Importance of Size and Ideology in the Formation of Governing Coalitions in Parliamentary Democracies', *American Journal of Political Science* 28, 671–92.

Mackie, T. T. and R. Rose (1990) *International Almanac of Electoral History*, 3rd edn (London: Macmillan).

MacRae, D. (1974) 'Consociationalism and Canadian Politics', in MacRae (ed.), *Consociational Democracy: Political Accomodation in Segmented Societies* (Ottawa: Carleton University).

Macridis, R. C. (1955) *The Study of Comparative Politics* (New York: Random House).

Macridis, R. C. (1968) *Modern European Governments: Cases in Comparative Policy Making* (Englewood Cliffs, NJ: Prentice-Hall).

Mahler, G. S. (1987) *New Dimensions of Canadian Federalism: Canada in Comparative Context* (Rutherford, NJ: Farleigh Dickinson University Press).

Mair, P. (1997) *Party System Change: Approaches and Interpretations* (Oxford: Clarendon Press).

Majone, G. (1991) 'Cross-national Sources of Regulatory Policy-Making in Europe and the United States', *Journal of Public Policy* 11, 79–106.

March, J. G. and J. P. Olsen (1976) *Ambiguity and Choice in Organizations* (Oslo: Universitetsforlaget).

March, J. G. and J. P. Olsen (1989) *Rediscovering Institutions: Organizational Factors in Political Life* (New York: Free Press).

March, J. G. and J. P. Olsen (1994) *Democratic Governance* (New York: Free Press).

Markoff, J. (1990) 'A Comparative Method: Reflections of Charles Ragin's Innovations in Comparative Analyis', *Historical Methods* 23, 177–81.

Markoff, J. (1996) *Waves of Democracy: Social Movements and Political Change* (Thousand Oaks, CA: Pine Forge Press).

Marradi, A. (1990) 'On Classification', in A. Bebler and J. Seroka (eds), *Contemporary Political Systems: Classifications and Typologies* (Boulder: Lynne Rienner).

Mayer, L. C. (1989) *Redfining Comparative Politics: Promise Versus Performance* (Newbury Park, CA: Sage).

Mayntz, R. and F. W. Scharpf (1975) *Policymaking in the German Federal Bureaucracy* (Amsterdam: Elsevier).

Mayntz, R. and H.-U. Derlien (1989) 'Party Patronage and Politicization of the West German Administrative Elite, 1970–1987: Toward Hybridization?', *Governance* 2, 384–404.

Mazey, S. and J. J. Richardson (1993) 'EC Policy-Making: An Emerging Europan Policy Style?', in D. Liefferink and P. Lowe (eds), *European Integration and Environmental Policy* (New York: Bellhaven).

McAdam, D., J. D. McCarthy and M. N. Zald (1996) *Comparative Perspective on Social Movements* (Cambridge University Press).

McCubbins, M. D. and G. W. Noble (1995) 'The Appearance of Power: Legislators, Bureaucrats and the Budget Process in the United States and Japan', in P. F. Cowhey and M. D. McCubbins (eds), *Structure and Policy in Japan and the United States* (Cambridge University Press).

McKenna, M. C. (1993) *The Canadian and American Constitutions in Comparative Perspectives* (Calgary: University of Alberta Press).

Meier, K. (1975) 'Representative Bureaucracy: An Empirical Assessment', *American Political Science Review* 69, 526–42.
Meijer, H. (1969) 'Bureaucracy and Policy Formation in Sweden', *Scandinavian Political Studies* 4, 103–16.
Mendez, J. L. (1996) 'Policymaking in American and Mexican States: Economic Development Policy in Pennsylvania and Nuevo Leon, unpublished PhD dissertation, Department of Political Science, University of Pittsburgh.
Meny, Y., P. Muller and J.-L. Quermonne (1996) *Adjusting to Europe: The Impact of the European Union on National Institutions and Policies* (London: Routledge).
Mesa-Lago, C. (1978) *Social Security in Latin America* (Pittsburgh: University of Pittsburgh Press).
Mesa-Lago, C. (1989) *Ascent to Bankruptcy: Social Security Financing in Latin America* (Pittsburgh: University of Pittsburgh Press).
Mierlo, H. J. G. A. van (1986) 'Depillarisation and the Decline of Consociationalism in the Netherlands, 1970–1985', *West European Politics* 9, 97–119.
Migdal, J. (1988) *Strong States and Weak Societies: State-Society Relations and State Capabilities in the Third World* (Princeton University Press)
Miles, W. F. S. (1988) *Elections in Nigeria* (Boulder, CO: Lynne Rienner).
Mill, J. S. (1846) *A System of Logic, Ratiocinative and Inductive* (New York: Harper).
Molutsi, M. and J. Holm (1990) 'Developing Democracy When Civil Society Is Weak: The Case of Botswana', *African Affairs* 89, 323–40.
Mooney, C. Z. (1996) 'Bootstrap Statistical Inference: Examples and Evaluations from Political Science', *American Journal of Political Science* 40, 570–602.
Moore, B. (1966) *Social Origins of Dictatorship and Democracy* (Boston: Beacon).
Moore, C. and J. J. Richardson (1989) 'The Politics of Unemployment: The National Context', in Moore and Richardson (eds), *Local Partnership and the Unemployment Crisis in Britain* (London: Unwin Hyman).
Moran, M. and T. Prosser (1994) *Privatization and Regulatory Change in Europe* (Buckingham: Open University Press).
Morris, D. M. (1979) *Measuring the Condition of the World's Poor* (New York: Pergamon).
Most, B. and H. Starr (1989) *Inquiry, Logic and International Politics* (Columbia, SC: University of South Carolina Press).
Mukarji, N. and B. Arora (1992) *Federalism in India* (New Delhi: Vikas).
Muller, P. (1985) 'Un schéma d'analyse des politiques sectorielles', *Revue française de science politique* 35, 165–89.
Nagata, J. A. (1975) *Pluralism in Malayasia: Myth and Reality* (Leiden: Brill).
Nagel, S. S. and V. Rukavishnikov (1994) *Eastern European Development and Public Policy* (New York: St Martin's).
Nakamura, R. (1987) 'The Textbook Policy Process and Implementation Research', *Policy Studies Review* 7, 142–54.
Naroll, R. and R. Cohen (1973) *A Handbook of Method in Cultural Anthropology* (New York: Columbia University Press).
Nieuwbeerta, P. (1995) *The Democratic Class Struggle in Twenty Countries, 1945–1990* (Amsterdam: Thesis).

Nordlinger, E. (1981) *The Autonomy of the State* (Cambridge, MA: Harvard University Press).
Norton, P. (1993) *Does Parliament Matter?* (Brighton: Wheatsheaf).
O'Donnell, G. (1978) 'Reflections on Patterns of Change in the Bureaucratic-Authoritarian State', *Latin American Research Review* 13, 3–39.
O'Donnell, G., P. C. Schmitter and L. Whitehead (1986) 'T*ransitions from Authoritarian Rule: Latin America* (Baltimore: Johns Hopkins University Press).
Olsen, J. P. (1987) *Organized Democracy* (Oslo: Universitetsforlaget).
Olsen, J. P. (1995) *The Nation State in European Context* (Arena Project, University of Oslo).
Olson, D. M. (1994) *Democratic Legislative Institutions: A Comparative View* (Armonk, NY: M. E. Sharpe).
Olson, M. (1982) *The Rise and Decline of Nations: Economic Growth, Stagflation and Social Rigidities* (New Haven, CT: Yale University Press).
Ostrom, E. (1990) *Governing the Commons: The Evolution of Institutions of Collective Action* (New York: Cambridge University Press).
Page, E. C. (1985) *Political Authority and Bureaucratic Power: A Comparative Analysis* (Brighton: Wheatsheaf).
Page, E. C. (1990) 'British Political Science and Comparative Politics', *Political Studies* 38, 438–52.
Page, E. C. (1992) *Political Authority and Bureaucratic Power: A Comparative Analysis*, 2nd edn (Brighton: Wheatsheaf).
Paige, J. (1975) *Agrarian Revolution* (New York: Free Press).
Pampel, F. C. and J. B. Williamson (1988) 'Welfare Spending in Advanced Industrial Democracies, 1950–1980', *American Journal of Sociology* 50, 1424–56.
Panebianco (1988) *Political Parties: Organization and Power* (Cambridge University Press).
Papadakis, E. and P. Taylor-Gooby (1987) *The Private Provision of Public Welfare* (Brighton: Wheatsheaf).
Parsons, T. (1939) 'The Professions and Social Structure', *Social Forces* 17, 457–67.
Pateman, C. (1980) *Participation and Democratic Theory* (Cambridge University Press).
Pempel, T. J. (1982) *Policy and Politics in Japan: Creative Conservatism* (Philadelphia, PA: Temple University Press).
Pempel, T. J. (1990) *Dominant Regimes* (Ithaca, NY: Cornell University Press).
Pempel, T. J. and K. Tsunekawa (1979) 'Corporatism Without Labor: The Japanese Anomoly', in P. C. Schmitter and G. Lehmbruch (eds), *Trends Toward Corporatist Intermediation* (Beverly Hills, CA: Sage).
Penniman, H. R. (1988) *France at the Polls, 1981, 1986: Three National Elections* (Durham, NC: Duke University Press).
Perez-Diaz, V. (1994) *The Return of Civil Society* (Cambridge, MA: Harvard University Press).
Peters, B. G. (1973) 'Political and Economic Explanations for Public Expenditures in the France, Sweden and the United Kingdom', *Midwest Journal of Political Science* 16, 225–39.

Peters, B. G. (1988) *Comparing Public Bureaucracies: Problems of Theory and Method* (Tuscaloosa: University of Alabama Press).

Peters, B. G. (1993) *The Politics of Taxation: A Comparative Perspective* (Oxford: Blackwell).

Peters, B. G. (1994a) 'Agenda-setting in the The European Union', *Journal of European Public Policy* 1,

Peters, B. G. (1994b) *American Public Policy*, 4th edn (Chatham, NJ: Chatham House).

Peters, B. G. (1995a) *The Politics of Bureaucracy*, 4th edn (New York: Longman).

Peters, B. G. (1995b) 'Overload in American Government', in R. Maidment (ed.), *American Democracy* (Buckingham: Open University Press).

Peters, B. G. (1996a) 'Institutionalisms Old and New', in R. E. Goodin and H-D. Klingemann (eds), *A New Handbook of Political Science* (Oxford University Press).

Peters, B. G. (1996b) 'Theory and Methodology', in H. A. G. M. Bekke, J. L. Parry and T. A. J. Toonen (eds), *Civil Service Systems in Comparative Perspective* (Bloomington: Indiana University Press).

Peters, B. G. (1997) 'Escaping the Joint Decision Trap: Policy Segmentation and Iterative Games in the European Union', *West European Politics* (forthcoming).

Peters, B. G. and M. O. Heisler (1983) 'Thinking About Public Sector Growth: Conceptual, Operational, Theoretical and Policy Considerations', in C. L. Taylor (ed.), *Why Governments Grow* (Beverly Hills: Sage).

Peters, B. G. and B. W. Hogwood (1991) 'Applying Population Ecology Models to Public Organizations', *Research in Public Administration* (Westport, CT: JAI Press).

Peters, B. G., M. K. McCulloch and J. C. Doughtie (1977) 'Types of Democratic Systems and Types of Public Policies', *Comparative Politics* 9, 327–55.

Pettersen, P. A. (1995) 'The Welfare State: The Security Dimension', in O. Borre and E. Scarbrough (eds), *The Scope of Government* (Oxford: Oxford University Press).

Picard, L. A. and M. Garrity (1994) *Policy Reform for Sustainable Development: The Institutional Imperative* (Boulder, CO: Lynne Rienner).

Pierce, R. (1991) 'The Executive Divided Against Itself: Cohabitation in France, 1986–88', *Governance* 4, 270–94.

Pierce, R. C. (1995) *Choosing the Chief: Presidential Elections in France and the United States* (Ann Arbor: University of Michigan Press).

Pierce, R. and P. E. Converse (1986) *Political Representation in France* (Cambridge, MA: Belknap Press).

Pierre, J. (1994) *Bureaucracy in the Modern State* (Cheltenham: Elgar).

Pierson, P. (1996) 'The Path to European Integration: A Historical Institutionalist Perspective', *Comparative Political Studies* 29, 123–63.

Pollitt, C. (1990) *Managerialism and the Public Service* (Oxford: Blackwell).

Pollitt, C. and G. Bouckaert (1995) *Quality Improvements in European Public Services* (London: Sage).

Polsby, N. W. (1968) 'The Institutionalization of the U.S. House of Representatives', *American Political Science Review* 62, 14–68.

Polsby, N. W. (1975) 'Legislatures', in F. I. Greenstein and N. W. Polsby (eds), *Handbook of Political Science*, vol. 5 (Reading, MA: Addison-Wesley).
Polsby, N. W. (1982) *What If? Essays in Social Science Fiction* (Lexington, MA: Lewis).
Pontusson, J. (1995) 'From Comparative Public Policy to Political Economy: Putting Institutions in Their Place and Taking Interests Serously', *Comparative Political Studies* 28, 117–47.
Popkin, S. L. (1979) *The Rational Peasant* (Berkeley: University of California Press).
Popper, K. (1959) *The Logic of Scientific Discovery* (New York: Basic Books).
Power, T. J. and M. J. Gasiorowski (1997) 'Institutional Design and Democratic Consolidation in the Third World', *Comparative Political Studies* 30, 123–55.
Pressman, J. L. and A. Wildavsky (1976) *Implementation* (Berkeley: University of California Press).
Pridham, G. (1986) *Coalitional Behavior in Theory and Practice: An Inductive Model for Western Europe* (Cambridge University Press).
Pross, A. P. (1992) *Group Politics and Public Policy*, 2nd edn (Toronto: Oxford University Press).
Przeworski, A. (1995a) 'Comments in Symposium on the Role of Theory in Comparative Politics', *World Politics* 48, 16–21.
Przeworski, A. (1995b) *Sustainable Democracy* (Cambridge University Press).
Przeworski, A. and H. Teune (1970) *The Logic of Comparative Social Inquiry* (New York: Wiley-Interscience).
Putnam, R. D. (1995) 'Bowling Alone: America's Declining Social Capital', *Journal of Democracy* 6, 65–78.
Putnam, R. D., with R. Leonardi and R. V. Nanetti (1993) *Making Democracy Work: Civic Tradition in Modern Italy* (Princeton University Press).
Pye, L. (1965) 'Introduction', in Pye and S. Verba', *Political Culture and Political Development* (Princeton University Press).
Quah, J. S. T. (1990) *In Search of Singapore's National Values* (Singapore: Institute of Policy Studies).
Rabinow, P. and W. M. Sullivan (1979) *Interpretive Social Science: A Reader* (Berkeley: University of California Press).
Radcliffe-Brown, A. R. (1957) *Structure and Function in Primitive Society* (New York: Free Press of Glencoe).
Ragin, C. C. (1987) *The Comparative Method: Moving Beyond Qualitative and Quantitative Strategies* (Berkeley: University of California Press).
Ragin, C. C. (1992) 'Introduction: Cases of "What Is a Case?"', in C. C. Ragin and H. S. Becker', *What is a Case?* (Cambridge University Press).
Ragin, C. C. (1994) 'Introduction to Qualitative Comparative Analysis', in T. Janoski and A. M. Hicks (eds), *The Comparative Political Economy of the Welfare State* (Cambridge University Press).
Ramage, D. E. (1995) *Politics in Indonesia: Democracy, Islam and the Ideology of Tolerance* (London: Routledge).
Ramirez, F. and J. Boli (1987) 'The Political Construction of Mass Schooling: European Origins and Worldwide Institutionalization', *Sociology of Education* 60, 2–17.

Reichard, C. (1997) 'Neues Steurungsmodell'': Local Reform in Germany', in W. J. M. Kickert (ed.), *Public Management and Administrative Reform in Western Europe* (Cheltenham: Elgar).
Rein, M. and L. Rainwater (1986) *Public/Private Interplay in Social Protection: A Comparative Study* (Armonk, NY: M. E. Sharpe).
Rhodes, R. A. W. (1997) *Understanding Governance* (Buckingham: Open University Press).
Richardson, J. J. (1984) *Policy Styles in Western Europe* (Hemel Hempstead: Allen & Unwin).
Riggs, F. W. (1964) *Administration in Developing Countries: The Theory of Prismatic Society* (Boston: Houghton Mifflin).
Robinson, W. S. (1950) 'Ecological Correlations and the Behavior of Individuals', *American Sociological Review* 15, 351–57.
Rogers, E. (1995) *The Diffusion of Innovations* (New York: Free Press).
Rogowski, R. (1995) 'The Role of Theory and Anomoly in Social-Scientific Inference', *American Political Science Review* 89, 467–70.
Rokkan, S. (1966) 'Votes Count But Resources Decide', in R. A. Dahl (ed.), *Political Oppositions in Western Democracies* (New Haven, CT: Yale University Press).
Rose, R. (1965) 'England: The Traditionally Modern Political Culture', in L. Pye and S. Verba (eds), *Political Culture and Political Development* (Princeton University Press).
Rose, R. (1989) *Politics in England*, 5th edn (London: Faber).
Rose, R. (1991) 'Comparing Forms of Comparative Analysis', *Political Studies* 39, 446–62.
Rose, R. (1992) *Lesson Drawing in Public Policy* (Chatham, NJ: Chatham House).
Rose. R. (1974a) *Electoral Behavior: A Comparative Handbook* (New York: Free Press).
Rose. R. (1974b) *The Problem of Party Government* (London: Macmillan).
Rose, R. and I. McAllister (1986) *Voters Begin to Choose: From Closed Class to Open Elections in Britain* (London: Sage).
Rosenberg, M. B. (1976) *Explaining Social Welfare Policy Development in Latin America: The Case of Costa Rica* (University of Pittsburgh: Center for Latin American Studies).
Roskin, M. G. (1991) *The Rebirth of Eastern Europe* (Englewood Cliffs, NJ: Prentice-Hall).
Roth, P. A. (1987) *Meaning and Method in the Social Sciences* (Ithaca, NY: Cornell University Press).
Rummel, R. J. (1972) *Dimensions of Nations* (Beverly Hills, CA: Sage).
Rummel, R. J. (1979) *National Attributes and Behavior* (Beverly Hills, CA: Sage).
Rummel, R. J. (1995) 'Democracy, Power, Genocide and Mass Murder', *Journal of Conflict Resolution* 39, 3–26.
Russett. B. M. (1964) *World Handbook of Political and Social Indicators* (New Haven, CT: Yale University Press).
Sartori, G. (1966) 'European Political Parties: The Case of Polarized Pluralism', in J. LaPalombara and M. Weiner. *Political Parties and Political Development* (Princeton University Press).

Sartori, G. (1970) 'Concept Misinformation and Comparative Politics', *American Politcal Science Review* 64, 1033–41.
Sartori, G. (1991) 'Comparing and Miscomparing', *Journal of Theoretical Politics* 3, 243–57.
Sartori, G. (1995) 'How Far Can Free Government Travel?', *Journal of Democracy* 6, 101–111.
Sartori, G., F.W. Riggs and Henry Teune (1975) *Tower of Babel: On the Definition and Analysis of Concepts in the Social Sciences* (Pittsburgh: International Studies Association).
Savoie, D.J. (1994) *Reagan, Thatcher, Mulroney: The Search for A New Bureaucracy* (Pittsburgh: University of Pittsburgh Press).
Savolainen, J. (1994) 'The Rationality of Drawing Big Conclusions Based on Small Samples: In Defense of Mill's Method', *Social Forces* 72, 1217–24.
Sbragia, A.M. (1992) *Euro-Politics: Politics and Policymaking in the "New" European Community* (Washington, DC: Brookings Institution).
Sbragia, A.M. (1992) 'Thinking About the European Future: The Uses of Comparison', in Sbragia (ed.), *Euro-Politics: Institutions and Policymaking in the New European Community* (Washington, DC: The Brookings Institution).
Sbragia, A.M. (1996) *Debt Wish: Entrepreneurial Cities, U.S. Federalism, and Economic Development* (Pittsburgh: University of Pittsburgh Press).
Scarbrough, E. (1987) 'The British Electorate Twenty Years On: Electoral Change and Election Surveys', *British Journal of Political Science* 17, 219–46.
Scarrow, H.A. (1969) *Comparative Political Analysis: An Introduction* (New York; Harper & Row).
Scheuch, E.K. (1990) 'The Development of Comparative Research: Towards Causal Explanations', in E. Oyen (ed.), *Comparative Methodology: Theory and Practice in International Social Research* (London: Sage).
Schmitter, P.C. (1974) 'Still the Century of Corporatism?', *Review of Politics* 36, 85–131.
Schmitter, P.C. (1981) 'Interest Intermediation and Regime Governability in Contemporary Western Europe and North America', in S. Berger (ed.), *Organized Interests in Western Europe* (Cambridge University Press).
Schmitter, P.C. (1989) 'Corporatism is Dead: Long Live Corporatism', *Government and Opposition* 24, 54–73.
Schmitter, P.C. and T.L. Karl (1992) 'The Types of Democracy Emerging in Southern and Eastern Europe and in South and Central America', in P.M.E. Volten (ed.), *Bound to Change: Consolidating Democracy in East Central Europe* (New York: Institute for East–West Studies).
Schmolders, G. (1960) *Das Irrationale in der öffentliche Finanzwirtschaft* (Cologne: Westdeutscher).
Schneider, B.R. (1991) *Politics Within the State: Elite Bureaucrats and Industrial Policy in Authoritarian Brazil* (University of Pittsburgh Press).
Scott, J.C. (1976) *The Moral Economy of the Peasant: Rebellion and Subsistence in Southeast Asia* (New Haven, CT: Yale University Press).
Self, P. and H.J. Storing (1963) *The State and the Farmer: British Agricultural Policies and Politics* (Berkeley: University of California Press).
Shaikh, A.M. and E.A. Tonah (1994) *Measuring the Wealth of Nations: The Political Economy of National Accounts* (Cambridge University Press).

Sharkansky, I. (1968) *Spending in the American States* (Chicago: Rand-McNally).

Sharman, C. (1994) *Parties and Federalism in Canada and Australia* (Canberra: Federalism Research Center, Australian National University).

Siegfried, A. (1930) *Tableau des partis en France* (Paris: Bernard Grasset).

Silberman, B. S. (1993) *Cages of Reason: The Rise of the Rational State in France, Japan, the United States and Great Britain* (University of Chicago Press).

Silverman, L. (1991) 'Beyond the Micro/Macro Distinction', *European Journal of Political Research* 19, 375–98.

Simeon, R. B. (1985) *Division of Powers and Public Policy* (University of Toronto Press).

Skocpol, T. (1979) *States and Social Revolutions* (Cambridge University Press).

Skocpol, T. (1979) *States and Social Revolutions: A Comparative Analysis of France, Russia and China* (Cambridge University Press).

Skocpol, T. (1984) 'Emerging Agendas and Recurrent Strategies in Historical Sociology', in Skocpol (ed.), *Vision and Method in Historical Sociology* (Cambridge University Press).

Small, M. and J. D. Singer (1982) *Resort to Arms: International and Civil Wars, 1816–1980* (Beverly Hills, CA: Sage).

Smelser, N. J. (1973) 'The Methodology of Comparative Analysis', in D. P. Warwick and S. Osherson (eds), *Comparative Research Methods* (Englewood Cliffs, NJ: Prentice-Hall).

Smith, F. J. and W. D. Craon (1977) 'Patterns of Cultural Diffusion: Analyses of Trait Associations Across Societies by Content and Geographical Proximity', *Current Anthropology* 16, 145–67.

Somers, M. R. (1995) 'What's Political or Cultural About Political Culture and the Public Sphere? Toward an Historical Sociology of Concept Formation', *Sociological Theory* 13, 113–44.

Sprague, J. (1982) 'Is There a Micro Theory Consistent with Contextual Analysis?', in E. Ostrom (ed.), *Strategies of Political Inquiry* (Beverly Hills, CA: Sage).

Steinmo, S., K. A. Thelen and F. Longstreth (1992) *Structuring Politics: Historical Institutionalism in Comparative Analysis* (Cambridge University Press).

Stepan, A. C. (1988) *Rethinking Military Politics: Brazil and the Southern Cone* (Princeton University Press).

Stepan, A. and C. Skach (1993) 'Constitutional Frameworks and Democratic Consolidation: Parliamentarianism and Presidentialism', *World Politics* 46, 1–22.

Stimson, J. A. (1985) 'Regression in Time and Space: A Statistical Essay', *American Journal of Political Science* 29, 915–47.

Stinchcombe, A. L. (1968) *Constructing Social Theory* (University of Chicago Press).

Stocking, G. W. (1984) *Functionalism Historicized: Essays on British Social Anthropology* (Madison: University of Wisconsin Press).

Strang, D. (1990) 'From Dependence to Sovereignty: An Event History Analysis of Decolonization 1970–1987', *American Sociological Review* 55, 846–60.

Strange, S. (1996) *The Retreat of the State: The Diffusion of Power in the World Economy* (Cambridge University Press).

Strom, K. (1988) 'Contending Models of Cabinet Stability', *American Political Science Review* 82, 923–30.

Strom, K. (1990) *Minority Government and Majority Rule* (Cambridge University Press).

Suleiman, E. N. (1974) *Politics, Power and Bureaucracy in France: The Administrative Elite* (Princeton University Press).

Suleiman, E. N. (1984) *Bureaucrats and Policy Making: A Comparative Overview* (New York: Holmes & Meier).

Suleiman, E. N. and H. Mendras (1995) *Le recrutement des élites en Europe* (Paris: Editions La Découverte).

Sullivan, M. J. (1996) *Comparing State Polities: A Framework for Analyzing 100 Governments* (Westport, CT: Greenwood Press).

Taagepera, R. and M. S. Shugart (1989) *Seats and Votes: The Effects and Determinant of Electoral Systems* (New Haven, CT: Yale University Press).

Tarrow, S. (1996) 'Making Social Science Work Across Time and Space: A Critical Reflection' in Robert Putnam's *Making Democracy Work*, *American Political Science Review* 90, 389–97.

Tate, C. N. (1987) 'Judicial Institutions in Cross-National Perspective: Toward Integrating Courts into the Comparative Study of Politics', in J. R. Schmidhauser (ed.), *Comparative Judicial Systems* (London: Butterworths).

Taylor, C. L. and M. C. Hudson (1972) *World Handbook of Political and Social Indicators*, 2nd edn (New Haven, CT: Yale University Press).

Tetlock, P. E. and A. Belkin (1996) *Counterfactual Thought Experiments in World Politics* (Princeton University Press).

Teune, H. (1968) 'Measurement in Comparative Research', *Comparative Political Studies* 1, 138–49.

Teune, H. (1990) 'Comparing Countries: Lessons Learned', in E. Oyen (ed.), *Comparative Methodology: Theory and Practice in International Social Research* (London: Sage).

Thelen, K., F. Longstreth and S. Steinmo (1992) *Structuring Politics: Historical Institutionalism in Comparative Analysis* (Cambridge University Press).

Thibaut, B. (1993) 'Presidencialism, Parliamentarismo y el problema de la consolidation democratica en America Latina', *Estudios Internacionales* 26, 216–52.

Thomassen, J. (1994) 'Empirical Research into Political Representation: Failing Democracy or Failing Models', in M. K. Jennings and T. Mann (eds), *Elections at Home and Abroad* (Ann Arbor: University of Michigan Press).

Tilly, C. (1975) *The Formation of National States in Western Europe* (Princeton University Press).

Tilly, C. (1993) *European Revolutions, 1492–1992* (Oxford: Blackwell).

Tocqueville, A. de (1946) *Democracy in America* (New York: Alfred A. Knopf).

Toonen, T. A. J. (1996) 'On the Administrative Condition of Politics: An Institutional Comparison of Administrative Transformation in the Netherlands', *West European Politics* 19(4), 17–3.

Tsebelis, G. (1990) *Nested Games: Rational Choice in Comparative Politics* (Berkeley: University of California Press).

Tsebelis, G. (1994) 'The European Parliament as a Conditional Agenda-Setter', *American Political Science Review* 88, 128–38.

Tuma, N. B. and M. T. Hannan (1984) *Social Dynamics: Models and Methods* (New York: Academic).

Tuohy, C. (1992) *Policy and Politics in Canada: Institutionalized Ambivalence* (Philadelphia: Temple University Press).

Tushnet, M. V. (1990) *Comparative Constitutional Federalism: Europe and America* (New York: Greenwood).

Tversky, A. and D. Kahneman (1974) 'Judgment Under Uncertainty: Heuristics and Biases', *Science* 185 (27 September) 1124–31.

Udy, S. H. (1958) 'Bureaucratic' Elements in Organizations: Some Research Findings', *American Sociological Review* 23, 415–8.

Uhr, J. (1992) 'Instituting Republicanism: Parliamentary Vices, Republican Virtues', *Australian Journal of Political Science* 28, 27–37.

Usui, C. (1994) 'Welfare State Development in a World System Context: Events History Analysis of First Social Insurance Legislation Among Sixty Countries, 1880–1960', in T. Janoski and A. M. Hicks (eds), *The Comparative Study of the Welfare State* (Cambridge University Press).

Van Ouvride, L. (1998) 'Policy Failure in Belgium', in P. Gray (ed.), *Policy Failure in Western Europe* (London: Routledge).

Vaughan, D. (1990) 'Autonomy, Interdependence and Social Control: NASA and the Space Shuttle 'Challenger'', *Administrative Science Quarterly* 35, 225–57.

Verba, S. (1967) 'Some Dilemmas of Political Research', *World Politics* 20, 111–28.

Verba, S. (1986) 'Comparative Politics: Where Have We Been, Where Are We Going', in H. Wiarda (ed.), *New Directions in Comparative Politics* (Boulder, CO: Westview).

Vickers, Sir G. (1965) *The Art of Judgment* (London: Chapman & Hall).

Von Mettenheim, K. (1995) *The Brazilian Voter: Mass Politics in Democratic Transition 1974–86* (University of Pittsburgh Press).

Vowles, J. (1995) 'The Politics of Electoral Reform in New Zealand', *International Review of Political Science* 16, 95–115.

Wallace, H. and W. Wallace (1996) *Policy-Making in the European Union* (Oxford University Press).

Wallerstein, I. (1980) *The Modern World System* (New York: Academic Press).

Warwick, P. and S. T. Easton (1992) 'The Cabinet Stability Problem: New Perspectives on a Classic Problem', *American Journal of Political Science*, 36, 122–46.

Weaver, R. K. and B. A. Rockman (1993) *Do Institutions Matter?: Government Capabilities in the United States and Abroad* (Washington, DC: Brookings Institution).

Webb, E. J., D. T. Campbell, R. D. Sechrest and L. Schwartz (1967) *Unobtrusive Measures: Nonreactive Research in the Social Sciences* (Chicago: Rand-McNally).

Webber, C. and A. Wildavsky (1987) *A History of Taxation and Expenditure in the Western World* (New York: Simon & Schuster).

Weber, M. (1949) 'Objective Possibility and Adequate Causation in Historical Explanation', in *The Methodology of Social Sciences* (New York: Free Press).
Weber, M. (1988) *Max Weber: A Biography* (New Brunswick, NJ: Transaction).
Weingast, B. (1996) 'Political Institutions: Rational Choice Perspectives', in R. E. Goodin and H.-D. Klingemann (eds), *New Handbook of Political Science* (Oxford University Press).
Welch, C. E. (1990) 'African Political Systems', in A. Bebler and J. Seroka (eds), *Contemporary Political Systems* (Boulder, CO: Lynne Rienner).
Welch, S. (1993) *The Concept of Political Culture* (London: Macmillan).
White, S. (1979) *Political Culture and Soviet Politics* (London: Macmillan).
Wiarda, H. J. (1981) *Corporatism and National Development in Latin America* (Boulder, CO: Westview).
Wiarda, H. J. (1985) *New Directions in Comparative Politics* (Boulder, CO: Westview).
Wiarda, H. J. (1997) *Corporatism and Comparative Politics: The Other Great "Ism"* (Armonk, NY: M. E. Sharpe).
Wickham-Crowley, T. P. (1991) *Guerillas and Revolution in Latin American: A Comparative Study of Insurgents and Regimes since 1956* (Princeton: Princeton University Press).
Wiesenthal, H. (1996) 'Organized Interests in Contemporary East Central Europe: Theoretical Perspectives and Tentative Hypotheses', in A. Agh (ed.), *The Second Steps: Parliaments and Organized Interests* (Budapest: Hungarian Centre for Democratic Studies).
Wildavsky, A. (1980) 'Policy as its Own Cause', in Wildavsky', *The Art and Craft of Policy Analysis* (London: Macmillan).
Wildavsky, A. (1987) 'Doing More and Using Less: Utilization of Research as a Result of Regime', in M. Dierkes, H. N. Weiler and A. B. Antal (eds), *Comparative Policy Research: Learning from Experience* (Aldershot: Gower).
Wilensky, H. (1974) *The Welfare State and Equality: Structural and Ideological Roots of Public Expenditures* (Berkeley: University of California Press).
Wilson, G. K. (1994) 'The Westminster Model in Comparative Perspective', in I. Budge and D. McKay (eds), *Developing Democracy* (London: Sage).
Wilson, W. (1898) *The State: Elements of Historical and Practical Politics* (Boston: D. C. Heath).
Wiseman, H. V. (1966) *Political Systems: Some Sociological Approaches* (London: Routledge & Kegan Paul).
Woolsey, T. D. (1893) *Political Science: or The State Theoretically and Practically Considered* (New York: Scribners).
Wright, D. S. (1988) *Understanding Intergovernmental Relations*, 3rd edn (Monterey, CA: Brooks/Cole).
Wright, V. (1997) Reshaping the State: The Implications for Public Administration', *West European Politics*, 17, 4, 102–37.
Young, C. (1982) *Ideology and Development in Africa* (New Haven, CT: Yale University Press).
Zelditch, M. (1971) 'Intelligible Comparisons', in J. Valker (ed.), *Comparative Methods in Sociology* (Berkeley: University of California Press).

Zhang, B. (1994) 'Corporatism, Totalitarianism and Transitions to Democracy', *Comparative Political Studies* 27, 108–36.

Index